How Behavioral Economics Influences Management Decision-Making

Perspectives in Behavioral Economics and the Economics of Behavior

How Behavioral Economics Influences Management Decision-Making

A New Paradigm

Kelly Monahan
Organizational Behavior Researcher, Regent University, Philadelphia, PA, USA

Series Editor
Morris Altman

ELSEVIER

ACADEMIC PRESS
An imprint of Elsevier

Academic Press is an imprint of Elsevier
125 London Wall, London EC2Y 5AS, United Kingdom
525 B Street, Suite 1650, San Diego, CA 92101, United States
50 Hampshire Street, 5th Floor, Cambridge, MA 02139, United States
The Boulevard, Langford Lane, Kidlington, Oxford OX5 1GB, United Kingdom

British Library Cataloguing-in-Publication Data
A catalogue record for this book is available from the British Library

Library of Congress Cataloging-in-Publication Data
A catalog record for this book is available from the Library of Congress

ISBN: 978-0-12-813531-0

Publisher: Candice Janco
Acquisition Editor: Graham Nisbet
Editorial Project Manager: Barbara Makinster
Production Project Manager: Swapna Srinivasan
Cover Designer: Matthew Limbert

Typeset by MPS Limited, Chennai, India

Contents

Preface

The goal of this book is to generate discussion around a new management paradigm in the 21st century firm. It is unlikely that all will agree with everything that is written, but nonetheless, it is necessary to challenge our most commonly held assumptions around management practices. Many other fields of study, such as medicine, engage in rigorous debate surrounding the assumptions they use to draw their conclusions and best practices. All too often, we, as business management theorists, fail to engage in the same level of debate, but rather continue to advocate for management behaviors based on a time and place that no longer resemble today's market conditions. To that end, this book seeks to begin the much-needed dialog and debate surrounding the role of the manager in today's organizations.

The role of the manager is shifting in profound ways as market complexities continue to present newfound challenges to the management of people in the workplace. This book considers an alternative paradigm, which is contrary to the dominant discourse found in many of today's leading management theories and activities. Today's dominant management perspectives focus on the behaviors associated with planning, controlling, organizing, and directing resources within organizations, which arise from a rational economic understanding of human behavior. However, within these pages, a new paradigm is presented, which hinges on the advancements made in recent decades within the field of behavioral sciences. Utilizing behavioral sciences creates an opportunity to bring humanity back to the forefront of management decision-making. In addition, recent behavioral science sheds light on the complexity and irrationality that arise in human decision-making, which necessitates a new understanding on how to manage people in the workplace.

This book is separated into two parts. The first half of this book builds the theoretical underpinnings necessary to form a new paradigm of management, while the latter half focuses on the pragmatic applications that the new paradigm presents to managers. Specifically, Chapter 1, The Changing Nature of Work: Macro-Level Considerations for Managers, examines five market forces, which fundamentally shifts the way people work, the structure of the workplace, and the way firms generate value. Chapter 2, Rational Economics and the Administrative Theory of Management, then seeks to challenge the dominant rational economic paradigm found in management theories in light of these new market conditions. In particular, key rational economic assumptions are questioned, including the irresistible pull to maximize one's own interests and the motivation to work for extrinsic factors. These rational assumptions have given rise to the role of management administration, which is namely to mitigate the rise of agency costs within firms. Chapter 3, Exploring Management Alternatives With a Behavioral Economic Lens, further challenges these dominant assumptions by considering empirical evidence in both laboratory and field experiments, which suggests that people do indeed work for more than financial gain and actively seek to collaborate and cooperate with others. With this newfound understanding of human motivation and decision-making in the workplace, Chapter 4, The Manager's Evolving Role, seeks to build a new theory around the role of the manager, which no longer has to rely on command and control styles of leadership to mitigate the costs of divergent interests in the workplace. Rather, social capital comes to the forefront as a key lever that managers in the 21st century can pull to align interest of individuals at the work. Within Chapter 4, The Manager's Evolving Role, a new paradigm and management framework is presented, which describes the new behaviors and skills necessary to lead in the future of work. In addition, a variety of heuristics and biases are examined, which impede the opportunity for managers to create both social and intellectual capital within their organizations.

Part II of this book seeks to apply the management framework by unpacking each of the core behaviors, along with their corresponding biases that can mitigate management performance. Chapter 5, Connecting: Bridging Across Networks to Attract New Talent Under Shared Objectives, explores ways managers must connect throughout a diverse ecosystem to hire the right talent at the right time for the organization. Chapter 6, Coaching With and Toward the Development of Expertise, considers the role of the manager as a coach and how the activities of goal-setting and performance management change in light of behavioral considerations. Chapter 7, Empowering: Building Reciprocity and Trust, examines the behaviors of empowering through the activities of employee engagement, along with specific heuristics that arise as power is leveraged in the workplace. Chapter 8, Adapting: Building Trust During Change Management, unpacks the management behavior of adapting by reexamining change management activities. Indeed, the latter half of this book will provide managers tools and case studies that leverage the new paradigm of management using behavioral sciences.

Understanding a new perspective on management can be challenging, but it is necessary for the further development of an organization's most valuable resource—its people. To that end, the author encourages readers of this book to dialog, debate, and question, not just the dominant discourse, but the new paradigm of management presented throughout these pages. Indeed, organizational success continues to hinge on the role of management within the firm and starting from a behavioral perspective may offer newfound insights previously left undiscovered in the traditional paradigm of management.

Dr. Kelly Monahan, PA.
Jan, 2018

Acknowledgments

The creation and completion of a manuscript is never a solo endeavor. Rather, manuscripts form in the midst of much dialog from colleagues and friends who generously lend their time to help develop the ideas needed to contribute to the broader narrative. To that end, the author would like to specifically thank my research assistant, *Kimberly Fazio*, for her dedicated efforts and research toward the development of this manuscript. Her advice, edits, and contributions were instrumental in the development and completion of this manuscript. Many of Kimberly Fazio's own experiences, insights, and fingerprints are woven throughout these pages.

In addition, the author would like to thank *Edward Monahan*, who provided thought-provoking dialog and debate, which further propelled the ideas presented in this book forward. His guidance and management experience were most helpful to the completion of this manuscript. Lastly, the author would like to express gratitude to *Kim* and *Ryan Torguson* for their continued support and friendship during the development of this manuscript.

Chapter 1

The Changing Nature of Work: Macro-Level Considerations for Managers

1.1 COMPLEXITY AND IRRATIONALITY INFLUENCE MARKETS, FIRMS, AND INDIVIDUAL BEHAVIOR

Management is the driving force inside an organization and the complexity and pressures they face competing in today's marketplace are profound. For example, the average lifespan of an S&P 500 company has diminished by more than 50 years (Gittleson, 2012). In the 1920s, firm survival rate was 67 years, while today few firms expect to survive for more than 15 years on the S&P 500. Furthermore, there is only one of the original organizations founded on the Dow Jones that exists today—all others have closed their operations, been acquired, or in some cases morphed into something entirely new. Simply put, a firm's chance of long-term survival is quite bleak in today's environment. However, it is argued that if a manager is able to strengthen the diffusion of knowledge in a firm through effective talent management, the firm's chance of survival will be much greater in today's complex markets.

While firm survival has always been challenging, the conditions by which they survive have drastically shifted. Some researchers have borrowed from military vernacular to describe the market conditions as *VUCA*, standing for volatile, uncertain, complex, and ambiguous. A term that derived in a military setting during the Cold War is now being applied to the environment by which firms compete. Indeed, one economist recently described the modern day financial markets as, "...sources of chronic instability, waves of speculation and bubbles" (Piketty, 2014, p. 214). There is growing consensus among business leaders and economists that markets are changing, which creates newfound challenges and opportunities for existing firms.

Rational economics predicts that all competitive markets will revert back to equilibrium. This is due to the assumptions of rationality and linear interactions between individual behavior and prices. However, few markets today actually behave in a way that reflects such predictability. If pure market rationality and equilibrium existed, our current systems would be much

How Behavioral Economics Influences Management Decision-Making.
DOI: https://doi.org/10.1016/B978-0-12-813531-0.00001-7

better at predicting and guaranteeing returns on stock markets. Therefore, rather than ascribing full rationality, behavioral economics predicts that individuals will make small deviations from rationality, which can cause unpredictable outcomes. The study of uncertainty, change and nonlinearity is referred to as *complexity theory*. Complexity theory emerged as mathematician and meteorologist Lorenz (1963) studied the turbulent flow in fluids, finding them surprisingly hard to predict. His research eventually showcased how the smallest change in one event creates unforeseen larger consequences in another. For example, Lorenz simply rounded an input in his 12-variable weather prediction model from .506127 to .506. This small rounding alternation dramatically changed the entire weather pattern. What was discovered, and then explained by complexity theory, was the interdependence between events that rarely followed a linear or predictable pattern. Complexity theory assumes interdependent relationships, which are hard to predict as a minor change in one can dramatically change the others. Therefore, unlike orthodox economic theories, complexity theory provides insights into the reciprocal relationship between markets, firms, and individuals. These relationships are best examined using nonlinear mathematic equations that account for feedback loops and interdependencies. These complex relationships are simply hard to model in economics because one is attempting to apply finite measurements to infinite possibilities (Levy, 2000). However, organizational reality is more often than not marked by complexity and uncertainty rather than predictable rationality.

Research seeking to explain these variations have resulted in entirely new inquiries into how markets and people *actually* behave. At a market level, complexity and chaos theories have been developed to explain why the economy is chaotic even when individuals are not. At a firm level, complex adaptive system frameworks have been developed to explain how firms adapt to their environment. At an individual level, behavioral economics has entered the forefront of discussions explaining human behavior and motivation. At the heart of these new streams of research is the idea that people exhibit bounded rationality, finite willpower, and limited self-interest in decision-making. These small variances in individual rationality can create significant changes in organizational level outcomes, which in part may explain the diminishing survival rates of firms. To this end, the assumption that markets and people exhibit fully rational behavior is increasingly been called into question in recent decades. This does not necessarily imply that neoclassical or orthodox perspectives are wrong, but rather may be incomplete. Uncertainty and complexity is simply an aspect of reality, which requires us to develop new ways of thinking around markets, firms, and individual behaviors.

Therefore, even in the midst of great advances in economics research, management theory has yet to be fully reexamined. Rather, a dominant logic based on the premise of rational economic behavior pervades many of today's management practices. Leading management practices are founded upon the assertion that markets, organizations, and individuals behave rationally, seeking to maximize their own self-interest. Unfortunately, this thinking does not accurately prepare managers for the unpredictable and often messy contexts facing individuals within today's changing market dynamics. Mintzberg (1973) argued that managers' behaviors are not nearly as systematic as assumed, but rather "their activities are characterized by brevity, variety and discontinuity." For these reasons, this book seeks to provide an alternative management paradigm, grounded in the assumptions of irrationality and complexity. This new perspective regards human behavior both individually and collectively as pliable and prone to deviations from rationality and self-interest. This book explores the irrational cognitions, which arise as individuals navigate the complexity of today's market conditions. In doing so, this book will provide a contemporary narrative of organizational success in a knowledge-driven economy, which ultimately calls for a shift in managerial mindset—shifting from a mechanistic-industrial worldview that favors planning, controlling, directing, and organizing resources, to one that seeks to motivate, coach, and develop intellectual capital by appealing to the intrinsic motivations of a firm's talent base. Human decision-making will continue to be at the forefront of organizational success; therefore, a manager's ability to navigate the hidden biases that impede their effectiveness will be instrumental to a firm's ability to survive in rapidly changing and complex conditions. As noted, small variations in behavior can lead to monumental consequences for firms. The complexity and irrationality managers face can lead to barriers which mitigate the productivity of the firm. Therefore, we must account for complexity and the nonobvious when examining managerial decision-making in the firm.

1.2 CHANGING MARKET CONDITIONS: GROWTH AND PRODUCTIVITY CONCERNS

A question that has concerned firm managers throughout the years is *how* to grow the firm. There are two productivity levers to pull for growth—technology and labor. Productivity is fueled by a change in one of those levers, as markets reward those firms, which are able to create or adapt quickly to change. Change is commonplace when discussing markets and firms since growth occurs from transformation. Furthermore, it is rarely the incumbent firm that produces the new idea or technology which sparks growth. Nearly a century ago, Schumpeter (1934) remarked that it was seldom the business that operated the stagecoaches to build the first railroad. This same holds true for today. Today's transportation systems continue to experience disruption by novel technology entrants. Many times incumbent firms fail to anticipate the new technology that will upend their business. However, it is this creative destruction caused by new firms' disrupting traditional ways of thinking which fuels economic progress. Politician Tom Barrett is credited for remarking, "Chaos brings uneasiness, but it also allows for creativity and growth."

Stated simply, market growth depends on change. However, the magnitude by which firms must change has certainly accelerated, thanks in part to advancements in technology, globalization, and lower barriers of entry into markets. Established firms now face a variety of competition, often from unexpected technology start-ups. As a result, wealth creation no longer solely derives from tangible sources, with the past four decades showing a rise in the value of intangible assets on firm's balance sheets (Tomo, 2015). Throughout this book, intangible assets are defined as the aggregate collection of a firm's nonphysical assets, such as intellectual property, business processes and methodologies, trademarks, and brand reputation. These are created from a firm's talent pool. This places great demand for knowledge and skilled workers in today's workplaces.

As a result of these changes, there is a need for renewed discourse regarding the role of management in the firm. If a manager seeks to grow firm value, do the current management assumptions still apply in a knowledge-driven economy? To examine this question, one must reconsider neoclassical economic assumptions of both the firm and managerial decision-making. It may be suffice to suggest that decades-old unchallenged assumptions must come under consideration in light of these unpresented changes.

Classical organizational theorists describe the theory of the firm as analogous to a theory of markets. Therefore, a firm in many ways responds and adapts to the changing conditions determined by the market. Market conditions are the characteristics, such as number of competitors, availability of skilled labor, and market growth rate, which enable or hinder a firm or new product's entrance. When the conditions of a market shift, this creates both opportunity and challenges for existing firms participating in the market. It is even more difficult for firms to survive without reconsidering, and many times reinventing their source of value and competitive advantage. Often the key to survival can be explained by the organization's ability to increase its productivity through effective change management. This can be evidenced by the fact that researchers have found as much as four times labor productivity difference between organizations in the 90th percentile compared to the 10th percentile (Syverson, 2011). Even when controlling for other variables, the total factor productivity (TFP) was nearly double. As shown in multiple studies conducted, the differences in labor productivity and markets persisted over time and across countries.

One of the two productivity levers can be used to explain for this phenomenon. More productive firms can be explained based on their technology investments or these differences can be explained by their talent management practices. This volume will argue the latter explanation—that as market conditions shift, management assumptions must too come under reconsideration. It will do no good to simply invest in additional technology to maintain equilibrium with the markets. Rather, attention must turn to the management of talent alongside technology investments. Recent research points to fact that digital transformation fails most often, not as a result of the technology, but as a failure of talent management practices (Kane, Palmer, Phillips, Kiron, & Buckley, 2015).

Many of our management practices derive from a time and place that no longer resembles today's marketplace or workforce. The rise of behavioral economics provides an alternative management perspective of the firm as it seeks to maximize efficiencies in changing conditions, caused in part by the growing emphasis and value of information and skilled labor. This chapter first seeks to examine some of the notable changing market conditions that face the 21st century firm manager. These trends will be discussed in light of their implications to managerial decision-making regarding labor productivity. A key question explored throughout is, how can managers help their people become more productive, and therefore grow the firm's value?

Piketty (2014) argues that modern growth can be defined as the increase in productivity through the diffusion of knowledge and skills. This perspective is called *new growth theory*, which describes the relationship between productivity growth and the diffusion of knowledge and skills. Stated in the context of new growth theory, a manager is able to grow the firm by increasing the firm's ability to create and utilize knowledge through the development of its people and technology. Therefore, in a rational and predictable economic environment, each available unit of capital would be invested where it is most productive, therefore producing continuous growth for the firm. However, we know that complexity and irrationality get in the way of predictable environments and rational resource allocations. Advancements in behavioral economics informs us that managers often make deviations from rational capital allocation decisions, often unintentionally curtailing productivity. Managerial decision-making is further complicated by the fact that technology and knowledge are often hard to measure. This deviation may partially explain why some economists have suggested that current statistics fail to represent the productivity growth one would expect in light of recent technological advancements (Gordon, 2016). Solow (1987) is famously known for quipping, "You can see the computer age everywhere but in the productivity statistics." Therefore, the deviation from rationality and questionable productivity growth requires a reexamination of our underlying management assumptions.

This book seeks to further explore the role managers have in the diffusion of knowledge and skills, which are key to increasing productivity and growth. In doing so, we seek to address the question, how can firm managers create value by further growing their firm's diffusion of knowledge and skills? Specifically, this question will be examined in light of a firm's arguably most important asset, its people. Ross (2016), leading authority and expert on innovation, remarked, "Among the world's most innovative countries and businesses there is an emerging cultural consensus on how best to strength their most critical resource: their people." It will be argued throughout that if a manager is able to strengthen the diffusion of knowledge in a firm through its people, the firm's chance of survival will be much greater. However, these ambitions are met with five changing market conditions. These changes will present headwinds or tailwinds depending on how well a firm manager can harness their growth potential.

1. Declining technology costs are driving a skills-biased workforce
2. The rise of intangible assets is increasing the value of data and information, which causes a firm to relentlessly focus on growing intellectual capital created by its people
3. Blurring industry lines form new types of competition, which disrupt traditional market boundaries
4. New forms of employment provide a continuum of labor, redefining the social contract between employer and employee
5. Firms are reorganizing by reducing hierarchy and looking to teams for decision-making, necessitating the formation of social bonds throughout the organization

1.3 DECLINING TECHNOLOGY COSTS ARE DRIVING A SKILLS-BIASED WORKFORCE

Competitive firms consistently seek to lower their labor costs, particularly in the area of noncore and routine tasks. This desire to decrease costs led many firms in the 1980s to offshore tasks, particularly in the areas of manufacturing, information technology, and customer service jobs. The ability to offshore tasks was based on the nature of the work, which was often defined by routine and low-skilled tasks. Overseas opportunities, specifically in developing countries, saw an increase in these routine-based jobs as firms were able to better compete in an environment of low wages. However, as wages increased in these developing countries, firms continued to seek lower costs of production. Advancements in technology have caused many firms to reevaluate their labor and technology mix. Rather than solely focusing on offshoring efforts as a way to decrease costs, firms are increasingly turning to technology. This, of course, has a tremendous impact to the labor markets.

The 1957 movie *Desk Set* portrays workers expressing concern over the installation of a new computer network, EMERAC (Electromagnetic Memory Research Arithmetical Calculator). In a relatively humorous screenplay, the writers hint to the growing fear among workers that computers may one day make certain professions irrelevant. Workers in the movie worry their "human brain work" will grow obsolete with the introduction of this new technology. Fast forward to the 21st century and this indeed may be the case. Frey and Osborne (2013) estimate that 47% of total U.S. employment is at high risk of automation over the next one to two decades. While economists continue to debate the exact percentage of jobs at risk, few argue that technology advancements are upending many of today's current professions.

While technology dissolving human labor has many times been met with fear (i.e., the Luddites uprising in the early 1800s against the mechanization of textile work or the Swing Riots of 1830 with agriculture workers protesting the rise of industrial machinery), the acceleration of technology in the 21st century, namely due to declining costs, has led to fundamental shifts in the labor market. As a result of declining costs of computer capital, the labor markets favor the skilled worker whose work is complemented by technology rather than replaced. In part, this can be explained by the strong link between human skills and technology adoption. Nelson and Phelps (1966) argue that higher skilled workers more easily evaluate and implement new technologies rather than resist their entrance into the workplace. Their economic growth model was built around the hypothesis that education or the acquisition of skills speeds technology diffusion. Skilled labor is characterized by the education and expertise a worker obtains. Doms, Dunne, and Troske (1997) provided empirical support for this hypothesis, showing that firms with more skilled workers were also using more advanced technologies. The reason for this relationship is that skilled workers have lower costs of acquiring new knowledge and therefore find it easier to change. This relationship rewards the highly skilled worker within the labor markets based on their ability to learn. The link between skilled labor and technology investment is key to understanding the labor market shifts in the 21st century.

If technology has traditionally upended the workplace, what makes this disruption different for today's manager? The answer can be explained by *Moore's law*. Moore (1975) predicted that the number of components per integrated circuit doubles every 2 years. This observation held true from 1975 until 2012 causing great technology advancements at decreasing costs. However, today we do see a level of saturation and slowing of progress in the speed of doubling. Nevertheless, the exponential rate of technology growth has had tremendous impact on the employment sector over the past several decades.

There is a shift within the knowledge-based economy that favors skilled labor. This shift is called *skills-biased technology change*, whereby technology is driving a premium for human skills, such as creativity, critical thinking, and empathy (Violante, 2016). Multiple researchers have found positive correlations between an increase in computer capital investment and the rise of skilled labor across industries. Link and Siegel (2007) argue that as much as 35–50% of the increase in growth in demand for highly skilled workers can be attributed to the investment in computers. As computerization continues to increase within firms, labor demands shift. Firm investments in computer capital tend to substitute low-skilled labor, while complementing high-skilled labor. Advancements in technology often leave certain acquired skills by workers obsolete, further driving down wages for low-skilled workers.

The ability of technology to replace workers can best be explained by the delineation of knowledge. Knowledge can be categorized into explicit and tacit knowledge. Explicit knowledge is the formalized, rule-based knowledge that thrives in well-defined contexts. Tacit knowledge is knowledge that cannot be formalized as it is socially constructed. Philosopher Michael Polanyi described tacit knowledge as, "knowing more than we can tell." This means that slight variations in meaning can occur, which often results in fluidity as new information is discovered. Explicit knowledge, on the other hand, is readily transferable and codifiable. Based on these definitions of knowledge, it should be of no surprise that computerization, and in particular automation, is taking over tasks that can be defined by explicit knowledge. Indeed, technology has commoditized explicit knowledge and routine tasks. However, even with the advancements in technology, tacit knowledge is hard to computerize as it relies on associative thinking and varied experiences. Even Frey and Osborne (2013) identify social intelligence tasks as a key bottleneck to complete computerization of jobs. As a result of these knowledge differences, leading experts advocate for a shift toward automating work, or explicit tasks, and humanizing jobs, those that rely on tacit knowledge. The ability of humans to cooperate and apply social skills, which relies on their tacit knowledge, will differentiate human productivity from technology.

The rise of technology upending jobs that rely on explicit knowledge is evidenced within the employment sector statistics. In 1900, the agriculture sector consisted of 41% employment, whereas in 2012 it was only 2%. The manufacturing sector reached its height in 1950, capturing 31% of the workforce, while in 2012 it was down to 18%. However, the sector which has experienced an even more dramatic flux of employment is the services. In 1900, only 31% of the total workforce worked in the services sector, and in 2012 the services represented 80% of total employment (Figure 1.1).

This has resulted in a dramatic change in the mere physical nature of work. Forty-six percent of American jobs require almost no physical demands on employees (Economist, 2011). The knowledge economy has shifted work from physically intensive labor conducted with workers' hands to knowledge-intensive work conducted with their minds. This alone has tremendous impact to the way that managers' consider the role of humans in the workforce. Yet, as will be discussed in chapter 2, many of our current management assumptions derive from a time of physical routine labor production.

In addition to the changing nature of work, one can drill further into the changing demands of jobs by examining the U.S. database of industrial

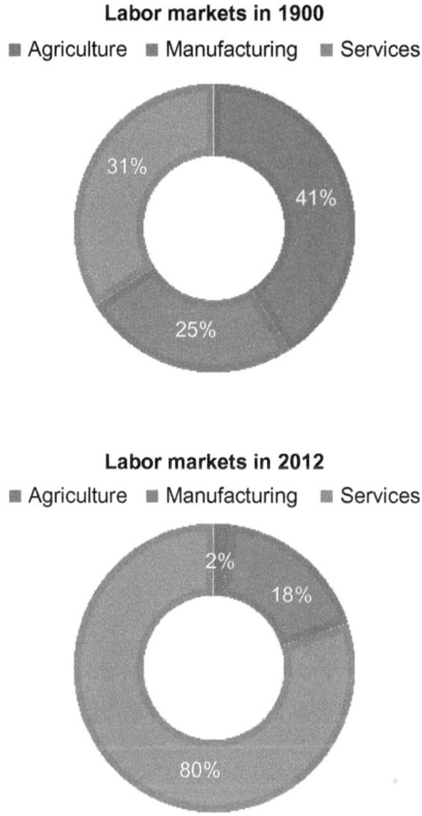

FIGURE 1.1 Pie charts for the labor force in 1900 vs 2012. *Source: Bureau of Labor Statistics.*

composition. This database provides two shifts that are noteworthy of concern. The first is the rise of the manager. In 1970, 5.9% of roles were classified as managers, rising to 14.4% in 2009. The rise of complexity in the workforce has necessitated the growth of managerial level functions. The second trend is the rise of nonroutine cognitive work. Beginning in the 1970s, the labor input of nonroutine cognitive tasks increased sharply relative to routine tasks. In addition, since 1980, virtually all job growth has occurred in occupations which rely on social skills. Social skills are those capabilities which allow employees to get along and coordinate well with others. These skills involve communication, listening, and empathy. Job roles that require high levels of analytical and mathematical reasoning but low levels of social interaction have experienced relatively flat growth. The highest growing jobs are for those employed in *both* high cognitive as well as high social skill occupations. This trend is driving a different type of skill premium in the workplace, one that favors both cognitive *and* social skills.

Research conducted by a leading consulting firm found that an employee having social skills contributes a 10% increase in median hourly earnings. Simply stated, labor markets favor employment and wages when a worker has both cognitive and social skills.

The extent to which a job contains high levels of repetition is negatively correlated with social skills. The more variety one is able to complete within their role, the greater opportunity to acquire *new* knowledge. Routine work does not require complex problem solving or creativity, which often results in lower investments in one's education. Therefore, technology continues to upend workers who do not have the right blend of problem solving, creativity, and social skills. However, further analyses reveals that social skills are complementary to cognitive skills. Both are required in order for one to experience wage growth in today's labor market. This is important as the market shifts from rewarding an either-or type of labor to a laborer that engages in both cognitive and social skills.

Why are we seeing this rise in the value of social skills in highly cognitive functions? Namely, social skills lower the transaction costs of doing business, as workers are able to better coordinate and share information quickly. As firms compete to create new knowledge, the ability of their workforce to work together becomes that much more important to productivity. This is supported by empirical research, which suggest a strong positive relationship between worker productivity and the effectiveness of interpersonal interactions. For example, Borghans, ter Weel, and Weinberg (2008) found that a worker's level of caring and directness with others was positively related to their level of productivity.

As technology costs continue to decline, firms increasingly compete for highly skilled and socially proficient workers. As a result, social skills remain high in demand within the labor market. Employers frequently list teamwork, collaboration, and communication skills as among the most valuable yet hard-to-find qualities of workers (e.g., Casner-Lotto & Barrington, 2006, Jerald, 2009). Therefore, employees purchasing power within the firm rises on account of acquired social skills. Stated simply, in knowledge-intensive environments, worker productivity continues to rely on one's ability to work well with others. Therefore, a manager's ability to attract, retain, and develop social skills throughout their workforce will help shape the firm's competitive advantage. However, as will be discussed in the next chapter, many of our management assumptions regarding talent are built upon an environment that favored unskilled workers on assembly lines. Many organizations are using these principles to manage and motivate their workforce, which may no longer work well in a skilled-bias environment. However, emerging lessons in behavioral economics can inform managers how to better recruit, retain, and develop a highly skilled workforce through the effective management of people.

SPOTLIGHT: Companies Respond to the Demand for Highly Skilled Workers

As the demand for highly skilled laborers continues to grow, how are organizations adapting? AT&T, an organization with approximately 280,000 employees, launched a major learning and developing initiative, *Vision2020*, which seeks to retrain and reskill their low-skilled workers in a digital age. This program is driven by the company's desire to become more agile against technology companies, who are disrupting their business model. Previously, their business model focused on competing in the telecommunications space. However, with new and unexpected competitive entrants, like Google, AT&T is forced to consider new technology applications such as cloud computing and digital networking as core customer solutions. However, much of their current workforce is not skilled in this domain. The *Vision2020* program hopes to close this skills gap by combining a hybrid learning format, offering both online and in-person courses on technology topics. In addition, AT&T's leadership recommends and allows employees to spend 5–10 hours a week in learning activities that help update their skillset. This learning and development program comes squarely from the market forces, which are quickly making routine, low-skilled work obsolete. *Vision2020* allows workers the resources to modernize their skills, benefiting both the firm and employee's marketability. Over time, AT&T seeks to align worker compensation and promotion to an employee's ability to learn (Hardy, 2016). Indeed, as noted in this example, learning will continually be at the forefront of a firm's competitive advantage.

Key Managerial Impact

Labor demands continue to shift in profound ways as technology replaces low-skilled routine work and complements highly skilled workers. As a result, declining computer capital costs create a premium demand for nonroutine cognitive workers. Tacit knowledge is the worker's competitive advantage over technology as explicit knowledge becomes automated. Continuous learning will be the primary focus for workers seeking to outpace technology advancements. This shift requires a reexamination of management practices as they derive from an environment, which favored unskilled routine labor.

1.4 THE VALUE OF INTANGIBLE ASSETS: THE RISE OF INFORMATION AND DATA IN A KNOWLEDGE ECONOMY

Economies shift as technology disrupts traditional ways of doing things. The late 1800s experienced a shift from agriculture to manufacturing. Manufacturing was then disrupted by the services industry in the 1980s. Today, we are in the midst of another shift, which emphasizes the value of intangibles, namely data and information. Today's largest market cap companies are increasingly valued by their ability to capture and manage information and knowledge, rather than by their ability to compete in a limited supply environment for a commoditized end product. Consider the difference just 15 years has made on the top five publicly traded companies by market cap. In 2001, the top five publicly traded companies by market cap were General Electric, Microsoft, Exxon, Citi, and Walmart. This diverse set of organizations represented a variety of industries, such as finance, diversified machinery, and retail, which represented the role of tangibles assets within the market. However, the 2017 top five list consisted almost solely of technology firms, Apple, Alphabet, Microsoft, Amazon, and Berkshire Hathaway (as of February 2017). This is of great economic importance as those companies with the largest market caps are those, in absolute terms, most valued by investors. The ability for firms to manage and grow their intangible assets continues to represent growth opportunities in the marketplace. In 1975, 17% of market value on the S&P consisted of intangible assets, often assets derived from physical inputs or natural resources rather than intangible sources. However, in 2015, 87% of the S&P 500 market value was due to a firm's intangible assets. This is a tremendous firm value shift that requires a new way of management thinking. Today's largest market cap companies are valued by their unique know-how rather than by their ability to compete for a physical resource in a limited supply environment. Market conditions favor those organizations who can capture and translate information into valuable services or products. Stated simply, firm growth can continue as long as firms keep coming up with new ideas to meet changing consumer demands. This is a new economic paradigm that requires a reexamination of both firm value creation and management practices.

While information has always been a valuable part of a firm's value creation process, its prominence has certainly warranted newfound management considerations. In previous industrial ages, work was completed by hand and often physically grueling. During the industrial era, workers would often convene on an assembly line, completing very specialized tasks to produce physical goods. Managers were tasked with "command and control" procedures to enforce that work was done as efficiently as possible. The main goal of the manager was to ensure compliance to a set of rules and procedures. This environment reflected the industrial era where firms competed on their ability to produce quickly and cheaply through capital investments and often the reduction or offshore of labor costs.

However, the knowledge economy disrupts this industrial way of thinking by placing a premium value on data and information—an intangible. Rather than managing workers who compete tangible tasks with their hands, organizations now seek talent who can design, innovate, and create new ideas using technologies. The traditional command and control style that dominated management in the industrial era will not work well in a knowledge-driven economy. The emphasis for managers is on maximizing the diffusion of knowledge and skills rather than establishing efficiencies in physical production. Therefore, growth and value is no longer solely captured by maximizing a firm's physical productivity, but determined by the firm's ability to capture and utilize data and information to compete in today's shifting marketplace.

What makes information unique from a firm's physical capital? Why should intangibles be managed differently from a firm's tangible resources? First and foremost is, information does not experience what economists refer to as *diminishing returns*. Traditional economies follow the assumption that simply adding more of the same capital investment will not lead to growth. Physical capital investments, at some point in time, decrease in their ability to produce valuable output, the more you add or invest. For example, adding a variable factor, such as workers, to a fixed factor, such as land, will eventually lead to less output for every new worker you add. There is only so much land to be toiled before you actually begin to increase the cost of production by adding additional workers. The notion of scarcity is prevalent in neoclassical economics. However, knowledge can be infinitely shared and reused, resulting in a possibility of limitless accumulation of information and ideas. Rather than the conception of scarcity, knowledge lives in the ideology of abundance. This allows knowledge to be subject to *increasing returns* as it is a nonrival good. In addition, some economists have argued that in a knowledge economy, the discovery of information leads to more information, further fueling innovation as knowledge is a nonrival good (Romer, 1990).

However, labor and capital are rival goods. As seen throughout the past couple of industrial revolutions, labor was replaced by capital when it was cost effective to do so. This was brought about by demand from consumers seeking the best possible product at the lowest possible cost. This put tremendous pressure on firms to optimize their overhead costs, with firms opting to replace labor for capital. While capital typically has much larger upfront costs (i.e., costs of purchasing a machine versus the salary of hiring an employee), it can be much cheaper in the long run.

These two components, capital and labor, are defined as rival goods in the resource decision-making process. Consumption of one of these goods prevents simultaneous consumption from another consumer of that same good. However, most information is nonrival as others can simultaneously consume its value. The value of information is sustained by the capital invested into the labor force. Therefore, the quality of a firm's workforce grows increasingly important to produce new knowledge. This creates an entirely new work paradigm for managers. It is no longer about managing a firm's ability to optimize their resource allocation among rival goods experiencing diminishing returns, but rather maximizing the growth of an abundant source of knowledge by investing the right capital alongside their workforce.

This has driven what many refer to as the *knowledge-based economy*. The knowledge-based economy can be defined as the intellectual capabilities and activities that lead to the unique know-how of the production of goods and services. In a knowledge-based economy, information creation and diffusion drives economic growth. Within the knowledge economy, there is greater dependency on intellectual capabilities rather than on physical inputs as knowledge drives the competitive advantage for the firm. Indeed, knowledge, ideas, and productivity are a direct result of the quality of the firm's labor force.

The rise of intangible value by no means diminishes the significance of products or services. Rather, firms that are able to apply intangible knowledge to the utility of their products and services are likely to be rewarded. Consider the following example. When you think of computers, which is the first company to come to mind? Xerox is unlikely at the top of your list. However, it was actually Xerox which first invented the graphical user interface for the computer along with the mouse. Nevertheless, it was Apple and Microsoft who profited from such inventions, not because of the product inventions themselves, but based on their firm's ability to incorporate new ideas and services around these inventions. It was Apple and Microsoft's applied knowledge that fueled their productivity and growth in the decades to come. Or consider the advent of the digital camera. The first digital camera was invented in 1975 by an engineer at Eastman Kodak. However, the firm's lack of capability to respond to this disruptive product, which appeared to compete with their highly profitable film business, left them far behind their competitors. In a knowledge economy, growth does not simply come from being the first to market with an actual invention, but rather by the ability to create and diffuse knowledge throughout the invention's lifecycle. Innovation transforms an invention into something useful for consumers. This usefulness relies on the creation of intellectual capital throughout the firm.

SPOTLIGHT: Dividing Labor into Value-Based Activities: Differentiating Between Highly Cognitive and Routine Tasks

In 2005, the pharmaceutical company Pfizer was under pressure to create new knowledge. Many of their existing patents for their pharmaceutical portfolio were nearing expiration and they were under tremendous pressure to reduce costs. However, leadership teams knew it would take more than simply cutting costs to reposition the company as a leader in the market. New knowledge would not simply come from cost reduction, but through their ability to better leverage their talent. An internal review of their talent strategy revealed that many managers were engaged in too much routine, noncognitive work. Too much of their work was stuck in processing data, filling out administrative work, and completing PowerPoint presentations. Rather than focusing on new knowledge creation, most were simply checking boxes to keep the business running. This was often referred to as the "grunt work" of management. Something

(Continued)

SPOTLIGHT: (Continued)

needed to change, but where would all of the work go? Though many of these noncognitive tasks were not considered core competencies or value-added, they still needed to be completed in order for the firm to be productive. To help address these concerns, the company created a program called PfizerWorks. Through the program, management was able to outsource various aspects of their "grunt work" in order to free up their time to complete more value-added activities. Within the first year of the program, over 60,000 employee hours were freed up and focused on highly cognitive work. Overall, the program was deemed successful and attributed to helping Pfizer create greater value in the market.

Miller & Wedell-Wedellsborg, 2013.

Key Managerial Impact

Within the knowledge-driven economy, value creation focuses less on a manager's decision-making with fixed resources and more on the ability to produce and apply knowledge. Knowledge is distinctly different from tangible assets in two profound ways—it experiences increasing returns and is nonrival. Therefore, knowledge creation and productivity will be a direct result of the quality of a firm's labor force. This requires a shift in industrial style command and control styles of leadership.

1.4.1 People Create Intellectual Capital

The rise of data continues to increase the amount of information available, raising the value of intangibles, while physical assets increasingly become commoditized. For example, every day, 2.5 exabytes of data is produced. Every minute, three million Google search queries take place; 140 million emails are sent; 5 million YouTube videos are viewed; 300,000 Facebook users update their status; 400,000 tweets are posted on Twitter; and Amazon.com sells 25,000 items. As a result, a question many are asking, is data the new oil in today's markets? The increasing emphasis on knowledge creation as the key differentiating factor, rather than physical assets, leads many to think so.

Oil dominated the markets in the 20th century. Yet, it was not the raw material itself, which generated competitive value, but the way in which the oil was refined. Much like oil, data is rather invaluable on its own. However, once data is refined and generated into intellectual capital, it is able to be used as a valuable and differentiating resource. Data, on its own, is much like a commodity, readily available; however, its application is the currency in today's knowledge-driven markets. The competitive advantage for firms resides in the applied insights derived from the data, and the ability of an organization to apply a large amount of readily available data into applicable knowledge largely depends on the quality of its workforce.

Various empirical studies link knowledge creation and firm productivity as a direct workforce outcome. For example, the Organization for Economic Co-Operation and Development (OECD) found that the creation of intellectual assets depends on the skill composition of a nation's labor force (2007). In addition, economic analyses by the Economic Policy Institute (2013) showed that higher productivity was associated with a more educated workforce. They conclude that a well-educated workforce is key to shaping prosperity at the state level. Schwab (2015), founder and chairman of the World Economic Forum, remarked that talent, not capital, is the primary driver of innovation and competitiveness in the 21st century. The growing dependence on a firm's workforce as the key differentiator leads to the skill-biased workforce trend discussed. The question now to consider is, what is intellectual capital and how do people create it in the workplace? We will explore both rational economic thinking as well as newfound behavioral insights to frame a new paradigm of knowledge creation and sharing in the workplace.

As will be discovered, managers must not seek to control the flow of information, but create environments that foster greater connection between individuals and groups. The growing value of knowledge suggests a new management paradigm, which seeks to create the conditions for people to relate to one another in such a way as to continually learn and create knowledge. This, however, requires further examination into individual and collective identities, power dynamics, and social relationships, which traditional economic and management literature has historically failed to account for. Rather than solely focus on knowledge creation as an individual task, this book argues for the enablement of interactions between individuals so that broader networks can form and transmit knowledge throughout the organization. Stated simply, knowledge creation is a complex endeavor, which encompasses the emergence of new ideas when multiple individuals come together and forge new connections. As a result, this will require managers to skillfully participate in relationship bridging across the firm to enhance individual and collective learning (Stacey, 2001).

1.4.2 What is Intellectual Capital?

Jack Welch believed, "an organization's ability to learn, and translate that learning into action rapidly, is the ultimate competitive advantage" (Slater, 1998). Welch recognized that competitive advantage relied less on a firm's tangible resources and more on the ability of people to learn and readily act on information to either respond to market shifts or create something new.

Competitive advantage is obtained by the ability of an organization's talent base to create and apply knowledge in the form of intellectual capital. Intellectual capital helps drive a firm's value creation and differentiation in the knowledge-driven economy. Intellectual capital consists of the organization's talent base, their organizational capital, and their external relational capital (Huang, Luther & Tayler, 2007).

1.4.2.1 Talent

Talent is comprised of employees' education, previous working experiences, and skillsets. Indeed, people drive the creation of intellectual capital. This has lead various researchers to define intellectual capital as "the total sum of everything known by everybody within a business" (Ornek & Ayas, 2015). Other researchers have referred to intellectual capital as the brain power of the organization (Stewart, 1991). However, as will be discovered, capturing knowledge within the firm's talent base is complex. Much of what is valuable to the firm is hard to transfer from and between individuals. Unlocking the expertise of an individual requires extensive interpersonal contact, consistent interactions, and ultimately trust (Goffin & Koners, 2011). Social interaction is a necessary component of effective knowledge transfer in the workplace. Ghoshal and Bartlett (1990) assert that business success or failure depends on how well individuals are able to share their expertise, learning, and resources across networks. As Simon (1991) remarked, knowledge is not given to the firm just because smart employees walk into the doors. Rather, knowledge must be actively sought out and acquired through effective management and a deep understanding of the social dynamics at work. Knowledge sharing is an inherently social process. Stacey (2001) referred to this as a complex response of relating to one another in order to share and create new knowledge. Therefore, intellectual capital creation derives and depends on relational contracts in the workplace, which will be further discussed throughout this book.

1.4.2.2 Organizational Capital

Organizational capital is the collection of intellectual assets that reside within the firm. These include the collection of intellectual property, such as patents, copyrights, trade secrets, and information technology systems. Organizational capital also includes the operating norms, philosophies, and culture which drives the business operations. Some researchers also refer to this as structural capital—or the internal environmental factors, which allow intellectual assets to be created and shared more efficiency. The value of these assets has increased over the past two decades with a significant increase in the filing of patents and trademarks (OECD, 2007). Often firms seek to develop their intellectual property through development of their talent base or externally acquire through a merger or buyout. The level of merger and acquisition activity set a new record in 2015, with over $4.7 trillion in dollars spent on acquiring firms (Picker, 2016). With firms actively seeking new ideas, products and people, mergers, and acquisitions are becoming an increasingly common form of acquiring knowledge in today's market.

1.4.2.3 External Relationships

Lastly, intellectual capital also captures a firm's external relationships within the market. This includes relationships with vendors, customers, and society at large. External relationships can be assessed based on brand perception as well as consumer and vendor loyalty. The stronger the brand perception and loyalty, the higher the prices a firm is able to charge for their products or services. However, this takes much trust and transparency to maintain the premium customer loyalty affords. As a result, firms rely on the growing amount of customer data for information on consumer attitudes, behaviors, and purchasing preferences. These data points become an important way of establishing relationships with potential and existing consumers. This firm's ability to translate these consumer data points into actionable insights largely depends on the quality of the workforce.

Therefore, while intellectual capital is typically categorized into three facets of intangible assets—a firm's talent base, their organizational capital, and external relationships—these all primary derive and are maintained by the quality of the workforce employed by the firm. Intellectual capital creation depends largely on the investment and management of a firm's talent base. As discussed, all else being equal, empirical research suggests it is the management of the intangible, namely people, that explain firm differentiation in the market.

1.4.3 Intellectual Capital Drives Firm Performance and Innovation

The management of intellectual capital within the firm drives overall firm performance and even individual innovative behaviors. For example, Smith et al. (2005) examined technology firms and found the rate of new product entry was dependent upon both the firm's talent base as well as the structural capital that resided within the firm. Firms with higher levels of intellectual capital were also faster to market with new products. Pragogo and Ahmed's (2006) study suggests that higher innovation performance within firms exists when a firm's people are supported with a strong organizational culture of people practices. As this research suggests, a firm's performance and ability to create new knowledge and innovation largely depends on the level of intellectual capital—namely its people and culture.

The benefits of intellectual capital creation extend beyond firm performance. The OECD credits innovative activities as the core driver of global economic progress and well-being (2007). The OECD points to various empirical evidence, which suggests innovation is linked to raising the standard of living at a national level, drives competitiveness at an organizational level, and is a necessary condition for improving individual productivity. In addition, innovative activities often result in lower prices for goods and services and higher wages for workers. Indeed, the economic literature suggests that investments in research and development produce an average of 30% return on investment for the firm (Frontier Economics, 2014). Not only that, but the knowledge spillovers achieved at a societal level are projected to be two to three times as large of a return on investment. The link between innovation, through the creation of intellectual capital, and growth is undisputed in both research and practice.

Key Managerial Impact

The creation of intellectual capital deals squarely with human cognitions. The ability and quality of people's decisions in the workplace precede the level of intellectual capital a firm can expect to generate. The growing emphasis on intellectual capital requires renewed discourse on how managers can create conditions for optimal human decision-making at work.

1.5 BLURRING INDUSTRY LINES: CREATING NEW RULES OF COMPETITION

"Airbnb is the largest hotel chain without owning a hotel room."

Alex Ross

Traditional economic and strategic management thinking assumes that industries are stable. However, today's blurring industry lines ask us to reconsider that assumption. Rather than playing by established rules with minimal disruption to market boundaries, firms are experiencing newfound competition across industry lines. As a result, firms must now focus their attention inward, seeking to create new knowledge and respond to changing customer demands. This is a shift in thinking as management decision-making historically relied on external cues.

Take for example a traditionally straightforward and well-defined industry, hospitality. Firms compete for customers based on their inventory of physical locations, amenities, price, and loyalty programs. It is an industry that was well established and often experienced mergers and acquisitions within its own boundaries (i.e., Marriott acquiring the Starwood chain). The real threat to larger firms was the possibility of acquisition by more efficient firms within the market. However, that threat now pales in comparison to the rise of new entrants coming from a completely different sector, namely technology. No longer is the hospitality industry confined to the physical location of hotels, but rather includes technology platforms, which connect customers with other individual homeowners. One of the largest disruptors to a well-established industry does not even own an actual hotel room.

Therefore, markets today can be best described as concentrate, disperse, and imperfect (Ross, 2016). They are concentrated in that many transactions are now redirected through a small number of technology platforms. However, they are dispersed as economic transactions have shifted from physical locations toward individual people which are connected through online platforms. They are imperfect because firms are no longer competing over identical goods. Airbnb showcases this market phenomenon by requiring all transactions to originate from a single technological platform, yet connecting customers with individuals located throughout the world. In addition, Airbnb competes on the basis of technology connectivity with the customer, rather than through physical inventory. This requires existing firms to focus less on establishing competitive advantage through increasing the quality of a product or even decreasing price, but rather by reestablishing the way it utilizes technology to connect with the customer. The hospitality industry, which was traditionally bounded by firms' abilities to compete over a product (hotel inventory) or service (loyalty program), no longer competes within that bound. Disruption, in the form of technology, has shifted consumer preferences toward peer-sharing, which completely transforms the hospitality market.

The question is, how did an entire industry fail to anticipate this large disruption to their market? A VP at a large hotel chain remarked, "We never foresaw our customers preferring to stay at stranger's home. This consumer preference shift completely blindsided us. In addition, we failed to have the technology infrastructure in place to quickly react."

Traditional strategic management decision-making derives from the assumption of stable external environments, which fails to account for blurring industry lines. This assumes that firms compete within well-defined boundaries and that markets will reward the most productive firm. Therefore, strategy is about positioning a firm's products within a particular industry, whereby all players play by the same rules. As a result, a firm's activities drive their core competencies and competitive advantage. This is accomplished by firms processing the information they receive from their external environment and translating it into an internal strategy. It can be classified as an outside-in approach to strategic formulation. The external markets direct the information gathering process.

However, this strategy assumes stable markets and industries, which technology entrants have proven false. The increase in globalization, the access to profound amounts of information, as well as the lack of stability creates boundary-less industries. These conditions often give new entrants into the market a competitive advantage. This also poses challenges to existing firms who are scanning their external environment to form their strategy. Rather, the blurring industry lines require firms to create knowledge from the inside and use this newfound knowledge to recreate their environments. Effective firm strategy now focuses on the process of creating and processing knowledge internally, as the instability of industry boundaries no longer provide the accurate external cues that can help inform a firm' competitive advantage. Rather than beginning with a firm's activities, which is common in most strategic planning, managers will now need to consider their firm's access and ability to process and form new knowledge. Once again, this hinges upon the quality of a firm's workforce (Figure 1.2).

The role of management will shift from positioning a firm relative to their environment cues to one relative to their ability to effectively process data and form new knowledge. This will require assessing their own internal talent and technological resources to determine how to best create new knowledge, seeking to disrupt traditional industry boundary lines. This often will result in utilizing the principles of *design thinking*, which positions the firm's outcomes around customers, rather than products or services. Design thinking begins with empathizing with a consumer's end state rather than scanning the external environment. Design thinking is contrasted with traditional strategic management decision-making in Figure 1.2. However, managers will need access to consumer data to effectively identify and respond to consumer needs. The call for consumer-driven thinking as the beginning point of strategy began as early as 1999 when Hagel and Davidson sensed a major market shift. Rather than the producers of goods and services having the power, it was the consumer who now had the power within the market. The authors argued that consumer data and information is a strong currency in the knowledge-driven economy and that it is the consumer who has the

Traditional Strategic Management

- An excerise of planning
- Organization centric
- Begins strategy with statements
- Orginates with top-down thinking
- Environmental constraints explored
- Goal driven–planning and controlling resources

Design Thinking

- An exercise of creating
- Human centric
- Begins strategy with questions
- Orginates with bottom-up user experiences
- Possibilities explored
- Hypothesis driven–tests, experiments, learns

FIGURE 1.2 Strategic management vs design thinking.

power to give or withhold it to the organization. A consumer becomes a producer and consumer at the same time with the exchange of their information. The challenge for firm management within this environment is the acquisition of consumer data, which often results after establishing trust with the consumer. Managers today will increasingly be called upon as design architects seeking to disrupt their business model by acquiring new sources of consumer knowledge by not only developing a quality workforce, but by also acknowledging the power of the consumer.

Key Managerial Impact

Management will continue to face mounting pressure to look beyond their industry lines and seek to position their firm around evolving customer outcomes. Strategy will increasingly rely on a firm's ability to look inward to disrupt existing boundaries by acquiring consumer data. As a result, managers will have to rely less on external cues and more on the quality of its people and data to create new knowledge and meet consumer demands.

1.6 NEW FORMS OF EMPLOYMENT: A CONTINUUM OF LABOR REDEFINES SOCIAL CONTRACTS

Labor markets are not immune to these discussed market shifts. A continuum of employment, which reconsiders the relationship between employer and employee, is on the rise. A contract or contingent workforce can be defined as nonstandard work arrangements between employer–employee. These nonstandard arrangements come in the form of temporary, contract, or other nonstandard forms of employment. This is type of work is also referred to as the gig economy, sharing economy and on-demand workforce. The nonstandard employment agreement involves a changing discourse in the nature of the social contract between employee and employer. In general, a *social contract* is defined as surrendering a part of individual freedom in exchange for the protection of rights. The idea of a social contract explains how the collective forms together to create a society, whereby each individual voluntary rescinds rights in exchange of the collective good. The key to a successful social contract relies on the sense of reciprocity. Individuals agree to work toward the common good, while the collective entity agrees to provide goods back to individuals. Traditionally, a social contract from an employer to an employee would offer security and a relatively predictable future in exchange for long-term employment. Employee commitment and loyalty derived from the ability of the firm to provide the worker a financially secure future in form of pensions, premium benefits, and increased wages. However, in the contingent workforce model, employee commitment will no longer derive from the safeguards employers offer. Management will have to rely increasingly on other forms of motivation to ensure quality of work. The value proposition of the employee–employer relationship is moving from security toward flexibility.

The idea of outsourcing work is in and of itself not novel. Organizations have historically sought to decrease their labor wages for noncore work functions. This included the move to many offshore locations or simply outsourcing to third-party services for these noncore tasks. Traditionally, this included services such as janitorial, administrative, and information technology support. However, the rise of the knowledge economy is giving rise to organizations increasingly looking toward contract workers for noncore functions, including knowledge-intensive tasks. The decreasing transaction costs of finding skilled labor, due to technology advancements, may explain the rise of the contingent workforce. Indeed, technology has reduced the barriers of entry as well as reduced costs in the talent acquisition process.

Traditionally, firms are built upon the notion that collective efforts make sense as a way to decrease the transaction costs of production. The costs of organizing internally makes sense when the costs of purchase is less than the market. However, the rise of contingent work has challenged these traditional forms of organizing work. This has profound implications for the division of labor within firms. Both the growing demand and supply of contingent workers is causing organizations to shift from role-based to skill-based work. Rather than outsourcing work to other organizations, increasingly firms are outsourcing work to individuals in the forms of contracts. Research suggests that contract work has risen to 16% of the workforce, up from 10% in 2005 (Sussman & Zumbrun, 2016). Some estimate that large organizations are contracting up 20–50% of their workforce. The rise of organizing work around contingent workers comes with both advantages and disadvantages to corporations and individuals as shown in Figure 1.3.

The compelling advantage to both organizations and individuals is the ability to tap underused capacity. This can come in the form of intangible assets, such as time, or tangible, such as a car or house space. This often leads to lower transaction costs as the worker simply uses capacity which would otherwise be wasted. In addition, organizations are able to have

Advantages	Disadvantages
Ability to tap into underused capacity	Lack of loyalty (i.e., many ride-sharing drivers work for both Uber and Lyft)
Lowers transaction costs	Certain type of contingent work can result in lower output quality
Provides agility and flexibility to both employer and employee	Lack of worker benefits, job protection, and stability
Certain types of contract workers report higher satisfaction	Can result in lower psychological ownership towards organization

FIGURE 1.3 The advantages and disadvantages of an alternative work arrangement.

greater control over their fixed labor costs, as contract-based work can flex according to market demands. However, this can result in a lack of loyalty toward the organization. An example can be found in the talent contract model transforming the transportation industry. Many drivers exploit their freedom by driving for both Uber and Lyft. There is little loyalty to the organization, but rather to their own interest. In addition, some organizations have struggled with maintaining a standard of quality with their contract workforce. Therefore, when a competitive advantage can be derived, many leaders rely on in-house talent to perform the tasks. This is likely due to the low psychological ownership that exists in the contingent workforce model. *Psychological ownership* is the feeling of ownership that an employee has toward an organization. Feelings of psychological ownership have been linked to higher levels of job satisfaction, employee engagement, and innovative behaviors. The challenge facing many managers is motivating a part of their workforce that may reside off the company's balance sheet. Yet, this continues to point toward a rise in specialization, where both individuals and firms devote their time and resources toward their core strengths. This in many ways allows new organizations to form, raise capital, and hire contingent workers to perform tasks that align to their individual strengths. Likewise, it allows organizations to focus their management energies toward their critical core functions.

Key Managerial Impact

The changing nature of employment continues to shift the role of manager within the firm from one who commands and controls resources to one who has to exert influence, often informally, to accomplish the required task at hand. Managers will have to reconsider the hiring, performance management, and development of a continuum of workers who come with different needs, preferences, and motivations.

1.7 REORGANIZING THE FIRM AROUND DIVISIONS OF LABOR

As technology disrupted the labor markets for the agriculture and then industrial era, technology continues to disrupt the labor markets and the way organizations divide work in a knowledge-driven economy. As many organizational leaders focus their attention and efforts to the implementation of new technologies, there is a potentially more important factor central to productivity—the way people respond and organize work around technology advancements. This is what Charles Babbage, an engineer and management philosopher, focused on during Britain's transformation from an agriculture to an industrial economy. While many other management theorist at the time considered the role of machinery as increasing productivity within the firm, Babbage instead focused on the people within the factory. Babbage observed a hidden economy underlying the visible industrial era, "the domestic economy of the factory." The domestic economy, which consisted of the management practices, people issues, and social relations, were critical to understanding the disruptive technologies transforming an entire nation's economy. Babbage advocated that productivity hinged upon the worker's response to the disruptive technologies and not necessarily the technologies themselves. A focus on the domestic economy remains a concern for today's managers facing similar, if not arguably, greater technology disruption.

The domestic economy of the firm considers the division of labor, a construct advocated for by Smith (1776) in *Wealth of Nations.* The division of labor remains central to many organizational behavior theories. Many people doing a simple and specialized task would yield much greater productivity than one single worker completing a project from start to finish. Smith famously noted that one worker could only produce one pin a day when completing the entirety of the process. However, dividing the making of a pin across several subset tasks would tremendously increase output. Yet, Babbage's thinking questioned whether Smith's original division of labor was all that was needed to understand productivity power. Could simply dividing small tasks across a labor force result in greater productivity power? Babbage's work emphasized that technology and even specialized and efficient workers did not guarantee effective firm productivity. Instead, it was the practice of effective management, or the domestic economy of the firm, which drove productivity.

Increasing specialization through the division of labor relies on the interdependency of people to complete work. Interdependency is amplified and put to the forefront of a knowledge-driven economy, where work is increasingly divided by expertise rather than by task. This is what Babbage referred to as the *division of knowledge*. A firm's long-term survival rests upon the effective passing of knowledge from one person to another within the firm. In addition, highly cognitive roles with little routine will struggle to find the same productivity power by dividing labor into simple routine subsets. Complexity challenges the simple learning by doing mindset of labor. Therefore, firms are responding to this pressure of knowledge flow by reorganizing the firm in two distinct ways that influence the role of the manager: a) the reduction of formal hierarchy and b) the increase in coordinated expertise through team-based structures.

1.7.1 Reduced Hierarchy

Leadership has always been at the forefront of the theory of the firm. Indeed, Chandler's (1977) work argued that a firm only exists with hierarchy. The costs of coordination is too high without a form of leadership structure.

Therefore, the perception of leadership in the firm can be a significant driver of financial valuation (Van Reenen, 2015). However, the discussed changing market dynamics are driving organizations to reconsider their formalized hierarchical structures. Do hierarchies drive agility and information flow in today's markets? Research suggests that hierarchies work well under simple and repetitive work conditions. When cognitions are not at the forefront of work, hierarchies help ensure consistent, predictable, and controllable results. However, in today's knowledge-driven economy, where cognitions are at the forefront of work, we see organizational redesign on the rise, namely in the form of "flatter" firms. Research finds that hierarchies actually mitigate effective information flow and worker satisfaction in highly ambiguous and complex environments. Rather than effectively coordinating communication among teams, research has found a negative effect between steep hierarchies and complex coordination.

The reduced form of hierarchies within firms can in part be explained by the increase in information technology. Milgrom and Roberts (1990) advocated for a reduction in hierarchical structure in organizations with the onset of information technologies. Technologies could now do some of the entry-level supervisory work, thus lessening the necessity of multiple layers of management to control agency costs. The rise of information technologies fundamentally upends the role of the traditional manager within a firm. Rather than relying on formalized authoritative measures to carry out the purpose of the firm, a manager must increasingly rely on informal mechanisms to influence workers to achieve the firm's mission. However, this also offers newfound opportunities to reestablish the working relationship between a manager and employee. One that was historically built upon compliance and adherence to process and rules, and can be renegotiated to one that cocreates based on the principles of trust.

1.7.2 Coordinated Expertise: Team Structures

A firm's existence requires dividing the collective effort of many into specialized parts to outperform the individual. Many firms are turning to the division of knowledge first to divide work. As a result, the emphasis is on individual strengths and their investment in education. However, this individual skill may render useless unless surrounded by complementary individuals. Therefore, many organizations are turning to team structures to complement their workers' efforts. Forming teams around skills and strengths allows the organization to remain flexible and agile to changing demands. In addition, team-based structures allow for decentralized decision-making and increasing autonomy, which in theory should allow for greater decision-making capacity, leading to more meaningful outcomes. However, this in actuality depends on how well workers work together. Therefore, this rise in flexible team structures makes the rise of social skills all the more important. Teams that are able to effectively work together are linked to higher levels of productivity, problem solving, and creativity. However, as will be discussed later, teams can also give rise to biases and groupthink, which actually mitigate the very thing teams are intended to do.

Some researchers see this team-based structure as analogous to the way Hollywood produces movies. Specialized skillset coming together in a team structure to create new knowledge and experiences is a model the entertainment industry has relied upon for decades. Dividing work among experts allows for agile teams who can easily form and dissolve as work necessitates. With each person bringing a unique perspective creativity often abounds. However, this puts newfound consideration on trust and psychological safety as one considers the domestic economy of the firm. Teams will increasingly be asked to work with outside experts or leverage workers across a continuum of employment, which will put the team in a constant state of forming. Creativity hinges on the trust the team has established among its members.

The rise of teams requires a mindset shift from one of individual consideration to one of collective concern. One's expertise can only be as good as the complementary skills coordinated around them. The role of the manager will increasingly be called upon to be as a social supporter and coordinator of complex knowledge transfer. This will require managers to reconsider existing performance management systems and learning mechanisms that today favor the individual and instead will need to also consider and support team performance. The rise of teams offers profound opportunities to leverage a division of knowledge; however, this also requires greater levels of trust and psychological safety among members coordinating a flow of knowledge.

Researchers at MIT studied various networks and structures for the effective flow of communication to solve a problem. In particular, the researchers were interested in the speed and accuracy the different network structures would have on information flow for problem solving. Mathematically, it was hypothesized that the circle-shaped structure would be the most effective. Removing layers should logically allow for a continuous and circular flow of information. However, and maybe to no surprise to individuals working in flat organizations, it was found that it was a star-shaped network that was most effective. The star-shaped network served as the most efficient structure for information to flow quickly and more accurately to solve problems. The researchers conclude that people require an integrator to help process the flow of complex information, but also require a short distance to that integrator. The integrator serves as a bridge to novel information coming in from another network. The integrator is able to quickly connect two relatively weak bonds by forming relationships between them (Figure 1.4).

Thus, a strong higher hieratical network was less effective than the star shaped, where participants were only one or two nodes removed from the

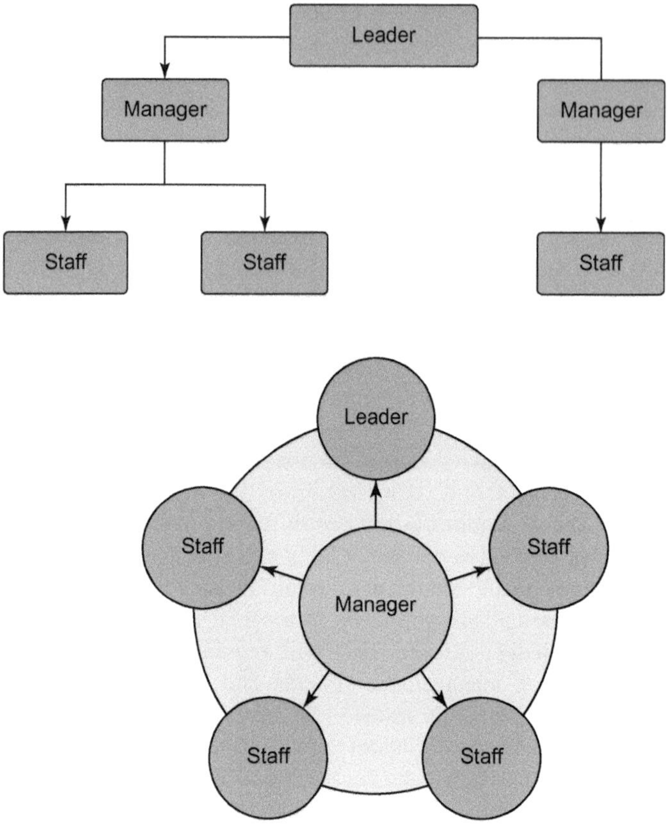

FIGURE 1.4 Layers of hierarchy restricts information flow compared to a star shape network.

center. As will be discovered throughout the book, the role of the manager shifts from one who seeks to control information to one who seeks to integrate the right people to each other.

In addition, multiple research studies show that diversity is a necessary component to knowledge creation within social networks. For example, very strong social bonds, which do not contain much diversity, often become victim to polarization and groupthink. The individual is not exposed to enough cognitively diverse information, and therefore, their access to novel information is weak. In fact, researchers find it is our weakest bonds, which promise the most access to novel thinking (Granovetter, 1973; Burt, 1992). These weak bonds are connected to others outside of one's network, and thus provide additional sources of information otherwise not found within one's network. The role of the manager is to bridge connections between various social networks to form links of new information flows. The connector is referred to as a *tertius gaudens*—a person who benefits from connecting two unrelated and even conflicting parties together. In fact, research shows that innovation often stems when two unconnected ideas come together. Johansson (2004) referred to this as the "Medci effect," which notes how innovation requires multiple and often distinct bodies of knowledge to intercept in order for new ideas to form. Within this line of research, the key to success depends on the combination and quality of diverse collaborations of networks within organizations coming together to create something that neither discipline could create on their own. A manager will increasingly be sought after to be the integrator and connect two unlikely people or ideas together to create intellectual capital in the firm.

Key Managerial Impact

Reorganization of the firm often removes the power and formality traditionally held by managers in strong hierarchical environments. No longer having to rely on authority granted by a chain of command, weakening ability to leverage extrinsic motivators and less opportunity to promote individual consideration requires managers to seek out newfound ways to manage an increasingly connected and disperse workforce. In addition, the manager will be sought after as key integrator, connecting both people and ideas together, to create intellectual capital in the firm.

1.8 CONCLUSION

While these discussed trends will continue to challenge existing firms in the market, a question that has puzzled economist is why are there performance difference in seemingly similar organizations? Why will some thrive under these imperfect market conditions, while others will struggle to keep their productivity either in equilibrium with the market, or even worse fall behind? Strategists have often argued it on account of differences in organizational capabilities, specifically deriving from management of the firm that differentiate seemingly similar firms (Gibbons & Henderson, 2012). Economists also agree that management practices are instrumental in understanding a firm's productivity (Bloom, Sadun, & Van Reena, 2014). Therefore, understanding how the role of management is transformed by the discussed market forces is of utmost importance.

In particular, the declining costs of technology give rise to the value of intangible assets, manifested through a firm's ability to manage their tacit knowledge. Rather than competing on products and services, organizations increasingly compete around their ability to manage information and knowledge. Traditional industry lines are thus disrupted by the entrance of nimble technology companies, disrupting existing firms' business models and giving more power to the consumer. This causes the organization to restructure around teams and seek newfound forms of employment in order to create new knowledge within the firm. As a result, the labor markets reward those workers with high cognitive and social skillsets (Figure 1.5).

These profound market shifts require a reexamination of management practices. As will be discussed later chapters, management practices derive from a time and place that no longer resemble today's organization or worker.

Changing Force	Organizational Consideration	Key Managerial Impact
Decreasing costs of technology	Leads to a skills-biased workforce	A reexamination of management practices as they derive from an environment, which favored unskilled routine labor. Continuous learning will be the primary focus for workers seeking to outpace technology advancements.
The rise of intangible assets on company's balance sheets	Increases the value of data and knowledge management, which requires a relentless pursuit of intellectual capital	Value creation will focus on a manager's ability to produce and apply knowledge. Knowledge creation and productivity will be a direct result of the quality of a firm's labor force. This requires a shift in industrial style command and control styles of leadership.
Blurring industry lines	New forms of disruption and competition arises	Management will continue to face mounting pressure to look beyond their industry lines and seek to position their firm around customer outcomes. Managers will have to rely less on external cues and more on the quality of its data and talent to meet these demands.
New forms of employment (i.e., gig economy)	Changing social contract between employee and employer	Shifts the role of manager from one who commands and controls resources to one who has to exert influence, often informally, to accomplish the required task at hand. Mangers will have to reconsider the hiring, performance management, and development of a continuum of workers who come with different needs, interests, and motivations.
Firm reorganization on the rise	Reduced hierarchy and more reliance on teams	No longer having to rely on chain of command authority, weakening ability to leverage extrinsic motivators, and less opportunity to promote individual consideration requires managers to seek out newfound ways to manage an increasingly shifting workforce.

FIGURE 1.5 The changing nature of work.

Many of our management assumptions were founded in an environment that favored the unskilled routine laborer. Firms sought to compete based on price and efficiency with managers seeking to control agency costs. However, market shifts are challenging some of our most commonly held assumptions around management. Indeed, the entire paradigm of management must come under a critical lens as todays' markets favor firms who are able to motivate, train, and develop a workforce, which creates new knowledge alongside technology investments. Growth and productivity are still a primary concern for the firm, but sustainable growth will focus on how well a manager can diffuse knowledge and skills by the development of a quality workforce.

REFERENCES

Berger, N., & Fisher, P. (2013). *A well-educated workforce is key to state prosperity. Economic Policy Institute*. Available from http://www.epi.org/publication/states-education-productivity-growth-foundations/.

Bloom, N., Sadun, R., & Van Reena, J. (2014). Management as technology? Available from http://cep.lse.ac.uk/textonly/_new/staff/vanreenen/pdf/2015aea_MAT.pdf.

Borghans, L., ter Weel, B., & Weinberg, B. (2008). Interpersonal styles and labor market outcomes. *Journal of Human Resources, 43*(4), 815–858.

Burt, R. S. (1992). *Structural holes*. Cambridge: Harvard University Press.

Casner-Lotto, J. and Barrington, L.: 2006, Are they really ready to work? Employers' perspectives on the basic knowledge and applied skills of new entrants to the 21st century us workforce., Report, Partnership for 21st Century Skills.

Chandler, A. (1977). *The visible hand: The managerial revolution in American business*. Harvard University Press.

Doms, M., Dunne, T., & Troske, K. (1997). Workers, wages and technology. *Quarterly Journal of Economics, 112*, 253–290.

Economist, April 7, 2011, p. 78.

Frey, C., & Osborne, M. (2013). The future of employment: How susceptible are jobs to computerization? *Technological Forecasting and Social Change, 114*.

Frontier Economics. (2014). Rates of return to investment in science and innovation. Retrieved from https://www.frontier-economics.com/documents/2014/07/rates-of-return-to-investment-in-science-and-innovation.pdf.

Ghoshal, S., & Bartlett, C. A. (1990). The multinational corporation as an inter organizational network. *The Academy of Management Review, 15*(4), 603–625.

Gibbons, R., & Henderson, R. (2012). Relational constructs and organizational capabilities. *Organizational Science, Vol 23*(5), 1350–1364.

Gittleson, K. (2012). Can A Company Live Forever? *BBC News*.

Goffin, K., & Koners, U. (2011). Tacit knowledge, lessons learnt, and new product development. *Journal of Product Innovation Management, 28*, 300–318.

Gordon, R.J. (2016). The rise and fall of American growth: the U.S. standard of living since the Civil War.

Granovetter, M. S. (1973). *The strength of weak ties, American Journal of Sociology, 78*(6), 1360–1380.

Huang, C. C., Luther, R., & Tayles, M. (2007). An evidence-based taxonomy of intellectual capital. *Journal of Intellectual Capital, 8*(3), 386–408.

Hardy, Q. (2016). Gearing up for the cloud, AT&T tells its workers: Adapt, or else. *New York Times*.

Jerald, C.D. (2009). Defining a 21st century education, Report, Center for Public Education.

Johansson, F. (2004). *The Medici Effect*. Cambridge, MA: Harvard Business Publishing.

Kane, G., Palmer, D., Phillips, A., Kiron, D., Buckley, N. (2015). Digital transformation: Becoming a digitally mature enterprise. MIT Sloan Management Review.

Levy, A. B. (2000). Errata in implicit multifunction theorems for the sensitivity analysis of variational conditions. *Mathematical Programming*, *86*, 439–441.

Link, A. N., & Siegel, D. S. (2007). *Innovation, entrepreneurship and technological change*. Oxford University Press.

Lorenz, E. (1963). Deterministic nonperiodic flow. *Journal of the Atmospheric Sciences*, *20*, 130–141.

Milgrom, P., & Roberts, J. (1990). Rationalizability learning and equilibrium in games with strategic complementaries. *Econometrica*, *Vol 58*(6), 1255–1277.

Miller, P., & Wedell-Wedellsborg, T. (2013). *The case for stealth innovation*. Harvard Business Review.

Mintzberg, H. (1973). *The nature of managerial work*. New York: Harper & Row.

Moore, G. (1975). Progress in Digital Integrated Electronics. *IEEE, IEDM Tech Digest*, 11–13.

Nelson, R., & Phelps, E. (1966). Investment in humans, technological diffusion and economic growth. *The American Economic Review*, *Vol. 56*(No. 1/2), 69–75.

Organisation for Economic Co-Operation and Development (OECD) (2015), Innovation and growth: Rationale for an innovation strategy. Retrieved from http://www.oecd.org/sti/inno/39374789.pdf.

Ornek, A. S., & Ayas, S. (2015). The relationships between intellectual capital, innovative work behavior and business performance reflection. *Procedia - Social and Behavioral Sciences*, *195*, 1397–1395.

Picker, L. (2016). A standout year for deals, in volume and complexity. The New York Times, DealBook. Retrieved from https://www.nytimes.com/2016/01/04/business/dealbook/a-standout-year-for-deals-in-volume-and-complexity.html.

Piketty, T. (2014). *Capital in the 21st Century* (p. 214) United States: Belknap Press.

Prajogo, D. I., & Ahmed, P. K. (2006). Relationships between innovation stimulus, innovation capacity, and innovation performance. *R&D Management*, *36*, 499–515.

Romer, P. (1990). Endogenous technological change. *Journal of Political Economy*, *98*(5), 71–102.

Ross, A. (2016). *The industries of the future*. Simon & Schuster.

Schumpeter, J. (1934). *The theory of economic development: An inquiry into profits, capital, credit, interest and the business cycle*. New Brunswick: Transaction Publishers.

Schwab, K. (2015). *The Human Capital Report*. World Economic Forum. Available from http://www3.weforum.org/docs/WEF_Human_Capital_Report_2015.pdf, preface.

Simon, H. (1991). *Administrative Behavior, 4th ed*. New York, NY: Free Press.

Slater, R. (1998). *Jack Welch & The G.E. Way: Management Insights and Leadership*, 12.

Smith, A. (1776). *Wealth of nations*. William Strahan, Thomas Cadell.

Smith, K. G., Collins, C. J., & Clark, K. D. (2005). Existing knowledge, knowledge creation capability, and the rate of new product introduction in high-technology firms. *Academy of Management Journal*, *48*(2), 346–357.

Solow, R. (1987). We'd better watch out. *New York Times Book Review*, 36, July 12 1987.

Stacey, R. (2001). *Complex responsive processes in organizations: Learning and knowledge creation*. New York, NY: Routledge.

Stewart, A.T. (1991). "Brainpower: Intellectual Capital is Becoming Corporate America's Most Valuable Asset and Can Be Its Sharpest Competitive Weapon. The Challenge is To Find What You Have – And Use It." Fortune. Available from http://money.cnn.com/magazines/fortune/fortune_archive/1991/06/03/75096/ access date: 08.02.2015.

Sussman, A. L., & Zumbrun, J. (2016). Contract workforce outpaces growth in Silicon-Valley style gig jobs. *Wall Street Journal.*

Syverson, C. (2011). What determines productivity? *Journal of Economic Literature, 49*(2), 326–365. Available from https://doi.org/10.1257/jel.49.2.326.

Tomo, O. (2015). Annual study of intangible asset market value from Ocean Tomo. *Web.*

Van Reenen, J. (2015). The economic importance of good management. *MIT. Podcast.* Available from http://ide.mit.edu/news-events-media/podcasts/ef2-economic-importance-good-management.

Violante, G. (2016). Skill-biased technical change. The New Palgrave Dictionary of Economics, 2nd Edition. Retrieved from http://www.econ.nyu.edu/user/violante/Books/sbtc_january16.pdf.

FURTHER READING

Davenport, T., & Rosner, D. (2016). November 11 *Decoding the path to purchase: Using autonomous analytics for customer mapping*. Deloitte University Press.

Hagel, J., & Singer, M. (1999). *Net worth: Shaping markets when customer make the rules.* Harvard Business Review Press.

Khoso, M. (2016). How much data is produced every day? *Northeastern Analytics Trends.* Available from http://www.northeastern.edu/levelblog/2016/05/13/how-much-data-produced-every-day/.

Weber, L. (2017). The end of employees. *The Wall Street Journal.*

Chapter 2

Rational Economics and the Administrative Theory of Management

2.1 DO WE STILL NEED MANAGERS?

As markets continue to shift and firms reorganize their talent models, the role of the manager is challenged. Some have argued that management is no longer needed as employees evolve into highly skilled workers. This is based on the idea that highly skilled workers perform best under the guise of self-management, rather than through traditional management structures (Hamel, 2011). There has been enough doubt cast upon the role of the traditional manager that a leading technology firm, Google, attempted to do away with it all together. Many of the organization's leaders were educated in the principles of engineering and exhibited a traditional command and control approach to leadership. The manager was present simply to ensure a job was accomplished and met all expectations. In 2002, Google, then a relatively small startup, deemed the management function as stifling innovation, creativity, and knowledge transfer. There was little time nor value attributed to the more human aspects of leadership, such as listening to employee concerns and developing career interests. As a result, Google decided to run a small experiment within a function of their organization by removing the management function completely and simply allowed teams to supervise themselves. Existing managers were then repurposed into individual contributors and everyone was seen as an equal in decision-making. Highly skilled workers can simply manage themselves, right?

The answer appears to be no, at least in large organizations. The longevity of the experiment lasted mere months before collapsing on itself. The problem? Employees did not know where to go for career advice, got lost navigating the firm, and could not figure out how to get an approval or even seek simple feedback on a project. Senior leaders, including the CEO, Larry Page, were bogged down with endless questions from employees on project approvals or needing expertise on a particular problem that would have historically been solved by a manager. There was no longer a filter between the organization's senior leaders and staff. A simple question or decision left

How Behavioral Economics Influences Management Decision-Making.
DOI: https://doi.org/10.1016/B978-0-12-813531-0.00002-9

employees bumping into each other seeking direction in every which way. The autonomy was too much to handle in a complex firm. The experiment concluded that there was an undeniable need for managers in order for the firm to be productive, even in highly skilled, knowledge-based organizations (Garvin, 2013). However, an examination into the way managers lead in the workplace required further investigation in a knowledge-driven and skills-biased environment. Is management still a function that should seek to command and control resources, or should it behave differently in light of today's markets that value intellectual capital?

Intellectual capital is all about people—the way they think, act, and solve problems together at work. Managers are increasingly called upon to create and develop people throughout the organization. The role of the manager has evolved from one that once simply administrated resources, often physical and financial assets, to one that must now coach and develop talent within the organization. This is a monumental shift in what organizations expect managers to do. The function of administrating resources through the activities of command and control may be outdated, but the role of a manager guiding people in a firm is certainly not. Yet, many top MBA programs are still built upon the activities of planning, controlling, directing, and organizing tangible resources. While managers must still occupy part of their time administrating workflows, many have argued that intellectual capital cannot be accomplished through this style of management (Stacey, 2001). Rather, recent research by Harvard suggests that managers who execute well on processes *and* talent management, such as crafting employee value propositions, setting clear and challenging goals, developing talent, and actively engaging in performance management activities, are outperforming their peers (Sadun, Bloom, & Van Reenen, 2017). Their research found the most notable performance differences in how many patents per employee were filled, the level of output change year over year, expenditures in research and development, as well as overall productivity and profits. The researchers conclude with the following: "If the world has really entered a "new normal" of low-productivity growth, as Robert Gordon and others have argued, pushing managerial capital up a level could be the best route out of performance doldrums" (p. 122). Therefore, management can be a key differentiating factor for companies operating in knowledge-driven economies.

As a result, it is argued that *people* may be one of the world's most underutilized resources in today's economy (Wartzman, 2017). Newfound attention is required on understanding how people think and behave at work, as intellectual capital, in part, depends on the effectiveness of employee's cognitions. The question is, how do people make decisions at work? What motivates employees to act in the best interest of the organization? Do management assumptions regarding human nature even matter at work? These questions and more will be explored within this chapter stemming from the dominant rational economic perspective. This viewpoint illuminates why the majority of management theory today is built upon the mitigation of agency costs within firms whose primary pursuit is shareholder wealth maximization. Furthermore, this type of management style and corresponding assumptions will be critiqued in light of the profound opportunities managers have in developing intellectual capital through the growth of their people at work.

2.2 THE SELF-FULFILLING NATURE OF SOCIAL SCIENCE THEORIES IN MANAGEMENT

> *"Nothing is more fundamental in setting our research agenda and informing our research methods than our view of the nature of human beings whose behaviors we are studying...It makes a difference to research, but it also makes a difference for the proper design of institutions"*
>
> Simon, 1985, p. 303.

The reality is the theory of management is one of social, psychological, and economic study. However, most of today's management theories derive from purely rational economic inquiry. This only reinforces the belief that people will behave in rational and self-interested ways. In addition, it presumes that the firm's sole existence is to maximize shareholder wealth. It also causes the theoretical underpinnings of management to be formed upon the principles of the scientific method. The scientific method is a form of investigation that is commonly associated with hard science studies, which seeks to understand natural laws through a well-defined process of hypothesis formulation, testing, and data analyses. While Aristotle is credited for informally beginning the scientific method by encouraging logical and deductive reasoning, he too recognized the limitations of this method, which could not extend beyond natural phenomena. The scientific method was most useful to explore things that "cannot be other than they are." But human decision-making and organizational phenomena is part of an emerging narrative that consists of multiple possibilities. Aristotle noted that "most of the things about which we make decisions, and into which we therefore inquire, present us with alternative possibilities...All our actions have a contingent character; hardly any of them are determined by necessity" (Aristotle, 350 B.C.E; Book I).

Management theories should contain possibilities that are ever changing as our interactions evolve and our understanding deepens of the organized complexity of relationships. However, management is more often than not approached from a natural or hard science perspective, rather than insightful inquiry into the possibilities of what yet could be. As Bennis and O'Toole (2005) quipped, "The problem is not that business schools have embraced scientific rigor but that they have forsaken other forms of knowledge." In addition, the real danger, as many scholars have pointed out, is that the ignoring of other "softer sciences" or humanities, is not only an inaccurate representation of the realities of management, but it also poses the danger of becoming self-fulfilling. This can unintentionally promote harmful theories through the process of a double hermeneutic. A *double hermeneutic* refers to the mutual interpretive interplay between what is being studied and the researcher's own interpretation of reality. Stated simply, the researcher and subject under investigation are cocreators of the phenomena. A researcher's perceptive cannot be separated from their interpretation of the observed behaviors under investigation. As Giddens (1984) remarks, "The findings of the social sciences very often enter constitutively into the world they describe" (p. 20). Since the researcher cannot fully separate themselves from the environment, they often unintentionally influence the outcome based on their choice of theory and language used throughout the investigation (Ferraro, Pfeffer, & Sutton, 2005).

Contrast this with the natural sciences (see Figure 2.1: *Comparing natural and social science inquiry*). Regardless of the researcher's interpretation, the natural world continues to exist without influence of the observer. It is simply a one-way relationship as the natural world does not change or adapt based on one's understanding of it. For example, if one believes the earth goes around the sun, it does not change what the earth or sun actually does. The natural sciences are beyond the control of humans and only scientific inquiry can help one understand the way things actually are. And, if the scientific inquiry is incorrect, it bears no influence over the actuality of the events. Human behavior, however, does not fall into this category. The human decision-making realm rarely follows predictable laws of science allowing for linear outcomes. Rather, the way in which people interact with others, the language they ascribed, and the actions they take help shape future outcomes. As Ghoshal (2005) argued, "a management theory – if it gains sufficient currency changes the behaviors of managers who start acting in accordance with the theory" (p. 77). Management and behaviors do not follow natural laws, but are usually outcomes of one's ideology. As a result, core assumptions about how and why people should work drive management

	Natural Sciences	Social Sciences
Types of inquiry	The study of natural phenomena (i.e., physics, chemistry, cosmology, biology)	The study of human behavior and societies (i.e., management, sociology, psychology, economics)
Emphasison	The physical world and the way things are	Human nature and social relationships
Causal inferences	Yes	Limited
Intentional explanation	No	Yes
Hypotheses	Can be proven and verified into a law	Can only be supported and cannot be applied universally
Self-fulfilling	No	Yes

FIGURE 2.1 Comparing natural and social science inquiry.

theories, which in turn drive management language, expectations, and behaviors in the workplace.

Assumptions about human nature have a significant influence over behavior. For example, does believing people are out to maximize their own interest actually influence the way people manage and behave at work? Surprisingly so, according to a growing body of empirical research. If we say people are self-interested, they tend to act like it. As economist Frank (1988) notes, "Our beliefs about human nature help shape human nature itself" (p. 237). The rational economic doctrine that people are simply self-interested are espousing management philosophies and practices that pit individuals against each other in hopes of creating a competitive market-like environment within organizations (Ferraro *et al.* 2005). Many of today's organizations are designed to promote competition, distrust, and natural selection. Ferraro et al. (2005) described the consequence of this assumption "in which an employee is merely a commodity that can be acquired, dismissed, or even traded, for instance, in mergers and acquisitions, with little consideration for anything except presumed corporate profitability and shareholder wealth" (p. 19). This is justified by rational economic thinking, which has long argued that the pursuit of self-interest in competitive environments produces socially optimal results. But, does it? Recent corporate scandals (i.e., Volkswagen emissions, Wells Fargo fraudulent accounts) and global economic recessions causes us to reexamine the reality of these core economic assumptions and their influence in today's organizations. As Keynes (1936) remarks, "The ideas of economists and political philosophies, both when they are right and when they are wrong, are more powerful than is commonly understood" (p. 383).

To illustrate the power of economic assumptions on behavior, consider the following studies. In a classical academic experiment, Marwell and Ames (1981) gave individuals 250 tokens and asked how many they were willing to invest on an "individual exchange" vs "collective exchange." Individual exchanges would be returned dollar-for-dollar, while the funds in the collective exchange would be pooled and multiplied by a factor greater than one and distributed evenly to all. The situation was set up to be a tragedy-of-the-commons, meaning the socially optimal result would be to put the entire amount into the collective exchange, but from an individual point of view, the most profitable strategy would be to put the tokens into the private account. Hence, one could easily maximize profit by receiving from the collective exchange, yet still placing all their money into the private account. The result? On average, economic students, who were exposed to self-interested behavior theories, put only 20% into the collective exchange, compared to other noneconomic students who put nearly half of their tokens into the collective exchange. What is more startling is what the researchers discovered by interviewing participant's after the experiment, in particular how their perception of fairness influenced the way they decided to distribute individual funds. Economic students were half as likely to be concerned with collective well-being when making their decision, finding fairness irrelevant in this context. This research suggests that these economic students did not consider collective concerns over their own private interests as part of the decision-making process. Yet, this type of self-interest thinking did not carry through in the other students from different disciplines. The authors conclude that, in general, excluding economic students, people "voluntarily contribute substantial portions of their resources to the provision of the a public good" (p. 307), which stands in contrast to the common held economic assumption that human nature is primarily self-seeking.

Additional experimental research has since been conducted, confirming the influence economic assumptions have on behavior. For example, Cadsby and Maynes (1998) found that business and economic students were much more likely to free-ride compared to nursing students. Carter and Irons (1991) confirmed that economic students were much more likely to keep resources for themselves in an ultimatum game compared to noneconomic majors. In fact, in another study, simply calling a game Wall Street rather than Community, dramatically influenced the behaviors of those playing (Liberman, Samuels, & Ross, 2004). As Mills (1940) concluded, "We influence a man by naming his acts or imputing motives to them" (p. 445). The way we assume and theorize about behavior can ultimately become self-fulfilling in social science inquiry. Therefore, it is of the utmost importance that business students and practitioners today reexamine their core assumptions regarding human nature in the workplace.

2.3 RATIONAL ECONOMIC THEORY

A rational economic-dominant discourse remains in the field of management, even in spite of changing market conditions which favor uncertainty, complexity, and knowledge flow. In fact, most management theories are built upon a time and place that holds little resemblance to the way companies compete today. Rather than driving efficiency and productivity through an unskilled workforce, firms are increasingly competing on their ability to manage knowledge and talent across networks. These market shifts require a newfound investigation into the role of management within the firm. This chapter seeks to reexamine two commonly held assumptions that have formed the dominant narrative around management, which is commonly considered a function of planning, organizing, controlling, and directing resources. The first assumption is at the individual level and prescribes the rationality of individuals at work. This assumption presumes that employees are first and foremost rational beings when it comes to decision-making and that they will actively seek to restrict their output due to an inherent dislike of work, which requires extrinsic rewards to align with the firm's interests. Many of today's leading performance management systems are built upon this notion. The second commonly accepted assumption is at the organizational level and reinforces that the sole purpose of the firm's existence is to achieve shareholder wealth maximization. This perspective carries the assumption that the primary goal of the firm centers around managing agency costs with an intent to derive profits on behalf of the owners of the firm. Unfortunately, these two core assumptions have been accepted as hard and fast laws built upon scientific inquiry, rather than the reality that they are simply pliable hypotheses with many alternatives yet to be explored. Both of these assumptions provide a rather incomplete view of today's worker or organization, which may ultimately misguide the actions of the managers seeking to navigate changing market conditions.

2.3.1 Individuals Pursue Their Own Interests

Rational economic theory is built upon the concept of *homo economicus* or the economic man. The concept of the economic man adheres to two main beliefs around human decision-making:

1. Individuals make rational decisions in a consistent manner to achieve well-defined preferences. Decisions are made without regard to outside influences, such as emotions or social pressures. Rather, the individual has access to all necessary information inputs and is able to logically sift through them to make an optimal choice.
2. The individual is a self-seeking agent, narrowly pursuing their own interests. Decisions are made to maximize their own satisfaction while exerting the least amount of effort. Incentives will drive human behavior and explains how people obtain what they want.

As a result of these ideologies, it is presumed that individuals will act in a consistent and logical manner, readily pursuing the maximization of their own utility, without the irrational pull of emotions or outside influences. A thorough cost-benefit analyses of all available information is presumed to be completed before any action. This ensures the rational actor meets well-defined needs, while minimizing the costs of their obtainment. An *Economist* article (1999) remarked that "Economists have typically described the thought processes of homo sapiens as more like that of Star Trek's Mr. Spock – strictly logical, centered on clearly goal and free from the unsteady influences of emotion or irrationality."

Outside influences are inconsequential to the rational actor who operates with seemingly unlimited mental capacity for positive decision-making. As a result, the *homo economicus* model of decision-making is atomistic in nature with a concentrated focus on the individual unit of analysis—often foregoing external stimuli such as social influences or environmental factors, which may hinder or enhance the cognitive processes of the individual. The rational economic literature is largely quiet on intrinsic and social influences, which may lead to irrationalities or deviations from utility maximization (Frey & Oberholzer-Gee, 1997). This helps explain why rational economics does not account for the possibility of irrationalities in preferences and decision-making. As Davis (2003) argued, the rational actor resides outside of the economic process—forcing the assumption that an actor's preferences are simply given and unchanged by the process of economic activity. Therefore, the individual's emotions, affective states, social influences, and even deeply rooted beliefs are not accounted for in the rational economic actor model of decision-making.

2.3.2 The Purpose of the Firm is to Seek Shareholder Wealth Maximization

The second dominant assumption within rational economics, from an organizational level, delineates the purpose of the firm. Most business schools today prepare managers to create shareholder wealth maximization, which emphasizes the duty and fiduciary responsibility of managers to ensure that the firm's owners are maximizing their investments into the organization. Historically, shareholders have been individuals; however, in today's marketplace, they are much more likely to be entities (70%), such as financial institutions, who own equitable interests in the firm. As a result, most shareholders are physically and psychologically distant from the companies they invest in (Bower & Paine, 2017). Therefore, the role of the manager to simply look after these investors interests by safeguarding and growing the firms' assets has simply become archaic. The idea of shareholder wealth maximization was first prescribed back in 1931 within the *Harvard Law Review*. Berle (1931) wrote, "the powers granted to the corporation or the management of the corporation – are necessary and at all times exercisable only for the ratable benefit of all the shareholders as their interest appears" (p. 1049). However, it was not until later, in the 1970s, when shareholder wealth maximization was largely accepted as the dominant discourse in management studies. Economist Milton Friedman (1970) wrote an essay in the *New York Times* arguing that "the social responsibility of business is to increase its profits." This assumption to solely pursue shareholder wealth arose during a time period of scarce financial markets as well as capital. Friedman's view was built upon the assumption that a competitive market focused on increasing financial capital would benefit society at large. However, this solitary focus on creating financial wealth has come at the expense of other forms of existing capital—including talent, social, and natural resources. It also has impacted the human experience of the wider definition of stakeholder—including employees, communities, and consumers.

Today's markets are completely different—with an abundance of financial capital and a new set of challenges being scarcity of qualified talent (highly skilled technical and socially proficient workers) and social capital (relationships, trust) (Roche & Jakub, 2017). Additionally, the average holding period for a share in a company has dramatically changed in the past three decades. In 1976, the average share was held onto for 5.1 years. Contrast that to 2015, when the average share was only held for 7.3 months. This shortening of shareholding places an entirely different timeframe on generating investor returns. In fact, society has taken notice. A recent survey suggests that only 7% of the US population believes the purpose of business is shareholder wealth maximization (Cone Communications, 2013). But, we continue to teach and expect managers to seek after shareholder wealth as if it were a natural law of business, regardless of market conditions. Rarely is this core assumption questioned, and maybe even more alarming, rarely do managers understand the impact this assumption has on their sense of purpose and role within the firm.

2.3.3 Managers Needed to Mitigate Agency Costs of Self-Seeking Individuals and Maximize Shareholder Wealth

How do these dominant economic assumptions influence our perspective of management? These core economic assumptions gave rise to the dominant discourse found within the administrative theory of management, which single-mindedly focuses on costs, controls, and efficiencies. Within the administrative theory of management, managers help enforce productivity of a self interested worker, while ensuring shareholders receive profits year over year. The administrative theory of management was grounded on the assumption of competitive markets and human rationality, which requires monitoring and incentives to minimize agency costs (Jensen & Meckling, 1976). *Agency costs* are costs that derive from conflicting interests between the firm owners and employees. Each time an employee acts in his or her own interest rather than the firm, costs are occurred. Adam Smith (1776) foresaw this emerging conflict of interest when writing, "*Negligence* and *profusion*, therefore, must always prevail more or less, in the management of the affairs of such a company." Jensen and Meckling (1976) would later describe managers as self-seeking individuals who would need to be incentivized and monitored in order to "limit the aberrant activities of the agent" (p. 5). An underlying assumption of agency theory is that employees will use firm's resources for their own consumption. In addition, agency theory is most fearful of a person shirking, or what is more commonly referred to in economics as free-riding. The job of management is to ensure free riding within the firm is limited as much as possible. Within rational economic theory, two tools are at their disposal—incentives and monitoring. Incentives would drive behavior while monitoring would ensure accountability. In other words, agency costs can be moderated by using fear and money. However, in the end, money was always recommended as a better tool, as Friedman (1970) argued it was the economic benefit received by both parties, which allowed for voluntary cooperation within markets and firms. Without this economic incentive, it was assumed human cooperation could only be achieved through coercion and fear.

Therefore, the role of the manager, as argued by Chandler (1962), is to ensure that employees are maximizing their productivity to the ultimate benefit of the organization's owners. The manager acts as a steward of another person's assets, ensuring agency costs are as low as possible when the owner is not around. This point of view considers employees as self-serving and naturally prone to act in deviant ways from the owner's interests. As a result, it is namely a pessimistic mindset that seeks to monitor and use extrinsic means for compliance to rules and adherence to organizational goals.

This pessimistic mindset runs deep throughout business management history. Classical management theories arose during the industrial era as more and more workers transitioned off farms and family businesses to factories and other forms of industries. The majority of workers at the time were considered laborers, operatives, or craft workers (Gordon, 2016). In fact, by 1910, nearly 40% of the workforce was comprised of blue-collar workers, 30% farmers, and less than 20% were classified as white-collared workers (HSBUS series Ba1034 through Ba1046). It is of no surprise, then, that the majority of theorists during this time period built management theories intended for the unskilled laborer who sought to actively restrict their output due to the unpleasant nature of the work. Quite frankly, work was disagreeable during this time period. Conditions were often bleak, and as will be discovered, the typical foreman, or manager of the time, used aggressive means to maintain order and compliance within factories. As a result, it could be argued that the rational thing for workers to do was minimize their output to preserve themselves as well as their income as jobs were scarce and unstable. Therefore, this primary assumption—the worker does not care to work, or what economists often refer to as disutility from work—ran deep within the management theories that would arise and provide the foundation for many other theories to be built upon. This assumption was further solidified in the mainstream press of the time. Labor relations were tense and headlines often proclaimed that the average worker sought more pay and less work. In addition, strikes were common and the overall relationship between labor and management during this industrial time period was described as "worse than at any time in history" (Williams, 1920). Something had to change with the way these newfound forms of organizations were operating.

The change began with Fredrick Taylor (1856–1915) who is often credited as the father of scientific management. Scientific management is a theory of management which seeks to use science to maximize productivity gains through the analysis and synthesis of worker tasks (Taylor, 1911). Prior to this, management was largely subjective with little to no formalization as a function or field of study. Taylor was instrumental in creating management into a formalized field of inquiry. However, Taylor held a fundamental belief that people by nature abhorred work and must be managed through entirely extrinsic means. Taylor (1911) believed, "The natural laziness of men is serious, but by far the greatest evil from which both workmen and employers are suffering is the systematic soldiering which is almost universal" (p. 20). *Soldiering* was a term used to describe the intentional restriction of output by a worker. As a result, the role of the manager was to create a system that maximized productivity of the worker or at least minimized the worker's ability to restrict their output. The manager did this by analyzing the "one best way" of doing a task within a certain time period and then setting very specific standards for productivity expectations.

In addition, Taylor believed the role of the manager was to be responsible for the comprehensive knowledge required to do the worker's role. This knowledge included the best way of how a job should be completed. This perspective resulted from a credence that many unskilled workers were simply unknowledgeable to know the best way to work. In particular, Taylor (1911) remarked that low-skilled workers were "so stupid and so phlegmatic that he more nearly resembles in his mental make-up the ox." However, Taylor was simply responding to the environmental context of his time to determine what he felt was the best way to manage resources, namely people, within the factory. His management principles thus flow from this pessimistic interpretation of the average unskilled worker of his time. Taylor (1911) believed that all knowledge must reside with the manager who was ultimately responsible for output, not the worker. It is no wonder that a command and control style of leadership emerged from this mindset. All accountabilities for output were given to managers, robbing the worker of any sort of intrinsic sense of accomplishments. As a result, the primary purpose of management was to ensure workers were maintaining a set level of productivity.

Compliance, or constant supervision, was an integral part of the role of manager during this time. Supervision primarily focused on tasks, processes, and resources, overlooking a key component—the worker herself. Rather, the worker was simply viewed as a biological machine, whose mind and emotions were better left outside of work. The focus was completely on the physical productivity of the worker and at times even sought to restrict the utilization of the worker's mind. As a result, the command and control style of leadership, though tracing its actual origins back to military, was commonly employed. Many companies during this time adopted these management principles and reported increases in not only productivity, but profits as well. Yet, as will be discovered, there were many pitfalls that would be discovered with Taylor's methods over the long term.

During the same time period, in France, Henri Fayol (1841–1925) was also formalizing the role and study of management. He led one of the largest steel and mining facilities in Europe (Williams, 2013). His management philosophies emerged from his direct experience as CEO. As a result, he viewed the firm from a top-down perspective. Like Taylor, he considered the management function from an engineering lens which sought to maximize productivity. Fayol developed a command and control style of management that focused on planning, directing, organizing, predicting, and controlling resources (Fayol, 1916). His writings on management almost exclusively focused on process and productivity, and often ignored the human aspect of work, such as individual differences, social dynamics, and motivations. Like Taylor, Fayol also believed that the manager was in control and central to the business's operations. While workers were given more consideration in Fayol's administrative management model, the primary focus and attention was on the very top levels of management. Fayol's context was that of a mining organization and he was often criticized for the generalizability of his findings to more complex and larger firms. However, Fayol's work and writings would help begin the study of administrative management by solidifying the planning, directing, controlling, and organizing of resources as management activities. Today, many MBA programs are still built around these activities as central to the role of a manager in a firm.

During the same time period as Taylor and Fayol, shareholder wealth maximization would rise within the business management discourse as a result of a ruling in 1919 within Michigan's Supreme Court's decision in *Dodge vs Ford Motor Company*. Henry Ford was the majority shareholder of his company, Ford Motors. Minority shareholders included Horace and John Dodge, who were starting a competing company, the Dodge Brothers Company. Needing additional capital to finance their startup, the Doge brothers were counting on dividends from their Ford Motor Company holdings. However, Henry Ford, well aware of this, decided to withhold dividends and instead justify the mounting cash as safe keep to lower consumer prices and even pay higher employees' wages. The Dodge brothers infuriated by this, sued the company for their owed dividends. The court decided in the favor of the Dodge brothers, though they did rule for a lower dividend payment to the brothers, allowing Henry Ford to also move forward with his plan to lower car prices and increase employee wages.

But, this is where the narrative for the purpose of business was altered. The judge was not amused by Ford's argument to use the organization as a charity. In fact, during his remarks, the judge made an offhanded remark to Henry Ford. "There should be no confusion. . .a business corporation is organized and carried on primarily for the profit of the stockholders. The power of the directors are to be employed for that end" (*Dodge v Ford Motor Co*, 1919, p. 684). The judge verbally noted this during the "mere dicta," which is a comment made in passing not relating to the court's decision on the ruling. To date, this is one of the only court cases that is used to legally position a firm as maximizing shareholder wealth. The state of Delaware, one of the modern-day authorities in corporate law, has never once validated the organization's purpose as such.

Yet, firms relentless pursue shareholder wealth and mitigate agency costs as if they were laws. This drive to align shareholder interests with management decision-making is increasingly accomplished through an increase in equity-based compensation for executives managing large firms. In 1984, zero percent of the median executive compensation at S&P 500 firms was equity-based, by 2001 it had risen to 66% (Stout, 2012). The American government also favored this type of thinking by amending the tax code in 1991 to encourage equity performance-based compensation. The result has created a widening gap between executive pay and their employees. In 1991, CEO's on average received 140 times that of their average employee. That number reached 500 times by 2003. Executives' interests are indeed closely aligned to shareholders, yet may never be further away from other stakeholders, such as employees and their local communities.

It was concluded by the end of the 1990s, "the triumph of the shareholder value criterion was nearly complete" (Gordon, 2007). This was then echoed in 2001 by Yale Hansmann and Kraakman (2001) whom wrote "Academic, business and government elites" agree "the ultimate control over the corporation should rest with the shareholder class; the managers of the corporation should be charged with the obligation to manage the corporation in the interests of its shareholders" (p. 440–441). By the turn of the century, shareholder wealth maximization was widely accepted and further propagated in mainstream press outlets as the legal responsibility of businesses, often justifying leaders' questionable behavior—such as ruthless exploitation of tax loops, massive employee layoffs, and pursuing strategies that would leave entire communities behind.

Ironically, Enron, was touted as an exceptional shareholder wealth maximizing firm in at least five of Harvard Business School case studies, as late as August 2001. Managers and employees were incessantly fixated on increasing stock price and applauded for doing so. The firm's entire culture embodied shareholder wealth maximization thinking—do whatever it takes to meet shareholder interests. However, as we now know, Enron collapsed due to its unethical pursuit of maximizing shareholder wealth by engaging in poor business decisions and accounting fraud. The relentless and single-minded pursuit of wealth left business leaders blinded to other purposes their firm may serve—such as job creation, consumer value, and sustainability.

Therefore, the dominant historical narrative for management can be summarized as follows: Individuals are primarily rational beings motivated to maximize their economic self-interest and will actively seek to restrict their output due to a natural distain toward work. As a result, agency costs arise, which represent the costs associated when individuals act contrary to the interest of the firm. To help keep agency costs down, managers must monitor and incentive employees. Additionally, management is needed to properly administer a firm's resources through the activities of planning, controlling, directing, and organizing of resources. This is all done for the sole benefit of maximizing the wealth of a firm's shareholder base.

Is this discourse wrong? Not necessarily, but it is incomplete and may not be sustainable as firms transition into a knowledge-driven economy. Are these natural laws that business phenomena follow? Absolutely not. These are ideologies that have helped shape the course of business decision-making and design over the past century. In many ways, these ideologies have become self-fulfilling prophecies into the 21st century. Unfortunately, this dominant narrative leaves no room for longer term consideration of other forms of incentives and capital outside of financial metrics. It leaves no diversity of thought for alternative ends to a business besides wealth creation. In addition, it lacks the fortitude to sustain the development of intellectual capital through a firm's talent base. As will be discovered, intellectual capital creation does not always develop by incentivizing employees and may actually be diminished by introducing extrinsic means at the expense of intrinsic motivators.

2.4 AN UNINTENTIONAL TUNNELING ON A TIME AND PLACE IN MANAGEMENT NARRATIVES

Many of today's leading management textbooks still primarily focus on Taylor's outdated scientific management principles and Fayol's management behaviors to inform how present-day managers should behave in the firm. In addition, the majority of management textbooks also assert that the primary purpose of the firm is to create shareholder wealth maximization. These core assumptions of business management are insufficiently challenged, much less considered flawed in light of new market opportunities. It is noted that this lack of rich historical discourse in business research results in much less citations and a bias toward the present, which neglects a proper understanding of the historical assumptions underlying today's research (Cummings & Bridgman, 2016). In addition, scholars argue that a forgetting of historical scholarship leads to a lack of innovative and creative discourse in management thinking and practices (Evans, 2008; Parolo et al., 2015). Recent research conducted from the London Business School noted that "Nine-tenths of the approximately 100 branded management ideas lost their popularity within a decade or so" (Birkinshaw, 2014). It is noteworthy to reinvestigate the origins of management thinking in order to rediscover insights for today's challenges.

Management thinking suffers from a narrow framing of the past. Indeed, recent management research showcases a narrow tunneling or anchoring upon a particular time period and researcher, which creates a dominant discourse in management (Cummings & Bridgman, 2016). In addition, this dominant thinking has made it hard for alternative theories to emerge (Donaldson & Walsh, 2015). This *anchoring bias* refers to human tendency to over-rely on a piece of information or data point to form judgments (Chapman & Johnson, 2002). Numerous research studies showcase how both relevant and irrelevant anchors can impede our ability to make decisions (Tversky & Kahneman, 1974).

To investigate this potential bias, management researchers Cummings and Bridgman (2016) recently conducted an expansive empirical study to determine how broad and wide the discourse of management thinking is in comparison to architecture and medical studies. In other words, they set out to determine if there was an unintentional anchor bias that may be limiting alternative management thinking. The fields of medicine and architecture were selected based on their similarity of stochastic professions, yet architecture and medicine do not seem to be suffering from a lack of innovative thinking in their respective areas. In medicine, for example, challenging core assumptions around how the body works and responds to its environment are key practices in the medical community, because doctors know it matters to societal-level outcomes. To illustrate this concept consider the following. Spontaneous generation theory was the leading discourse for centuries prior to the discovery of germ theory in 1859. Historical research suggests that universities began training in the practice of medicine in the 13th century meaning the belief of spontaneous generation theory spanned eras. This assumption taught that hygiene was not a potential cause of germs or disease transfer. It was only through much empirical evidence and debate taking place within the medical community that they deemed the previous spontaneous generation assumption obsolete and even harmful to patient outcomes. The medical community was then able to build an entirely new set of medical behaviors around a new assumption—hand washing matters to patient outcomes.

Cummings and Bridgeman also found within their research "that management and business history has a far more limited geographical and temporal perspective than either of its two comparator fields of inquiry" (p. 254). While the other fields of inquiry enjoy a broad range of geography, the majority of management thinking derives primarily from the United States during the industrial era. One of the compelling conclusions was that "medical and architecture history is more able to than business history shift historical focus so as to move with the problems or interests of the times" (p. 255). This is due to the fact that the majority of business articles possess an intense bias toward the timeframe of 1900–1920 in the United States. This historical narrowing discourse, or anchor, can unintentionally create a misrepresentation of the broader management function. This limits the innovative evolution for future management thinking. In addition, it perpetuates the anchor effect, whereby the majority of management thinking points back to a specific time and place, rather than expand the scope to include additional times, places, and events that reside outside of this 20-year time period.

Stated simply, business management has anchored its thinking upon a time and place that no longer resembles today's environment. Indeed, early

20th century management thinking may not hold much truth for the complexities faced in the 21st century context. In addition, this anchoring has caused far too many students to overestimate the success of the Taylor and Fayol narratives of business, while largely ignoring historical challenges that have rose alongside these dominant perspectives. As business management historians Wren and Bedeian (2009) point out, "True, there had been others, but their ideas remained in the shadow of the intellectual offspring of Fayol and Taylor" (p. 439). It may be time to explore these figures who often remain in the shadow of dominant business theories to determine a better way to manage and create intellectual capital throughout the firm.

2.5 MANY HISTORICAL MANAGEMENT THEORISTS EXPRESSED SKEPTICISM, YET REMAINED IN THE SHADOWS

This unintentional tunneling on management history back to this industrial time period, and in particular back to this idea of scientific management, has omitted alternative perspectives also rising long before and during this same time period. While many management researchers unintentionally anchor upon Taylor and Fayol's thinking as the origin of management, if one looks further back into history and even considers other perspectives during their time, alternative assumptions about people at work appear. There is much more to the story than people will only work for pay and always act in their own self-interest. In addition, there is compelling role context and social dynamic often at play, which limits the classically held assumption that people inherently dislike work.

2.5.1 Historical Perspectives Before the Industrial Revolution

While management is a relatively new academic discipline, people have long sought to organize and manage their labor since the beginning of mankind. Many examples exist long before Taylor and Fayol entered the management scene. For example, Ancient Greeks recognized that worker productivity could be achieved through enhancing the environment through music (Glotz, 1926). Confucius (552–479 BC) encouraged the Chinese bureaucracy to cultivate the moral nature of people to secure cooperation rather than relying on rewards and punishments—a similar debate that we still face today (Wren & Bedeian, 2009). The ancient Romans would institute one of the first checks and balance systems, recognizing the limitations of absolute control and power. These are just a few of the many historical examples one could consider as a starting point for organizational management well before the Industrial Revolution.

In addition, the idea of the purpose of business was remarkably different prior to the Industrial Revolution. The early colonial settlers would enter into commerce with the goal of serving God, others, and their communities. John Winthrop declared in 1630 that "we must entertain each other in brotherly affection. We must be willing to abridge ourselves of our superfluities, for the supply of others' necessities. We must uphold a familiar commerce together in all meekness, gentleness, patience and liberality." The socially acceptable business person existed to serve the community's interests, not their own. Modern-day business ethics Professor Rollert (2017) described the conviction of the present-day management narrative as "a radical change in the way we look at each other and the broader human world" ultimately expressing concern that "orienting commercial conduct exclusively toward self-interested ends can imperil a community and the integrity of one's conscience."

Even Adam Smith realized that mankind was limited in their pursuit of self-interest based on *moral sentiments*—or the desire to be respected by others (Smith, 1759). Social influence limited the extent to which individuals could act as self-interested agents. British social reformer, Robert Owen, in the late 19th century described the key to worker and management relations as one founded on interpersonal relationships and trust, not mere economic transactions. He found greater productivity could be achieved through listening, educating, and meeting worker needs. Owen was a resounding advocate for improving the relations between managers and workers during this time by elevating the needs of the worker. He also sought out innovative ways to do so, such as providing meals, dancing lessons, and other recreational activities to the workforce.

During this time period in America, Henry Varnum Poor, a leading analyst of the railroad industry during the mid-1800s, also sought to understand the managers role in increasing worker productivity. He found communication and information flow between workers and management as imperatives to unity and worker productivity. He believed that management should be "the soul of the enterprise, reaching and infusing life," further cautioning "Wherever there is lack of unity there will be a lack of energy – of intelligence – of life – of accountability and subordination" (Chandler, 1956, p. 157). Furthermore, Henry Varnum Poor anticipated the dangers of "regarding man as a mere machine, out of which all the qualities necessary to be a good servant can be enforced by the mere payment of wages. But duties cannot always be prescribed, and the most valuable are often voluntary ones" (Chandler, 1956, p. 155). The emphasis prior to the 20th century was on using business to serve the needs of others—"the idea that a stable economic system could indeed be organized along the lines of self-interest would have seemed absurd" at this time (Rollert, 2017).

2.5.2 The Response to Scientific Management: Turnover, Low Morale and Even Outlaw

However, the rise of the Industrial Revolution would bring new assumptions regarding the role of commerce in a society. Along with changing assumptions, scientific management grew as the leading management solution to worker productivity and shareholder wealth generation. However, scientific management was met with much resistance from employees at the time of its inception. In 1919, over four million American workers, or one-fifth of the nation's workforce, went on strike (Boyer et al., 2001). Turnover at leading manufacturing firms, such as the Ford Motor Company, were reaching 380%. In addition, absenteeism was consistently at 10% of the workforce per day (Wood & Wood, 2003). This should come as no surprise as worker's reactions to scientific management, who marked the role of the manager as one who distrusts employees, restricts autonomy and lessens both the individual and collective intentionality on the job. This was a consequence of viewing workers as a biological machine who were there to complete singular tasks. In addition, it was believed the worker could only be incentivized through pay since much of the work at the time was repetitive, noncognitive and lacked any meaning back to the overall system. One Ford employee is recorded as saying the following when scientific management was introduced at the plant,

> *"Once a Ford employee had learned the special spasm expected from him he can go through life without a single thought or emotion. When the whistle blows he starts to jerk and when the whistle blows again he stops jerking, and if that isn't the simple life, what is?"*
>
> Cowan, 1997, p. 189.

But, after numerous labor revolts, the United States government deemed scientific management as potentially dehumanizing and was not to be adopted at their government arsenals. At the heart of their concern with the Taylor system of management was his primary notion of the firm's existence. Taylor (1911) states during the court proceedings to the Commission on Industrial Relations that "All employees should bear in mind that each shop exists first and last and for all time for the purpose of paying dividends to the owners" (p. 795). The committee formed by the government seeking to investigate scientific management concluded,

> *"This complete elimination of all consideration for the welfare of the employees, that the manufacturer may profit, seems to be the fundamental principles of this obnoxious system. The committee further showed that the introduction of the system will be the means of overworking and enslaving the men...and the most serious objection of all was that it denied the employees a voice in determining the conditions under which they shall work...under no circumstance will they aid and abet in the introduction of any system that would reduce them to mere soulless machinery, mechanical in action, denuded of thought and which would rob them of their manhood"*
>
> Wilson, 1916, p. 1107–1108.

2.5.3 What Do Workers Really Want? Going Undercover to Find Out

Needless to say, while scientific management provided albeit an alternative to subjective management, it indeed was not openly embraced by many, simply due to its oversight of the humanness of the worker. During this labor unrest of the early 20th century, a less known management theorist took a different approach to understand the perils facing the relationship between the worker and manager. Rather than following Taylor's method of scientific management, Whiting Williams became one of the world's first undercover bosses, preferring to form his assumptions around the worker by firsthand experience and observation. While he believed in the use of data to help managers make better decisions regarding resources, he also believed management was grounded in the humanities, and relied heavily on individual intentionality, choices, and social influences. As such, Williams (1920) noted, "People cannot be interviewed for their feelings. The interviewer can only listen, and then try to understand because he is not only hearing but experiencing and sympathizing" (p. 1). Much like Ghoshal (2005) who would share many of William's same concerns regarding the use of scientific management research decades later, Williams's primary research collection method was to observe the worker firsthand, before forming assumptions.

Whiting William's travels led him around world to a variety of industries—working right alongside the common laborer of his time. He quickly realized that the lack of stability for work led to much personal hardship among the working class. Williams (1920) described it as impacting the psychological and emotional well-being of the worker. He attributes the rise of unions as a direct result of the lack of empathy and disconnection from management, not as a result of workers actively seeking to restrict their output. In addition, he correlates worker satisfaction and productivity with the worker's ability to find meaning by a thorough justification of why their work matters. From his perspective, an individual's job defined their sense of worth and identity within social society (Wren & Bedeian, 2009). As a result, Williams connected many local societal ills (such as the rise of the Klu Klux Klan) with worker anger stemming from poor working conditions.

Both Taylor and Williams observed soldiering from workers; however they differed dramatically in what caused the worker's restricted output. Taylor ascribed soldering as resulting from the inherent laziness of man. Williams, on the other hand, believed it to be a symptom of the poor working relationship between manager and employee. As a result, their approaches to improving worker productivity varied greatly. Taylor would turn to the stopwatch to ensure worker compliance, while Williams would advocate infusing meaning to the average labor's workday to increase productivity.

Like Taylor, Williams recognized that extrinsic means were indeed important to the worker. Yet, Williams observed that money was simply a means to a greater end—individual worth and meaning as well as the means of social comparison. He wrote, "Not one of them all but is anxious to find two things between the start and finish of his daily stint of labor. The first of these is the dollars and cents required for his daily living. The second is the usefulness, and hence the dignity and self-respect required to make that daily life worth living. The wise employer today realizes that he cannot prosper unless his co-workers find these two things" (Untitled manuscript, p. 2). Much like behavioral economists would discover decades later, Williams also found that money was never considered in the objective but rather in comparison to others. "We give the dollar altogether too great an importance when we consider it the cause. . .the dollar is merely an especially convenient and simple means for facilitating the measurement of a man's distance from the cipher of insignificance among his fellows" (1920, p. 323).

Williams (1921) expressed much concern with the principles of scientific management, which seemed to distance the worker from their craft and with their fellow workers. "Within this new and multiplex organization, the specialization of men's daily jobs has taken them off into the remote separateness of economic and psychological cells" (p. 1). As a result of the assembly line and growing emphasis on noncognitive routine work, the average worker was increasingly becoming disconnected from the larger cause or purpose of the firm. This in return would make it harder for the worker to justify their output. It would also lessen their ability to find meaning and social identity within their workplaces. Williams urged managers to consider the connection between worker's self-respect and their productivity. In the end, he encouraged less use of the stopwatch and management by fear, and more focus on understanding the motivations of the worker, which he predicted would lead to better productivity. In addition, he also encouraged management to invest in the development of the worker's skillset by teaching them a variety of skillsets, encouraging job rotations, giving them additional responsibilities, and proactively increasing their knowledge of the industry. Williams held the hypothesis that individuals not only inherently wanted to work, but would exceed manager expectations when their sense of meaning, belonging, and fairness were met. He recommended that the role of management was to help meet these needs. Williams states, "In large measure, the successful leader of men in industry is the executive who follows a variety of methods to convey to each of his associates the one unmistakable sincere message of the value of the worker's own indispensable contribution to the work of the organization as a whole, and the indispensable value of the organization, in turn, to him" (Untitled manuscript, p. 5).

During this same industrial era, Albert Barnes, founder of A.C. Barnes Company in 1908, also employed an alternative strategy to scientific management. Barnes was fascinated with psychology and the basis of human values. Barnes believed that the study of the arts and the involvement in adult learning could bring about better worker experiences for those often engaged in industrial work. As a result of this conjecture, Barnes began instituting a 6-h work day at his factory. He also put up dozens of exquisite artworks within the factory, encouraging workers to learn to connect human nature with art by observing and discussing the paintings. Barnes used art as a way to connect workers with a shared sense of humanity. In addition, he encouraged all of his workers, regardless of race, to engage in active dialogues around literature, philosophy, and art. To help foster the workers' development, Barnes established a library within the factory as well. Indeed, Barnes was able to apply his psychological knowledge of human needs to secure employee commitment and productivity. The financial performance of his company served well under his management style. Barnes created a remarkable profitable factory within 5 years and would later sell the business for $6 million dollars in 1929. Unlike Taylor, both Barnes and Williams had an underlying assumption that the development and growth of the common worker would lead to not only better organizations, but better societies. They both saw work as a means to meet and fulfill fundamental human needs. The goal of the manager was to facilitate these conditions for knowledge, development, and growth.

2.5.4 The Rise of Social Dynamics in Management Thinking

In the late 1920s, another researcher was seeking to unlock what might drive higher productivity and performance from employees. Researcher Elton Mayo believed that environmental conditions could be altered in such a way to improve human performance. This included increasing the lighting, adjusting the temperature, ensuring workstation cleanness, and instituting a host of breaks during work. Unfortunately, his experiments are dominantly known for the discovery of what is referred to as the *Hawthorne effect.* The Hawthorne effect is the psychological phenomenon that humans will improve their performance as a result of increased attention from others watching, including supervisors, colleagues, or clients. While Mayo's writings led to many human relations improvements in the workplace, an often-unknown finding, which may contain even greater relevance, was discovered by Mayo during this time. While many initially assume the Hawthorne experiments discovered the power of observation on productivity, two other important, but lesser known, attributes of the experiment contributed to increased worker productivity.

The first was the desire of the workers to belong to a work group. Elton Mayo wrote, "The desire to stand well with one's fellows, the so-called human instinct of association, easily outweighs the merely individual interest and the logic of reasoning upon which so many spurious principles of management are based. The working group as a whole actually determined the output of individual workers by reference to a standard that represented the group conception (rather than management's) of a fair day's work. This standard was rarely, if ever, in accord with the standards of the efficiency engineers." In other words, Mayo allowed workers to form small working units and set their own standards of work. The pressure to be respected by others and ensure all was fair led the group to enforce their own norms, which often superseded the original standards set by management. In addition, these working groups brought about a sense of community and belonging, which further fueled productivity.

The second contributing factor to increased productivity was that Mayo actively engaged the workers during the experiments—asking for their input and relaxing supervisory regimen on the workers. The workers felt a sense of involvement in the experiment and findings as Mayo continuously sought their input for ways to improve the study. In many ways, Mayo's findings were simply a translation of what the common worker expressed during this time, which still holds true today. Workers need to feel a sense of belonging, involvement, and purpose in order to unlock greater levels of productivity. In the end, the recommendation of Roethlisberger and Dickson (1939), who summarized these findings of the Hawthorne experiments, determined it was the manager's responsibility to maintain equilibrium in the many social systems which arise in organizations. The emphasis of the manager was on relationship management, not efficiencies.

Another key figure to write about the advantages of groups and social systems during this time period was management theorist, Mary Parker Follett. During her time, Follett advocated for cooperation, not competition within workplaces. She saw business as an interrelation of many stakeholders—including customers, employees, communities, and shareholders whom needed to cooperate with one another to succeed. These interests could only be met through the intentional integration of individuals working together for a larger purpose beyond themselves. In Follett's view, "Man discovers his true nature, gains his true freedom only through the group" (p. 6). As a result, employees who felt connected to a larger and shared purpose would extend themselves, because their interests aligned to others. In order to align interests, she encourage integrative unity, which sought to find solutions by confronting diverse perspectives, rethinking initial assumptions, openly sharing information, and viewing problems as "ours," not "yours." The diversity of thought shared during times of cooperative conflict, she argued, would bring innovative approaches to solve more complex problems and unleash greater creativity in the workplace. It would also help fulfill individual identities as they were able to express themselves and work toward creative resolve with others.

Follett saw the role of organizational leadership to not only increase profits, but also inform a larger purpose and narrative for the firm's existence. This overarching shared purpose among individuals would act as the invisible leader in most situations, guiding decision-making. The role of the manager would be to interweave individual and group responsibilities in a variety of complex situations into this larger purpose. Her argument was that managers do not manage single elements, but complex interrelationships; not persons, but situations. In addition, her view of power was novel at the time. Rather than assuming managers have absolute power-over individuals, Follett encouraged that managers adopt a power-with mentality. Power would be situational and reside with the person who has the most knowledge and experience for a particular situation. The situation would guide the power dynamics, as different situations require different knowledge, and managers would actively participate by connecting the right individuals to each other and dealing with any conflict that may emerge. "To Follett, the essence of good human relations was creating the feeling of working with someone rather than working under someone" (Wren & Bedeian, 2009, p. 317). Yet, much of her work remains in the shadows, though Wren and Bedeian (2009) observes, "Follett uncannily presaged many of today's management thinkers in advocating participative management, the benefits of teams (i.e., groups), cooperative conflict resolution, and that authority should go with knowledge" (p. 321).

2.5.5 Contemporary Management Concerns on Administrative Theory

By the mid-1950s, Foyl's administrative theory of management began experiencing strong criticism. Simon (1957), and then Drucker (1974), remarked that some of the worst mistakes in management derive from imposing a mechanistic model of a universal organization upon a living business. In reality, people within an organization often deviate from rational and predictable behaviors, which administrative management was founded upon. Of particular concern today is applying Fayol's emphasis on the unity of command and control, which stressed hierarchy and singularity of responsibilities. While this may have been appropriate during the industrial era, critics now remark that this indeed may be dysfunctional to organizations who seek to bring out a diversity of thought, personal contact, and cross-functional collaboration (Simon, 1957). In particular, Barnard (1938) and Simon (1957) argued that Fayol's administrative theory of management was excessively formalistic and built upon nonoperational analyses. Yet, many of today's leading organizations still suffer from the silos and lack of knowledge transfer that administrative theory of management has rendered.

During the 1960s, Douglas McGregor, a management researcher, also began to actively critique the assumption that people disliked work, cautioning the impact it was having on management behaviors. McGregor believed this core assumption was driving a restriction of human development, learning, and innovative behaviors. He strongly encouraged adoption of an alternative assumption—that people enjoy work under the right conditions. He divided these two competing assumptions about human nature into Theory X, noting that people inherently dislike work and should be managed through command and control, versus Theory Y, which believed people inherently enjoyed work and managers should support and actively participate in the workers development, trusting them to execute on the day-day tasks assigned.

Also, recognizing the over emphasis on rational assumptions and management administration in business studies, Robert Gordon and James Howell published a report on the state of business education in 1959. Within their report, they called upon academics to also consider the very important role of social studies. "Of all the subjects which he might undertake formally, none is more appropriate for the businessman-to-be than human behavior…The very nature of the firm and of the manager's role in the firm suggests that every person anticipating a responsible position in a modern business enterprise needs a substantial amount of knowledge of human behavior" (p. 166). Solely focusing on administrating resources and not considering the importance of human behavior, social dynamics, and alternatives to self-seeking behavior has indeed been questioned throughout the past decades. However, much of these concerns remain on the fringe of the dominant discourse being overshadowed by the administrative theory of management.

Lastly, one of the leading contemporary voices critical on the theory of administrative management is Professor Henry Mintzberg. Mintzberg went into the field to observe managers firsthand across a variety of industries and organizations to form his theories on management. As a result, Mintzberg (1989) observed management more as an art that required synthesis of information, listening to people and often engaging in emergent actions dictated by complex environments. Real managers in real organizations rarely followed rationality, linearity, and predictability as was described in administrative theory of management. Instead, the three attributes Mintzberg (1989) saw as effective management were interpersonal behaviors, processing information, and leveraging information to make decisions. To summarize, managers engage in multiple roles and behaviors depending on the need at hand. These skillsets could not be learned through rational thinking or even analyses, but instead must be practices and experienced in order to develop. As a result, Mintzberg (2004) went on to write *Managers, Not MBA's* to lament the fields current focus on administrative activities, which simply does not lead to successful management in today's complex, interpersonal, and information focused firms.

2.5.6 An Alternative Purpose of the Firm Debated Throughout the 20th Century

Not only has the theory of administrative management been actively debated since its inception, but the premise of shareholder wealth has also faced similar apprehensions. Throughout the last 100 years, many have questioned whether the job of managers is to solely increase shareholder wealth by managing agency costs—in the courts, in practice, and in rigorous academic debates. Scholars recently posed the following riddle in a leading management conference and published article.

Justice is to law, as medicine is to health as business is to...

What is your own response to this question? What would you put forth as the purpose of the firm? In some cases, the dominant and socially acceptable answer depends on who and when this question has been posed.

2.5.6.1 The Purpose of the Firm Debated in Academia

The public debate of the firm's purpose began with Berle's (1931) argument in the *Harvard Law Review*, which proposed that the single purpose of the firm was to increase shareholder returns. However, Berle's argument faced a strong opponent. Dodd (1932) strongly disagreed with the shareholder primacy theory presented by Berle. Dodd openly debated with Berle's thesis in the *Harvard Law Review* and argued for a "view of business corporation as an economic institution which has a social service as well as a profit-making function" (p. 1145). Dodd recognized that shareholders were important, but that the purpose of the firm must extend beyond their needs. This includes pursuing benefits to the larger society by providing jobs for employees, producing quality products and services for customers and overall contributions to the welfare of the community. Dodd was a very early proponent of what would later be referred to as stakeholder theory. Interestingly, Berle (1954) conceded to Dodd's point of view in his work, *The 20th Century Capitalist Revolution* writing,

> *Twenty years ago, the writer had a controversy with the late Professor E. Merrick Dodd, of Harvard Law School, the writer holding that corporate powers were power in trust for shareholders while Professor Dodd argued that these powers were held in trust for the entire community. The argument has been settled (at least for the time being) squarely in favor of Professor Dodd's contention (p. 169).*

For a short time period, it appeared that a broader view of the firm would include more than just shareholders. Behavioral economists would also enter into this debate in the mid-1950s, questioning whether the notion of maximization was even feasible for organizations. Simon (1957) as well as Cyert and March (1963) advocated for *satisfying profits*, not maximizing them as the purpose of the firm. They argue that in reality, managers pursue multiple goals and can only strive toward satisfactory attainment across a variety of factors—such as sales, profits, customer satisfaction, and employee well-being. Simon (1957) also referred to individual behavior as *satisficing*—choosing a good option, but not necessarily the one that maximizes. It was postulated that the firm also satisfices by attempting to achieve numerous goods, one of which is profit. Management success is achieved by reaching satisfactory levels of several goals over time. To maximize one goal would come at too high of a cost to other goals, thus negating performance in the long run. As the firm becomes increasingly efficient in pursuing multiple goals, R.H. Day argues that the satisficing strategy actually achieves longer term wealth maximization as a result.

However, by the late 1950s, the rational economic thought of the Chicago School began to dominant management thinking and repurposed the theory of the firm to maximize shareholder value. The Chicago School emphasized a small number of theorems regarding human decision-making and instead focused on the creation of mathematical and scientific models to describe the power of free and competitive markets. Economics, in particular, would be severed from its humanities roots during this inquiry and solely focused on scientific research techniques (Khurana, 2007). Management of the firm would be viewed as a rational and technical activity that should be closely monitored, removing much of the autonomy managers had traditionally experienced in a broader stakeholder view of the firm. In addition, the entire focus of management studies began to focus on improving expertise through the creation of rational decision-making, rather than educating on the idea of social obligations.

The Chicago School also went against the dominant Keynesian economic discourse at the time, which advocated for government intervention, and instead insisted that free markets with little to no government involvement produced the best outcomes. Their primary assumptions were that markets are stable, people behave rationally, and prices are the best allocator of resources. Even when questioned regarding the legitimacy of these assumptions, Friedman (1953) argued that it did not matter if assumptions were unrealistic as long as the goal of science was achieved, which was to achieve successful qualitative prediction. As a result, the Chicago School was able to develop shareholder wealth maximizing models to showcase, how in theory, a society would benefit at large of such a pursuit.

The primary driver of the Chicago School was a deep-seated belief that human liberty could only be found in competitive and free markets. The Chicago School downplayed the fear of monopolies and corporate greed, and instead feared the government becoming too involved in the economy. Friedman (1982) voiced that "private unregulated monopolies" were the lesser of two evils compared to "government regulation and ownership" (p. 29). The Chicago School not only steadily produced their economic philosophy of rationality and competitive free markets in leading academic journals, but also positioned their perspectives in mainstream publications, books, and radio shows. The Chicago School of thought would go on to be recognized with a groundswell of Nobel prizes and actively participated in government policy decision-making. Combine this with the economic impasse of the 1970s and the collapse of communism signified by the fall of the Berlin Wall, and by 1990, shareholder wealth maximization emerged as the unquestionable dominant assumption that guided nearly all management theories. Managers no longer served a broader stake of constituents, but should only seek to engage in activities that maximized financial firm value.

The Chicago School of thought would go unchallenged in the mainstream literature for decades, apart from a few daring voices who remained outside the school's dominant voice. As Khurana (2007) remarks, "Under the sway of the new economic orthodoxy [Chicago School], any suggestion that the corporation was subordinate to any societal institution other than shareholders was increasingly regarded as soft-minded and suspect" (p. 304). However, one of those cautionary voices was British economist Schumacher (1973), who expressed great concern over the stifling of human souls for the pursuit of economic gain. He wrote a book focused on revisiting *Economics as if People Matter*, cautioning, "The substance of man cannot be measured by Gross National Product" further adding, "The modern economy is propelled by a frenzy of greed and indulges in an orgy of envy, and these are not accidental features but the very causes of its expansionist success. The question is whether such causes can be effective for long or whether they carry within themselves the seeds of destruction." Schumacher (1973) also worried about the self-fulfilling nature of the undisputed pessimism regarding human behavior in businesses. He wrote,

> *"If human vices such as greed and envy are systematically cultivated, the inevitable result is nothing less than a collapse of intelligence. A man driven by greed or envy loses the power of seeing things as they really are, of seeing things in their roundness and wholeness, and his very successes become failures. If whole societies become infected by these vices, they may indeed achieve astonishing things but they become increasingly incapable of solving the most elementary problems of everyday existence."*

In the end, Schumacher concludes that the current dominant economic discourse is simply irrational to the ultimate pursuit of societal well-being by confusing the means with the ends. The current economic model upholds consumption and wealth as the primary ends rather than as a means toward well-being. The rational economic aim should be the maximization of human well-being, which results in the least amount of consumption. This notion was of course in the minority at the time of publication.

However, by the turn of the century, a multitude of corporate scandals would once again bring shareholder wealth maximization into question. In a landmark article written by the late Sumantra Ghoshal (2005), he fervently bemoaned the blind acceptance of the shareholder wealth maximization model as the only acceptable path to profitable business practice. This blinded faith in supervising agency costs and assurance in stable markets led to a fundamentally negative view of individuals at work. The outcome was devastating to Ghoshal who attributed the unethical business meltdowns (i.e., WorldCom, Enron) of the early 2000s as stemming from these assumptions. Rather than promoting voluntary cooperation, he argued business environments were simply built on mechanical compliance models, which were not working in practice. He viewed the growing undercurrent of the dehumanization of business practice as a direct result of these cynical sentiments.

> *"Combine agency theory with transaction costs economics, add in standard versions of game theory and negotiation analysis, and the picture of the manager that emerges is one that is now very familiar in practice: the ruthlessly hard-driving, strictly top-down, command-and-control focused, shareholder-value-obsessed, win-at-any-cost business leaders" (p. 85).*

In addition, Ghoshal (2005) attributed the desire for scientific approaches as a cause for neglecting to explain corporate performance by the "choices, actions and achievements of individuals" (p. 77). His primary concern with the commonly held assumptions of his time was that it led to an amoral perspective of the firm, easily justifying the many unethical management practices arising in business. Self-interest assumptions became the socially acceptable norm, and even required for success (Miller, 1999). Unethical behavior became easily justified by the rationale that "everybody does it" (Green, 1991). As a result, Ghoshal (2005) strongly advocated for new assumptions of human nature in economic and management theories that recognized deviations from self-interest and promoted the common well-being of the stakeholders in which the business sought to serve.

Even newer academic research cautions the short-term approach to maximizing shareholders may actually be having the inverse effect. Stout (2012) wrote, "Perhaps most disturbing, far from having proven itself a governance cure, the increasing influence of shareholder value thinking on business law and practice has been accompanied by, if anything, a decline in American corporate and economic performance" (p. 104). However, more recent empirical research suggests that a long-term orientation toward multiple goals has recently been shown to positively correlate with job creation, market capitalization, economic profit, earnings, and revenue (Barton, Manyika, & Willamson, 2017). Researchers analyzed over 615 nonfinancial organizations to determine if a difference existed between short-term pursuit of wealth generation compared to long-term goal pursuits. These long-term organizational behaviors were measured by looking at investment spending, earnings quality, and margin growth. From their sample, the researchers identified 167 companies (27% of the sample) as exhibiting long-term behaviors. Not only were positive economic correlations found, but the difference was staggering in company performance between those who pursued long-term behaviors with those that pursued short-term wealth maximization. For example, the long-term companies created 132% more jobs, 81% more economic profit, and 58% higher market capitalization after 2008. The researchers suggest that nearly $1 trillion in US GDP could have been created, along with another 5 million jobs, had all organizations within their population sought out long-term behaviors. This research supports the idea that Simon (1957) suggested decades earlier—firms which seek out multiple longer-term goals, willing to satisfice in the shorter term, are much more likely to generate financial growth.

2.5.6.2 The Purpose of the Firm Debated in Courts

In 1968, another case, *Sklensky v. Wrigley*, would be brought to court to determine how to best address and balance the interests of shareholders. Decades earlier, during the *Ford Motor Company vs Dodge* case, it was ruled in the favor of shareholders. This time an outcome favoring a larger group of stakeholders would rule. The Chicago Cubs president was approached by a shareholder to install lights at Wrigley Field to begin conducting night time games to increase profits for shareholders. However, the president strongly disagreed as he felt baseball was a daytime sport and lights would have deteriorating impact to the surrounding neighborhood. Installing lights to host nighttime games, while likely increasing profits, would negatively impact other stakeholders of the business. The president objected to this and insisted he was making the best possible decision for the business and community. The judge ruled in favor of the president noting that it was "not satisfied that the motives assigned to the directors are contrary to the best interests of the corporation and the stockholders...because they showed no fraud, illegality or conflict of interest in making that decision." In other words—the company was still making a profit and handling the affairs of the business in a legal and satisfactory manner, even if it meant shareholder wealth was not maximized in every decision made. This ruling was a shift, which considered businesses as broader in scope than simply securing additional profits for shareholders.

2.5.6.3 Businesses Respond to Shareholders Throughout the Century

The larger stakeholder ideology of the firm was supported by a majority of companies in the early and mid-20th century. Though as some have argued, it was less about altruistic motives and more about keeping unions at bay. Williams (1920) noted that the sharp rise in union membership was simply a direct result of an overall lack of concern over employee needs. As a result, companies scrambled to enlarge the social contract and strengthen the relationship between the firm and employee. During this time, employees across the country reaped numerous benefits, including increases in company-sponsored retirement funds, shortened working hours, increased health care coverage, and stability of employment (Wartzman, 2017). Organizational leaders quickly realized that communities, consumers, and employees were also key stakeholders in securing financial success and capturing employee loyalty apart from unionization. In 1951, the chairman of Standard Oil of New Jersey declared, "The job of management is to maintain an equitable and working balance among the claims of various directly affected interest groups…stockholders, employees, customers and the public at large."

Yet, satisficing firm behavior came under scrutiny in the mid-1980s when a series of hostile takeover bids began. As Ward (1997) points out, profitable companies like Gillette and Disney were targeted as organizations who could become even more profitable if their single pursuit was on wealth maximization. Useem (1996) describes the shift corporate executives began to feel. He notes, "Your days of satisficing are over, from now on, you must maximize. If you don't, we will." This fear was then realized when 13 CEOs of Fortune 500 companies were dismissed between April 1992 and August 1993. This trend continued as Charan and Colvin (1999) report that CEO dismissal rates tripled between 1980 and 1999. In 2005, Donaldson, while skeptical of alternative theories of the firm wrote, "I am confident about this: Today's top executives, in America, at least, are exceedingly obsessed with shareholder value, in ways that their predecessors were not." As a result, companies now actively seek leaders, not to be stewards of an organization's longer-term health and vitality, but to single mindedly pursue shareholder wealth maximization, often resulting in leadership behaviors, which are, emotionally detached from their companies as living institutions. Solansky (2014) notes this is a large shift in societal expectations of business leaders. "The emphasis of leadership effectiveness has drastically shifted from an age-old assessment of leadership that aspires to wisdom, to a current day assessment of leadership that aspires to compete to achieve market efficiencies and maximum organizational profits" (p. 40).

As a result, the overemphasis in both academia and changing U.S. legislation, shareholder price is upheld as the ultimate barometer in resource allocation decision-making, even when it is contrary to the resources' intended use. For example, consider the research conducted by the Senate Permanent Subcommittee in October 2011, which analyzed the outcomes of the American Jobs Creation Act of 2004. The review sought to determine how well companies managed their funds received via the tax break, which carried the mandate to utilize the funds toward employee and firm development, rather than shareholders. In 2004, this government policy allowed U.S. multinational companies to take a temporary but significant tax break on their foreign profits. Rather than taxing foreign profits at a 35% corporate tax rate to bring back to the U.S., companies were only taxed at a rate of 5.25%. The mandate of the act was to use these dollars on worker hiring and training, R&D, infrastructure, capital investments, and provide overall financial stability for the purposes of job retention and creation. It was strongly stated that that companies should not use these funds for stock buyouts or increases in executive compensation packages. The intent was to earmark these dollars for U.S. worker growth and development. As a result of the tax break, companies brought $312 billion dollars back to the United States.

However, nearly 8 years later, it was discovered in an investigative report that the top 15 companies whom took advantage of this tax break actually cut more than 20,000 workers and slowed their pace of research and development spending. Yet, those same 15 companies saw executive compensation packages increase 27% from 2004 to 2005 and another 30% from 2005 to 2006. In addition, stock buybacks increased 16% from 2004 to 2005 and 38% from 2005 to 2006. The study concluded that the 840 companies who took advantage of the American Jobs Creation Act of 2004, associated between 60 and 92 cents in payments to shareholders on each dollar brought back to the United States. The dominant emphasis on maximizing shareholder wealth and aligning executive compensation based on agency theory seemed to exert too great a hold on these business leaders who undeniably did little to boost worker development.

As executives' compensation continues to be aligned with shareholder price, a practice that was once illegal in the 20th century, has come to the forefront of modern-day business practices—share buybacks. The practice of allowing organizations to buyback their shares was made legal in 1982, right around the same time agency theory was dominating the academic discourse on management. It has been recognized as a defense strategy by leading firms who may be slow to adopt to changing market structures. In November 2016, Goldman Sachs projected share buybacks to rise 30% in 2017, representing $780 billion dollars. One of the problems voiced with adopting this strategy is that executive compensation can rise even as business performance slumps, as a share buyback will typically inflate share price and earnings per share. Even if business is in a slump, the buyback will at least temporarily result in stock price inflation.

Of course, not all buybacks are a defensive strategy and can be effectively used when a company is perceived to be undervalued in the market. Yet, its sharp increase in use has caused some to question the opportunity cost at stake. Those same dollars could be invested in research and development or worker learning and growth to create a longer-term competitive advantage in the market. As a result, Lazonick (2015) believes this type of resource allocation strategy actually undermines innovation, promotes unstable employment practices, increases inequality, and lowers worker productivity. He refers to this as a "downsize and distribute" strategy, rather than a "retain and reinvest" mindset. Downsize and distribute stems from shareholder wealth maximization thinking, seeks to drive costs down, and use the costs savings to payout shareholders. Constrast to the retain and reinvest mindset, which seeks to primarily use capital to invest in production capabilities of its labor force. This echoes Robert Bookings who stated nearly a century earlier, "Capital, not labor, should be treated by management as a commodity."

In addition, Lazonick (2017) argued for a new perspective on the role of shareholders in business decision-making. He advocates, "As a rule, public shareholders do not invest in a corporation's productive capabilities; they simply buy shares outstanding on the market, hoping to extract value that they have played no role in helping to create" (p. 1). Therefore, Lazonick does not suggest that shareholders are the only ones that inherit risk when investing in a business. Rather, taxpayers and employees inherit as much, if not more risk, in the business. As a result, they are as equally due to the residual cash made from the business endeavors. For example, Lazonick (2015) argues that the National Institute of Health, which is funded by taxpayer dollars, has an annual operating budget of $30 billion. Part of this multibillion dollar budget is used to finance for-profit organizational efforts in helping with research endeavors. Those dollars given to organizations are not simply accountable to shareholders, but also to taxpayers. In addition, Lazonick shows how employees, while engaged in a transactional relationship with an employer, which is assumed to be assessed at fair market value, assumes much risk in the breaking of such contracts through layoffs or a lack of investment in the individual's development. Therefore, Lazonick warns that it is more than just shareholders who are at risk with business decision-making and as a result businesses need to reconsider the role of seeking to only maximize value for one of its constituents.

Other voices in business have expressed growing concern over the role that shareholder wealth maximization has had on individual and organizational behavior. For example, some research suggests that this sole pursuit of shareholder wealth has turned corporate behavior to resemble sociopathic tendencies (Bakan, 2005). Jack Welch, once a leading voice for the dominant discourse, declared shareholder wealth maximization as, "the world's dumbest idea" and "insane." In addition, current Unilever CEO, Paul Polman, recently decried the shareholder wealth maximization model by stating, "Too many companies are running their business into the ground, I would argue by being myopically short-term focused on the shareholder. We're going back to where it should be...I do not work for the shareholder, to be honest. I work for the customer." (Buckley & Chung, 2017, p. 48–49). Nevertheless, the emphasis on maximizing shareholder returns remains the dominant discourse in the purpose of public corporations (see Fig. 2.2 for a chronological timeline of the purpose of the firm debate).

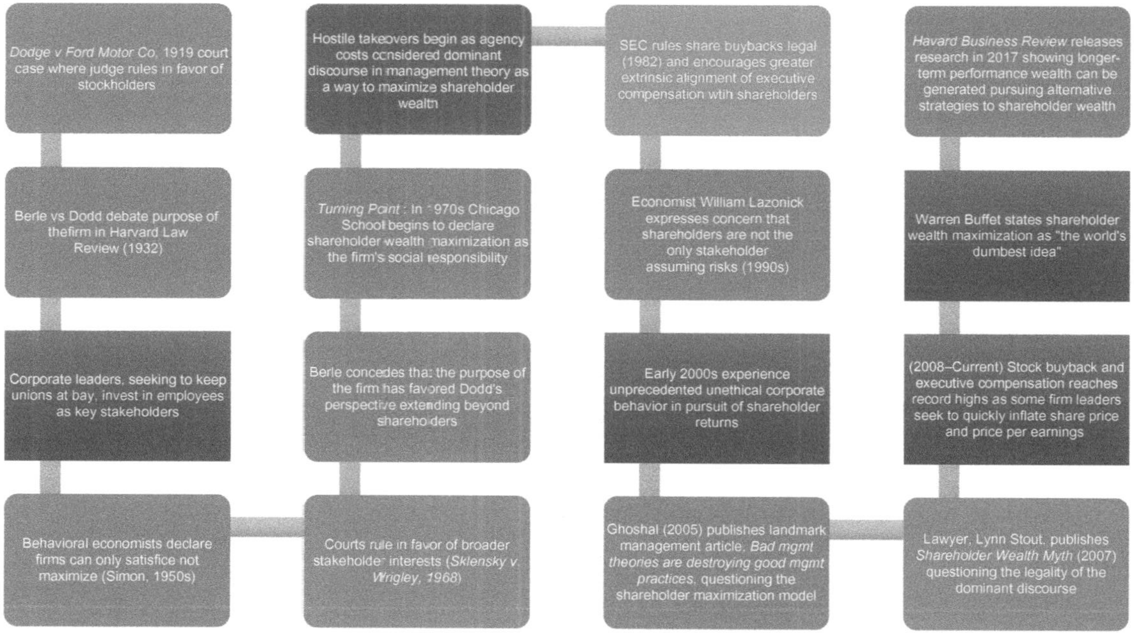

FIGURE 2.2 Chronological timeline of the purpose of the firm debate.

2.6 CONCLUSION

In the end, it is important to note that "shareholder primacy is a managerial choice – not a legal requirement." It is not a natural law that managers must follow to guarantee success of the firm. And, it is important to note that this pursuit may not even lead to its intended outcome. Rather, managers have a variety of tools and means at their disposal to maximize the purpose of their firm. By exploring the historical origins of today's management practices, we are able to unpack both historical and contemporary criticism that have arisen throughout their inceptions. In addition, we are able to explore an alternative assumption that people do have an inherent desire to express themselves through their work when certain needs are met. We will now turn our attention to ways managers can leverage alternative assumptions to drive productivity and knowledge creation in their firms. As will be discovered, if managers are able to better leverage individual's intrinsic drive toward meaning and belonging, the command and control style would be deemed ineffective in today's knowledge-driven environments. Rather, a new theory of management decision-making arises that seeks to not only maximize the short-term wealth of the firm, but seeks longer-term sustainability of the organization through the development of its workforce. With the constant pressures facing many firm managers as it relates to shareholder wealth maximization, exploring alternative paradigms may better safeguard managers against the inherent biases that arise during shortsighted and narrowly framed decision-making contexts. Advancements in behavioral science alongside the changing market conditions require a critical examination into the administrative theory of management decision-making and behaviors.

But, make no mistake—business has and always will be the lifeblood of a nation's pathway to prosperity. The role of business in society can lead to greater economic freedoms, social mobility, wealth, and drive innovation. It was the role of business that accelerated the economic growth experienced in the 20th century, bringing along a host of quality of life improvements. In addition, work can provide immense meaning to individual's lives as they seek to contribute to larger societal concerns. Business can be used as a powerful force for both economic and individual growth.

Yet, these rational assumptions guiding management decisions discussed in this chapter will likely not sustain us in the 21st century as businesses face newfound challenges. To challenge the dominant discourse that drives human behavior and beliefs that will help shape society's well-being is commonplace in other disciplines. Consider the example within the field of medicine and its importance to societal health. The medical community not only reassess assumptions, but even deems traditional theories as obsolete through further explorations. Similar to medicine, the field of business contributes greatly to societal outcomes—through the development and sale of goods, services, and knowledge. It is businesses that propel society forward. Yet, the business community lacks the same level of rigorous debates of core assumptions that the medical community practices. As a result, our dominant management theories may be less helpful in describing and shaping 21st century effective management of the firm, which could ultimately impact societal level outcomes. We will now turn our focus on exploring the alternative assumptions that may better guide manager decision-making in knowledge-driven economies.

REFERENCES

Aristotle. (350 B.C.E.). Rhetoric, Book I, Part 2. Translated by W. Rhys Roberts. http://classics.mit.edu/Aristotle/rhetoric.1.i.html

Bakan, J. (2005). The corporation: The pathological pursuit of profit and *power*. Free Press.

Barnard, C. (1938). *The functions of the executive*. Cambridge, MA: Harvard University Press.

Barton, D., Manyika, J., & Willamson, S. K. (2017). The data: Where long-termism pays off. *Harvard Business Review*, May-June Issue.

Bennis, W., & O'Toole, J. (2005). How business schools lost their way. *Harvard Business Review*, May Issue.

Berle, A. A. (1931). Corporate powers as powers in trust. *Harvard Law Review*, *44*, 1049–1074.

Berle, A. (1954). *The 20th century capitalist revolution*. New York: Harcourt Brace.

Birkinshaw, J. (2014). Do we still need managers? *Business Strategy Review*, *25*, 6. Available from https://doi.org/10.1111/j.1467-8616.2014.01042.x.

Bower, J. L., & Paine, L. S. (2017). The error at the heart of corporate leadership. *Harvard Business Review*, May-June Issue.

Boyer, P. S., Dubofsky, M., Monkkonen, E. H., Numbers, R. L., Oshinkey, D. M., & Rosenberg, E. S. (2001). *The oxford companion to United States history*. Oxford University Press.

Buckley, T., & Chung, M. (2017). *If unilever can't make feel-good capitalism work, who can? Bloomberg Business week*. Available.from https://www.bloomberg.com/news/features/2017- 08-31/if-unilever-can-t-make-feel-good-capitalism-work-who-can.

Cadsby, C., & Maynes, E. (1998). Choosing between a socially efficient and free-riding equilibrium: Nurses versus economics and business students. *Journal of Economic Behavior & Organization*, *37*(2), 183–192.

Carter, J. R., & Irons, M. D. (1991). Are economists different, and if so, why? *Journal of Economic Perspectives*, *5*(2), 171–177.

Chandler, A. D. (1956). *Henry Varnum Poor: Business editor, analyst, and reformer*. Cambridge, MA: Harvard University Press.

Chandler, A. D. (1962). *Strategy and structure: Chapters in the history of the industrial enterprise*. Cambridge: MIT Press.

Chapman, G. B., & Johnson, E. J. (2002). Incorporating the irrelevant: Anchors in judgments of belief and value. In T. Gilovich, D. Griffith, & D. Kahneman (Eds.), *Heuristics and biases: The psychology of intuitive judgment* (pp. 120–138). Cambridge, UK: Cambridge University Press.

Charan, R., & Colvin, G. (1999). Why CEOs fail. *Fortune*, *21*, 69–78.

Cone Communications. (2013). *Cone Communications/Echo Global CSR Study*. Cone Communications, LLC.

Cowan, R. S. (1997). *A social history of American technology*. New York: Oxford University Press.

Cummings, S., & Bridgman, T. (2016). The limits and possibilities of history: How a wider, deeper and more engaged understanding of business history can foster innovative thinking. *Academy of Management Learning and Education, 15*(2), 250–267.

Cyert, R. M., & March, J. G. (1963). *A behavioral theory of the firm*. Englewood Cliffs, NJ: Prentice-Hall, Inc.

Davis, J. B. (2003). *The theory of individual in economics: Identity and value*. London: Routledge.

Dodd, E. M. (1932). For whom are corporate managers trustees. *Harvard Law Review, 45*, 1145–1163.

Dodge v Ford Motor Company., 170 N.W., 684. (Mich. 1919).

Donaldson, T., & Walsh, J. P. (2015). Toward a theory of the firm. *Research in Organizational Behavior, 35*, 181–207.

Drucker, P. F. (1974). *Management: Tasks responsibilities, practices* (p. 559) London: Heineman.

Evans, J. A. (2008). Electronic publication and the narrowing of science and scholarship. *Science, 321*(5887), 395–399.

Fayol, H. (1916). *General and industrial management*. Martino Fine Books.

Ferraro, F., Pfeffer, J., & Sutton, R. (2005). Economics language and assumptions: How theories can become self-fulfilling. *Academy of Management Review*, 8–24.

Frank, R. (1988). *Passions within reason: The strategic role of emotions* (p. 237) W.W. Norton & Company Publishing.

Frey, B., & Oberholzer-Gee, F. (1997). The cost of price incentives: An empirical analysis of motivation crowding-out. *American Economic Review, 87*(4), 746–755.

Friedman, M. (1953). *Essays in Positive Economics*. Chicago: University of Chicago Press.

Friedman, M. (1970). The social responsibility of business is to increase its profits. *The New York Times Magazine*.

Friedman, M. (1982). *Capitalism and freedom*. Chicago: University of Chicago Press.

Garvin, D. A. (2013). How Google sold its engineers on management. *Harvard Business Review*, December Issue.

Ghoshal, S. (2005). Bad management theories are destroying good management practices. *Academy of Management Learning and Education Journal, 4*(1), 75–91.

Giddens, A. (1984). *The constitution of society* (p. 20) Cambridge: Polity Press.

Glotz, G. (1926). *Ancient Greece at work*. New York: Alfred A, Knopft.

Gordon, J. (2007). The rise of independent directors in the United States, 1950–2005: Of shareholder value and stock market prices. *Stanford Law Review, 59*(6), 1465–1568.

Gordon, R. (2016). *The rise and fall of American growth*. Princeton University Press.

Green, R. M. (1991). When is "everyone's doing it" a moral justification? *Business Ethics Quarterly, 1*(1), 75–93.

Hamel, G. (2011). First, let's fire all of the managers. *Harvard Business Review*. Available from https://hbr.org/2011/12/first-lets-fire-all-the-managers.

Hansmann, H., & Kraakman, R. (2001). The end of history for corporate law. *Georgetown Law Journal, 8*(2), 439–468.

Jensen, M. C., & Meckling, W. H. (1976). Theory of the firm: Managerial behavior, agency costs and ownership structure. *Journal of Financial Economics, 3*(4), 305–360.

Keynes, J. M. (1936). *The general theory of employment, interest and money* (p. 383) UK: Palgrave Macmillan.

Khurana, R. (2007). *From higher aims to hired hands: The social transformation of American business schools and the unfulfilled promise of management as professions*. Princeton, NJ: Princeton University Press.

Lazonick, W. (2015). Stock buybacks: From retain-and- reinvest to downsize-and-distribute. *Center for Effective Public Management at Brookings*. Available from https://www.brookings.edu/wp-content/uploads/2016/06/lazonick.pdf.

Lazonick, W. (2017). The Functions of the Stock Market and the Fallacies of Shareholder Value. Institute for New Economic Thinking Working Paper Series No. 58. Available at SSRN: https://ssrn.com/abstract=2993978 or https://doi.org/10.2139/ssrn.2993978.

Liberman, V., Samuels, S. M., & Ross, L. (2004). The name of the game: Predictive power of reputations versus situational labels in determining prisoner's dilemma game moves. *Personality and Social Psychology Bulletin, 30*(9), 1175–1185.

Marwell, G., & Ames, R. E. (1981). Economists free ride, does anyone else? Experiments on the provisions of public goods, IV. *Journal of Public Economics*, 295–310.

Miller, D. T. (1999). The norm of self-interest. *American Psychologist, 54*(12), 1053–1060.

Mills, C. W. (1940). Situated actions and vocabularies of motive. *American Sociological Review*, 904–913, December.

Mintzberg, H. (1989). *Mintzberg on management*. Free Press.

Mintzberg, H. (2004). *Managers, not MBA's*. San Francisco: Berrett-Koehler.

Parolo, P. D. B., Pan, R. K., Ghosh, R., Huberman, B. A., Kaski, K., & Fortunato, S. (2015). Attention decay in science. *Journal of Infometrics, 9*(4), 734–745.

Roche, B., & Jakub, J. (2017). *Completing capitalism: Heal business to heal the world*. Berrett-Koehler Publishers.

Roethlisberger, F. J., & Dickson, William J. (1939). *Management and the worker*. Cambridge, MA: Harvard University Press.

Rollert, J. P. (2017). When making a profit was immoral. *Chicago Booth Review*. Available from http://review.chicagobooth.edu/economics/2017/article/when-making-profit-was-immoral.

Sadun, R., Bloom, N., & Van Reenen, J. (2017). Why do we undervalue competent management? *Harvard Business Review*, 122, September–October Issue.

Schumacher, E. F. (1973). *Small is beautiful: Economics as if people mattered*. New York: Harper & Row.

Simon, H. (1957). *Administrative behavior*. New York: The Free Press.

Simon, H. (1985). Human nature in politics: The dialogue of psychology with political science. *American Political Science Review, 79*, 293–304.

Smith, A. (1759). *The theory of moral sentiments*.

Smith, A. (1776). *The wealth of nations*. Scotland: William Strahan and Thomas Cadell.

Solansky, S. (2014). Education and experience impact leadership development psychological empowerment. *Leadership & Organizational Development Journal, 35*(7), 40.

Stacey, R. *Complex responsive processes in organizations: Learning and knowledge creation*. London: Routledge.

Stout, L. (2012). *The shareholder value myth*. San Francisco: Berrett-Koehler Publishers.

Taylor, F. W. (1911). *The principles of scientific management* (pp. 44–46). New York: Harper & Brothers, 59.

Tversky, A., & Kahneman, D. (1974). Judgment under uncertainty: Heuristics and biases. *Science, 185*, 1124–1131.

Useem, M. (1996). *Investor capitalism: How money managers are changing the face of corporate America*. New York: Basic Books.

Ward, R. D. (1997). *21st century corporate board*. New York: Wiley.

Wartzman, R. (2017). *The end of loyalty: The rise and fall of good jobs in America*. New York: Hachette Book Group.

Williams, C. (2013). *Management* (7 ed.). South-Western Cengage Learning.

Williams, W. (1920). What's on the workers mind?

Williams, W. (1921). Untitled manuscript. Box 9, MS 3580. *The Western Reserve Historical Society*.

Wilson, D. D. (1916). Halting the Taylor system. *Machinists' Monthly Journal*, *XXIII*(11), 1107–1108.

Wood, J., & Wood, M. (2003). *Henry Ford: Critical evaluations in business and management. Volume 1*. London: Routledge.

Wren, D. A., & Bedeian, A. G. (2009). *The evolution of management thought* (6th ed.). John Wiley and Sons.

FURTHER READING

Buckley, T., & Campbell, M. (2017). The fresh scent of success. *Bloomberg Business Week*.

Gergen, K. J. (1973). Social psychology as history. *Journal of Personality and Social Psychology*, *26*(2), 309–320.

Giddens, A. (1987). *Social theory and modern sociology*. Cambridge: Polity Press.

Gordon, R., Howell, J. (1959). Robert A. Gordon, James E. Howell; The education of American business men: A study in University-College programs in business administration, prepared for the Ford Foundation.

(1916). Industrial relations. Final report and testimony submitted to Congress by the Commission on Industrial Relations. Vol I. Washington Government Printing Office.

Kiechel, W. (2012). The management century. *Harvard Business Review*. Available from https://hbr.org/2012/11/the-management-century.

Mayo, E. (1975). *The social problems of an industrial civilisation*. Routledge and Kegan Paul, 1949; later ed with appendix.

McGregor, D. (1960). *The human side of enterprise*. New York: McGraw-Hill Book Company.

(1999). Rethinking thinking. The Economist, Retrieved September 17, 2017 from http://www.economist.com/node/268946

Schein, E. (2010). *Organizational culture and leadership* (4th Ed.). Jossey-Bass.

Williams, W. (1927). Box 8: Manuscript "Man and mine the coal mine".

Chapter 3

Exploring Management Alternatives With a Behavioral Economic Lens

3.1 EXPLORING ALTERNATIVE ASSUMPTIONS OF PEOPLE AT WORK

Chapter 2, Rational Economics and the Administrative Theory of Management, critiques two core assumptions, which are grounded in rational and transactional cost economies that drive many management decision-making in today's firms. The first assumption, that people are primarily rational decision-makers and actively seek to restrict their output, creates the need to appropriately incentivize individuals to align with firm goals. The second assumption is that the purpose of the firm is to pursue shareholder wealth maximization. Under this guise, a manager's core task is to mitigate agency costs and they do so through the activities of planning, directing, organizing, and controlling resources.

But, what if these assumptions were wrong or even just incomplete? And, as a result, unintentionally shaping poor management behavior across firms. Advancements in behavioral economics may offer alternatives of what drives people beyond rationality, and ultimately shed newfound light on the role of managers at work. The role of the firm and management is important to get right as business is fundamental to societal well-being. The importance of the role of business in achieving individual freedom and prosperity is profound. For example, Porter and Stern (2015) looked at the relationship between social progress and economic growth across 133 nations and found a strong correlation between the two activities ($r = 0.78$). Not only can economic growth provide positive societal level outcomes, work can provide immense meaning to individual's lives as they seek to contribute to larger societal concerns. Therefore, getting the underlying assumptions about people at work right is key to effective management in today's complex environments.

This chapter seeks to provide alternatives to the commonly held rational assumptions of people at work, in the hopes of generating a new narrative

How Behavioral Economics Influences Management Decision-Making.
DOI: https://doi.org/10.1016/B978-0-12-813531-0.00003-0

around the role of management in the firm. The following alternatives are explored:

1. Individuals are influenced by outside factors in the decision-making process, including their own biases and social factors.
2. Individuals are motivated by intrinsic factors at work, but these may be easily crowded out by external incentives.
3. The purpose of the firm can extend beyond shareholders wealth to seek sustained value for stakeholders.

These alternatives are grounded in idea that people do not operate under perfect knowledge or are always able to make decisions in their best interest. As a result, these behavioral economics management alternatives consider the often conflicting or overriding presence of psychological, social, and emotional factors in individual and group decision-making. In particular, behavioral economics provides an insightful look into the inner lives of individuals making decisions, while also expanding the individualistic perspective to include social factors.

3.2 BEHAVIORAL ECONOMICS: THE INNER LIFE OF INDIVIDUALS

Advances in both behavioral economics and psychology seek to deal with the realities-facing individuals within organizations. The behavioral economics literature, while still relatively young, seeks to investigate the inner life of the individual, which does not always predictably respond to incentives. While the mathematic modeling may not be as advanced as rational economic theories, it is distinguished for its reflection of real life decision-making. Yet, the influence of the inner life of individuals at work remains neglected in organizational studies (Ashkanasy&Jordan, 2008). Business consultant Whiting Williams (1957) urged business leaders at Johnson & Johnson to recognize, "the unbelievable importance of the worker's feelings and experience rather than his logic or reasons as factor in all his viewpoints and attitudes" (p. 2). As discussed, rational economic thinking is relatively mute on the concepts of feelings and emotions in the workplace. However, behavioral economics considers both the inner life of the individual through psychological research, as well as the environmental factors, through sociological research, which often conflict or override rational thinking and behaviors. While one may assume human rationality prevails, quite the contrary is suggested in the research.

Rather than assume markets, firms, and individuals operate with perfect knowledge, behavioral economists recognize reality often resembles imperfect knowledge conditions, uncertainties, and limitations. At the firm level, behavioral economists Cyert and March (1963) argued it is awkward to assume perfect knowledge in the theory of the firm, but contend managers must assume the exact opposite, being forced to make decisions in the midst of uncertainty. This is further complicated at the group and individual level, when knowledge is often censored or withheld due to social influences. And as other studies suggest, people make best guesses and take shortcuts to arrive at decisions (Kahneman, 2011). Rarely are individuals able to operate under certainty, either due to their own limitations or the constraints imposed by the environment. Therefore, individuals frequently confront an imperfect environment and face their own limitations for navigating its complexity. As a result, decisions rarely reflect the best choice amongst a known set of alternatives, but rather represents an alternative that simply satisfices (Simon, 1957).

This change in assumption about rationality and perfect knowledge marks a newfound understanding of the role of the manager in a knowledge-based environment. It also enlarges the influence of an individual's inner life on the interaction with others within organizations. Neoclassical economics assumes the autonomy of atomistic individuals remains unchanged by interaction with others, and that the cognitive process for individual choice is privately governed by the rational desire to seek out their best interest, uninfluenced by the preferences of others. However, as will be demonstrated throughout, this is rarely the case in organizations (Thaler, 2015). Rather, complex processes of relating occur between individuals, which cause irrationalities in individual preferences and decision-making (Stacey, 2001). Rather than simply seeking maximum utility, individuals often assess fairness, levels of reciprocity, and sometimes just act out of human generosity towards others with no anticipated returns (Delton, Krasnow, Cosmides, &Tooby, 2011), none of which are accounted for in rational economics.

Therefore, behavioral economics considers how the individual's inner life and environment can tax or enhance one's ability to rationalize and learn in the workplace. As we will explore, humans have a finite capability to deeply engage in rational cognitive decision-making. This causes an individual to not only take shortcuts, but also rely on the environment for behavioral cues. The creation of intellectual capital hinges upon the limitations of human cognitions and the constraints of the environment through the presence of social influences. Thus, the social dynamics help explain individual cognitions at work and is recognized in behavioral economic studies, which rely on both laboratory and field settings. Studies prove how group member decision-making often differs from what an individual may have decided on their own (Bougheas, Nieboer, Sefton, 2015).

We will now turn our attention to the growing body of literature that explains how *real* people behave in *real* firms, facing the limitations of their own intellectual capacities, the influence of affective states, the reliance on environmental cues and, at times, the motivation to act beyond their own individual utility maximization. We will explore an alternative to the *homo economicus* model, which will provide newfound explanations for how knowledge and intellectual capital is created and shared within today's firms (See Fig. 3.1 for a contrast of industrial and knowledge based management styles.). This alternative view, which seeks to understand employee behavior in the firm will shed light into the circumstances affecting individual decision-making and offer greater depth for mangers to integrate these limitations into their quest to maximize knowledge sharing within the organization.

3.3 ALTERNATIVE 1: AN INDIVIDUAL'S ABILITY TO ACT RATIONALLY IS BOUND BY COGNITIVE LIMITATIONS, EMOTIONS, AND THE INFLUENCE OF OTHERS

Thus far, we have explored the limitations to the assumption that people always make decisions to maximize their own utility. This is not to say that people do not behave rationally, but there is often so much more to the story. It will be explored that an individual's own cognitive limitations are brought on by periods of fatigue, affective states, or mindset, which influence effort levels and outcomes. In addition, while much of the decision-making conversation centers around the individual, rarely do individuals create knowledge in a vacuum. Instead, people react to information signals from others, sometimes choosing to censor their own individual preferences in order to follow along with the group.

3.3.1 Cognitive Limitations to Learning and Rationality

Simon (1957) argued that rationality was bounded by the complexity of the environment and the limits of one's own humanity. While the brain only comprises of 2.55% of a human's body weight, it accounts for nearly 20% of the body's energy (Hardiman, 2012). Given the toil thinking has on the body, the

	Industrial Revolution	Knowledge Economy
Type of Worker	Primarily low skilled labor that thrived on routine and predictability	Highly skilled; generates ideas and drives innovation
Role of Manager	Command and control of resources; relies on incentives for compliance	Integrates and fosters innovation; seeks to increase social and intellectual capital
Organizational Emphasis	Shareholder wealth maximization; capital accumulation	Sustained collective value across stakeholders; people, profits and planet
Economic Lens	Rational Economic Theory; Natural Law	Behavioral Economics; Social science
Primary Management Theory	Administrative, manage agency costs	Behavioral, create stakeholder value
Shareholders	People; invest up to 5 years	Institutions; invest < 1 year

FIGURE 3.1 Evolution of workers and firms.

brain has developed a series of shortcuts or heuristics to quickly make decisions and conserve energy. Kahneman (2011) famously coined this as thinking fast, which relies on "System 1" thinking. System 1 thinking is automatic and requires little, if no effort, or conscious control. However, thinking slow, or "System 2" thinking requires intentional effort and deliberate attention (Stanovich & West, 2000). Psychologists over the years have coined this dichotomy of how the brain works in numerous ways, all of which recognize the distinction between an autopilot vs intentional response. For example, De Bono's (1970) work focused on vertical compared to lateral thinking, while Frederick (2005) focused on intuitive and reflective thinking. Neuroscientists tend to examine a person's working memory compared to their longer-term memory recall. Other studies refer to the dualistic nature of the brain as top-down or bottom-up processing (i.e., Wolfe, Butcher, Lee, & Hyle, 2003). Regardless of the terminology used and the nuances that ensue, the recognition within the psychology literature of dualistic human thinking and its limitations have been well-known for quite some time.

Therefore, in order to understand intellectual capital creation, it is important to understand *how* people learn and create knowledge. Learning and knowledge creation requires individuals to engage in slow thinking—Deliberate, thoughtful, and intentional processing. Learning is often captured by changing one's mind on a particular idea through the acquisition of new knowledge. However, three distinct cognitive limitations emerge as individuals engage in learning and knowledge-oriented activities: Cognitive dissonance, confirmation bias, and decision-fatigue.

3.3.1.1 Cognitive Dissonance

In many cases, learning requires people to face cognitive dissonance. Cognitive dissonance refers to the phenomena of having to recreate a core mental model or belief. A mental model captures the understanding surrounding the way something works in the real world. Mental models are often described as the images and representations one creates to interpret reality around them. Dissonance occurs when one is faced with information conflicting with their existing mental model. For example, imagine having the belief that the sun orbits around the earth, only to be presented with evidence to the contrary. A state of dissonance immediately occurs. This can be an uncomfortable exercise for many. Festinger (1957) argues irrational behavior can often be explained by the strong motivator to maintain cognitive consistency. People may actively ignore rational facts and logic in order to avoid the discomfort that cognitive dissonance can bring.

Learning directly causes a disruption to cognitive consistency by presenting an individual with something new or different. This causes the person to have to exhibit additional energy and effort towards integrating new information into already existing mental models. This mental model shift requires slow thinking, which often has to override the reactive fast thinking part of the brain. Fast thinking constantly seeks to recognize and confirm what it believes to be true in order to maintain consistency of thought. While this conserves energy, it also restricts the ability for learning.

The effort required to overcome the discomfort of learning can be paralyzing. Recent research confirms cognitive dissonance as the leading barrier towards new knowledge attainment. Dechawatanapaisal and Siengthai (2006) surveyed 162 participants undergoing change across three organizations, finding cognitive dissonance as a direct impediment to the acquisition of new knowledge during a change initiative. Many employees remarked, "this isn't the way we do things" when confronted with new information. The implication for management is to consider practices that moderate the unpleasant experiences often required to create new knowledge in the workplace, since people are inherently wired toward maintaining cognitive consistency. Indeed, a strong obstacle to rational thought and learning in the firm is the individual's innate desire to avoid cognitive dissonance.

3.3.1.2 Confirmation Bias

Another obstacle to learning new information is something called confirmation bias, whereby individuals only seek out information that confirms preexisting beliefs, while remaining blind to contradictory data. In 1979, Stanford University conducted an experiment with 48 undergraduate students, showing empirical evidence for confirmation bias (Lord, Ross, & Lepper, 1979). Half of the students selected to participate were pro-death penalty and the other half of the students were anti-death penalty. The researchers provided two fictitious studies to both groups of students—One in favor of the death penalty and the other showcasing data against using the death penalty.

The results showed that the two groups significantly differed in their perception of the reliability of the studies. The group that was pro-death penalty believed the pro-death penalty article to be well-written and researched, while quickly pointing out the flaws of the contrarian point of view study. Likewise, the anti-death penalty group highlighted the flaws with the pro-death penalty research and found validation in the anti-death penalty study. In addition, after reading both studies, the students' previous views became ever stronger during post-experiment analyses. Being exposed to contrary data only seemed to confirm their initial perspective. The conclusion is that tendencies towards System 1 thinking can be very hard to override—Even when challenged with logical and rational data.

3.3.1.3 Decision-Fatigue

Another hindrance to an individual's cognitive processing is fatigue. Decision-fatigue is the phenomena that describes the lowering of quality of decision-making that results from the continued act of deciding. In other words, the more an individual engages in System 2 thinking, the more this part of the brain fatigues with its use. As a result, System 1 kicks in to conserve energy and the individual ends up taking shortcuts in further decision-making scenarios or even simply determines to follow the status quo to avoid further depletion. This was highlighted in a recent empirical study of a court judge's rulings on granting parole (Danziger, Levav, & Avnaim-Pesso, 2011). Over 1100 of the judges cases were reviewed in a year timeframe. To the surprise of the researchers, it was not the prisoner's ethnic background, crime committed, or sentence that predicted whether or not they was granted parole. Rather, it was the time of day that the case was heard. Parole was granted at a rate of 70% in the morning, however, by the late afternoon the percentage of cases granted parole was under 10%.

What was happening in this real-life scenario? The constant demand for decisions comes at a biological price to the decision-maker. Decision-fatigue, also known as ego depletion, had lessened the mental ability of the judge to continue to make complex rational decisions. As a result, he was much more likely to choose the easier status quo option, which is what the judge unintentionally did by late afternoon. The impact of decision-fatigue has been highlighted multiple times in various laboratory experiments. For example, in one laboratory experiment researchers split participants into a decider and nondecider group (Baumeister, Bratslavsky, Muraven, & Tice,1998). The decider group had to make numerous decisions over what product they would choose to purchase, often being forced to make a variety of complex trade-off decisions. The nondecider group simply observed the various products available and offered their opinion, not being forced to make any decisions. These participants were then asked to see how long they could keep their hand in an ice-cold bucket—An exercise that causes the brain to engage in intentional System 2 willpower and self-control. The decider group was only able to keep their hand in the water for an average, 28 s, while the nondecider group was able to maintain self-control longer and kept their hand in an average of 67 s.

Another study demonstrated the decision-fatigue effect by asking participants to resist the temptation of eating a bowl of M&M's and cookies, which was placed right in front of them. After resisting this temptation, the participants were given a specific task to complete and it was observed that the participants were much less likely to stay focused on the task and more easily gave up. This was true in another study where participants were asked not to show any emotion while watching a tear-jerker movie. Afterwards, these participants were much more readily to give up during a complex task activity in the laboratory than their counterparts not exposed to the movie. Indeed, one's cognitive processing and ability to remain rational, is subject to fatigue and limitations.

Behavioral economist Simon (1957) summarized the limitations of an individual's cognitions as bounded rationality. Bounded rationality reflects the limitations of one to make decisions in their best interest. These limitations often come in the form of cognitive depletion, confirmation bias, and decision-fatigue. Therefore, behavioral economists assume a finite level of cognitive resources for the individual decision-maker. Managers in organizations should also consider this truth when leading individuals and teams to help safe guard organizational outcomes.

3.3.1.4 Status Quo Bias

These three cognitive limitations inherently lead to the status quo bias, a disposition towards regularity, which makes innovation and knowledge transfer so difficult in practice. Humans favor towards apathy in light of cognitive dissonance, discomfort, and fatigue, which makes the status quo a powerful and satisficing alternative for individuals. Rather than change, many individuals and organizations pursue stability.

An example illustrated by research showed that individuals rarely change their healthcare benefit options, even when organizations provide newer and better alternatives. While newer employees were most likely to select the better and newer option, legacy employees tended to persist with original healthcare options selected years prior. Changing plans requires information seeking activities, which weighs stronger than the economic incentive to change to the more cost-effective option. This points to the question of using economic incentives as a means to create knowledge, learn, and change behaviors in the workplace. Their effectiveness may be less beneficial than most rational economists suggest.

There may be no greater concern for managers seeking knowledge creation within their firms than employees resisting and overcoming the status quo bias. The status quo bias plagues many once successful large firms by the pull to keep doing what it did to attain success in the first place. Kotter (2008) stated, "Great leaders understand that historical success tends to produce stable and inwardly focused organizations, and these outfits, in turn, reinforce a feeling of contentment with the status quo" (p. 56). Today's managers must recognize the comforting pull of the status quo and mitigate its impact by considering the decision-maker's sources of dissonance and fatigue.

3.3.1.5 Pardon the Interruption: The Distractions on Rational Cognitions

Realizing the cognitive limitations to an individual's learning, what are the other obstacles encountered in the quest for knowledge creation within the organization? Consider the following empirical study, which uncovered the impact a physical distraction can have on learning. An elementary school in New Haven, CT was experiencing a discrepancy in pupil academic performance between classrooms, but were puzzled as to the cause behind this problem. The principal ensured the curriculum taught was consistent and all the students had the same opportunity to succeed, however, half of the students continued to fall behind in their studies. The school even switched the teachers from the high-performing classrooms to the low-performing classrooms, but to no avail. A research team was brought in to observe and determine what was impacting the student's performance. When the research team set-up in a classroom on the same side as the lower performing students to conduct their study, they complained that their environment was too loud. This one side of the school directly faced a set of train tracks, exposed to the noise of the trains rattling by. The team quickly realized that the other side of the school faced away from the tracks, less prone to the noisy distraction. The team concluded it was the physical location of the classroom, not the students themselves that was to blame for the lower performance. While it was discovered that learning was negatively influenced by the noisy trains, the researchers were startled to discover the magnitude of the noise's influence on learning outcomes. The research found that the students who sat on the side of the building facing the tracks were an entire grade year behind their classmates. The constant noise disruption created by the rattling trains impeded the student's ability to accurately retain information. The city of New Haven responded by installing noise cancellation pads in all the classrooms facing the tracks. The result? The students quickly caught up to their classmates and the school now experiences equal learning outcomes regardless of classroom location.

If the presence of a physical noise can influence a person's cognitions, what about the presence of internal distractions? In ground breaking research, Mullainathan and Shafir (2013) discovered the presence of internal distractions are just as loud as noisy trains passing by. They summarize the phenomena as a psychological state of scarcity. "Scarcity itself captures attention via a bottom-up process. This is what we mean when we say it is involuntary, happening below conscious control. As a result, scarcity, too—Like trains or sudden noises—can pull us away even when we are trying to focus elsewhere." As a result, the presence of an unmet need within the individual—Such as hunger, looming deadlines, a lack of strong relationships—can pull cognitions away from the task at hand. Simply facing a state of scarcity can take a toll on one's ability to think rationally.

This state of scarcity is often attributed to what psychologists refer to as *cognitive load*—The total amount of information that one's working memory can hold at one time (Sweller, 1988). Scarcity can create a high cognitive load by unconsciously pulling away our attention towards an unmet need, limiting the capacity to process additional information. For example, psychologists have shown that dieters struggle completing a very simple task when shown a picture of food. The picture of food invokes a mental response that temporarily blinds participants to the task at hand. As we have learned, the human mind only has a finite amount of rational resources to devote to System 2 tasks such as learning and these finite resources are easily interrupted, often unconsciously, by the mind drawing away focus to address some type of unmet and more urgent need. The internal life of an individual is marked with interruptions that disrupt rational thought and managers can help identify, navigate, and mitigate these types of inner challenges.

3.3.2 Emotions Can Limit or Improve Learning

Another distraction leading to limitations in rational decision-making arises when one considers the role of emotions in decision-making. Cabanac (2002) defines emotions as the conscious mental activity that can be characterized by the intensity and degree of pleasure or displeasure it causes on the individual. Emotions hold a much more powerful influence over individual decision-making and preferences than rational economists accounts for. For example, research has shown that one's affective state, primed by having the participant recall a happy or sad memory, significantly influenced their belief on whether or not they could complete the required task (Bandura, 1997). Individuals who recalled a sad memory were less likely to believe they could complete the task throughout the experiment. Whereas those who had invoked a positive memory, prior to task completion, were much more efficacious and successful during the experiment (Kavanagh & Bower, 1985). The objective reality of whether or not the person could complete the task was null and void by whether the person had simply recalled a happy or sad memory.

Emotions often invoke a physiological response, which arouses the nervous system with various states. Many neuroscientists have discovered that emotions and cognitions are inextricably linked (Damasio, 1994) as they influence one's ability to think "logically" or "rationally". For example, positive emotions are correlated with openness to new ideas, problem solving, and better recall of information, while negative emotions restrict one's openness to knowledge. Managers cannot simply focus on encouraging employees to think more rationally, without considering the emotional component of decision-making. As Hess (2014) states, "People are emotional. Organizations are emotional environments" (p. 59). It would be unwise for managers not to consider the impact one's emotions has on creating and sharing knowledge with others in the workplace.

3.3.2.1 *Rationality Hijacked by the Amygdala*

Emotions can and do override the ability to learn new information and behave rationally. The interruption of one's top-down attention, by a bottom-up process can be a powerful inhibitor to learning. Top-down processing refers to the perception of one's environment by relying on cognitions, while bottom-up processing refers to the perception of sensory information or stimulus, which are coming in from the environment. Emotions that occur through a bottom-up process are much harder to control as a stimulus occurs and emotions are sparked. However, emotions that occur through a top-down process, where the individual is able to create space between the stimulus and response are more likely to be rational. However, all too often, individuals operate from a limited capacity to control these often unwelcome bottom-up interruptions.

For example, constraints on time, attention or resources invokes an emotional biologic response. When in an aroused emotional state, one is often hijacked by the amygdala, which overrides more logical thinking and instead forces the individual to react to an immediate need. The amygdala is the part of the brain that acts as the processing and memory center for stimuli and emotions. It is directly connected to the prefrontal cortex, the area of the brain that is involved with one's highest intellectual capabilities. The amygdala functions outside of conscious thought, and is connected to the limbic system, which operates as the mechanism for survival. When the amygdala senses a stimulus that causes fear, such as a lion in the road or giving a speech to a crowded room, it activates a stress hormone, called cortisol, which causes the body to prepare for a fight or flight response. A low to medium level of cortisol is linked to positive learning outcomes, however a high level of cortisol is shown to impede learning, memory, and cognitive function (Goleman, 1997).

Various empirical studies show that students with high levels of anxiety struggle to pay attention and received lower test scores than their less anxious classmates (Black, 2005). This may be explained by the biological response that fear triggers within the body and mind. Stress creates a chaotic and non-coherent heart rate, which in return produces non-coherent patterns in the brain (Hannaford, 2005). Sometimes, one will remark that they simply "just can't think straight" under high anxiety situations. This is due to the fact that stress has sabotaged the ability of the prefrontal lobe to function at full capacity (Goleman, 1997).

However, smaller doses of stress invoked in a safe environment actually lead to greater productivity, learning, and creativity. When the prefrontal lobe is able to stay in control, or regulate the emotional response, stress can be a positive influence. For example, Bailey's (2001) study links a calm, but alert state with one's ability to recognize patterns, make sense of the environment and solve problems. In addition, an individual who experiences this alert but calm state is better able to relate and empathize with others. A key component of learning, as Stacey (2001) discusses is the ability to relate to one another. The right level of stress can help facilitate healthy relating to one another in the workplace.

Therefore, emotions are a powerful enabler or restrictor to learning. An individual constantly assesses the relationship between a stimulus and their effects trying to form cause and effect relationships between behaviors and outcomes (Hess, 2014). Fear creates nothing more than a classical conditioning learning environment that invokes a stressful response, ultimately not conducive to knowledge creation. Fear appeals to a lower order cognitive state that simply responds to a fight or flight stimuli. While in the short-term is may produce quick results, longer term it is disastrous to learning, knowledge development, and creativity. Research shows that rational thinking is best accomplished when people are in an environment that proactively seeks out critical thinking, are able to bring their authentic self to the situation, has the permission to take risks and not be punished for mistakes. In other words, fear is not provoked in these environmental conditions. Maslow (1972) stated learning occurs "to the extent that he or she is not crippled by fear and to the extent he or she feels safe enough to dare." Fear may be one of the single biggest inhibitors to learning. Today's managers must actively seek to create environments that foster just enough stress to invoke a positive emotional and alert response, without allowing individuals to be hijacked by their amygdala.

3.3.3 Mindsets Influence the Learning Outcome

Another influence on one's decision-making, long recognized by psychologists, is the internal attitude or mindset that the individual possesses regarding their ability to control outcomes. In particular, Bandura (1997) showed how one's level of self-efficacy—The belief in one's ability to organize and implement a course of action leading to desired outcomes, influences their information seeking activities, and performance outcomes. While affective states, such as attitudes and moods influence beliefs, consider a powerful inhibitor to successful performance in the fixed mindset research conduct by Dweck (2006). Her research concluded that learning outcomes are predicted upon whether or not participants believe they can create change. A fixed mindset is represented by the assumption that people's traits are static. A growth mindset on the other hand is manifested as the core assumption that people are malleable. Various empirical studies with school-aged children show that children with a growth mindset are much more likely to persist in the face of failure and exert greater effort towards obtaining their goals.

The research completed in the classroom was also carried over into the workplace to assess the impact a manager's mindset would have on their ability to make analytical decisions. Wood and Bandura (1989) completed a simulation for managers to complete, but prior to that primed them into one of the two mindsets. The first group was trained on how difficult it is to create change and that organizations are fixed entities. The other group was shown examples of how malleable organizations and people are. The fixed mindset group struggled completing the task at hand. This was due to their decreasing levels of efficacy and inability to utilize strategic analytical strategies as time progressed. The researchers conclude that the mindset one has creates a bias towards their self-regulatory mechanisms governing cognitive functioning. Those that are growth-oriented are better able to control their circumstances by utilizing stronger analytical thinking tools and setting self-directed goals. However, the bias towards fixed beliefs inhibits the performance of individuals by creating erratic decision-making patterns and lessening their organizational aspirations. In addition, further research confirms that viewing abilities as static in nature impedes skill development and actually diminishes one's interest in the task at hand (Jourden, Bandura, &Banfield, 1991). While one's mindset alone does not predicate success, it does influence the ability of the individual to learn and persist in the face of difficulties. A fixed or growth mindset can exhibit either a tax on cognitive reasoning or an enhancement to one's efforts towards overcoming obstacles.

Either way, the research has clearly linked one's mindset with their cognitive capacity and perceived ability to be successful.

3.3.4 The Influence of Others

Thus far we have focused on an individual's own cognitive limitations. We will now turn our attention to the influence of others in the decision-making process. In particular, two distinct features of a group cause deviations from one's own individual preferences: Informational signals and self-censoring.

3.3.4.1 Information Signals

Information signals are transmitted through one's verbal and nonverbal communications, which convey information about one's preferences and attitudes towards a phenomenon. These signals have a tremendous influence on knowledge sharing because individuals are social learners (Bandura, 1997). People are wired to actively seek out information signals from others to help determine behavioral norms in a particular context. As a result, other people's opinions, information, and behaviors hold a great influence over one's individual preferences. Individuals rarely make a decision without obtaining input from the necessary information signals. A study by *Forbes* found that 81% of consumers across industries rely on friends and family to inform a purchasing decision. Within the same study, 38% of moms admitted that other women simply liking products on social media directly influenced their brand preference.

Individual preferences are easily swayed. Consider the following MIT study, which sought to determine the influence information signals had on individual preferences. Specifically, the researchers looked at how an individual's song selection would be influenced by others (Muchnik, Arai, & Taylor, 2013). The control group was not given any information on others' downloads and simply chose to download songs based on their own preferences. However, the treatment group, also free to choose to their own songs were given an additional piece of information in the form of a popularity bar, noting the amount of times others had also selected the song. Rational economic theory would suggest this should hold little, if any, influence on the individual's choice. Yet, this additional information held significant influence in this study. The treatment group was greatly influenced by the downloads of others. Therefore, the stronger the information signals released by the group, the more likely the group's preferences are to undermine an individual preference.

When was the last time you felt your preference was undermined by the influence of others? Maybe you were swayed by an influential leader's opinion or were persuaded to agree with the majority on a business decision. Often, the strength of information signals depends on:

- The number of people within the group whom agree on the same point of information.

- Perceived expertise of an individual.
- Your own level of admiration or intimidation of others in the group.
- The amount of perceived power one holds.

Information signals are strong hidden influencers throughout organizations that can enhance or derail individual decision-making. Even if you knew something to be absolutely true, how quickly could you be swayed by others? Before answering that, consider the following classical psychology study (Asch, 1940). The research experiment simply asked participants about the length of the lines on notecards. There were clearly longer and shorter lines drawn on the cards. This was not a trick question or optical illusion. But, here is what was alarming: Individuals were swayed at least once when given unanimous group information suggesting that one of the lines was shorter, though this was obviously false. This information signal, in the form of a group observation, overrode one's own perception of what was true (See sidebar: Abilene Paradox). As Sunstein and Hastie (2014) note, "If people will ignore their own visually clear perceptions of simple straight lines and defer to others, then surely they are likely to defer to others on the hard and complicated questions that face businesses." (p. 436).

The Abilene Paradox

Many times, making a sub-optimal decision is simply a result of poor group communication and the desire to not "rock the boat". An example is illustrated by the Abilene Paradox, where a group of people make a decision contrary to the preferences of many, if not all, of the individuals in the group (Harvey, 1974). The illustration describes a family making an undesired trip to Abilene, Texas for dinner, because everyone believes the majority of the group wishes to go. The drive is long and the weather uncomfortably hot. Rather than voicing a contrary opinion, all individual members take the hot journey to a mediocre dining facility. This results in a negative experience and outcome for all the individuals who realize upon their return, they all preferred to simply stay home that evening for dinner, but then question why no one said anything. The group members start pointing fingers saying they were simply following along with what the majority had voiced. Come to find out the majority was all self-censoring. This occurred because they were misreading the information signals from each other and irrationally decided to go along with the majority. Managers would be wise to actively solicit contrary opinions from the group before making an unwanted trip to Abilene.

The phenomenon of information signals overriding individuals own rationality in group setting is referred to as herding behavior. Herding behavior is marked by a lack of individual decision-making, which causes people to act and think like the majority around them. Herding behavior is usually characterized by the gravitation of individuals to similar preferences based solely on the fact that the majority is engaged in the behavior. Underpinning herding behavior is a fear of missing out, a phenomenon commonly known as *FOMO*, which is amplified in social media contexts. This fear is exasperated when the majority appears to be doing something that an individual has not yet taken part of. This type of individual irrational thinking can lead markets astray and cause them to perform in unexpected ways. For example, the dot-com bubble of the 1990s occurred, in part, by herding behavior. Rational investors would have seen that the majority of so called "hot" start-ups were actually not producing any revenues, much less profits. Yet, the herding instincts drew in thousands of investors during the initial public offerings. Individuals were anxious to not pass up on this opportunity that seemingly so many were taking advantage of. The dotcom bubble quickly became a bust when the speculation of easy and quick capital turned out to be nothing more than misplaced overconfidence in the majority's speculation of dotcom success. A fear of missing out can cause even the most rational individual to join the herd.

3.3.4.2 Self-Censoring

It has been observed that information signals can cause a social dilemma within individuals. What if the information signals are in conflict to an individual's preference? The social pressures can cause an individual to keep quiet and not share information in order to protect their own reputation. The self-censoring of individual cognitions, which occurs in group settings is a notable reason why dysfunctional groups arise and poor decisions are made. A rational individual will consider the social costs for stepping out of line with the majority or most powerful person in the group. If the costs are too high, the individual will self-censor their own cognitions in group settings. If the environment lacks psychological safety research shows the flow of information will be restricted. The lack of openly diverse dialog can lead to devastating organizational results. As more and more individuals self-censor, groupthink will occur. Groupthink is defined as irrational decision-making, which occurs when individuals prefer group harmony over their own rational cognitions. Consider one of the most infamous examples noted in history—The invasion of Cuba at the Bay of Pigs. President Kennedy laid out a flawed plan of attack, and not one of his closest advisers said a word. Many held private concerns and did not agree with the President's plan, however, censored their apprehensions. As history shows, the attack went forward and failed, with devastating consequences to the United States government. Sorensen (1965) launched an inquiry into why none of Kennedy's advisers expressed their concerns or doubts in a plan riddled with flaws. While Kennedy's advisers privately held reservations over the invasion, no one "pressed, partly out of fear of being labeled "soft" or un-daring in the eyes of their colleagues" (p. 306). This story illustrates that the more individuals self-censor and withhold private cognitions, the likelihood for groupthink arises, making irrational, or even destructive decision-making highly probably.

Key Managerial Impact

Individual rationality and the ability to privately make decisions to maximize one's utility is constantly under attack by one's own limitations, emotions, mindset, and the influence of others. It may better serve managers to recognize that people are bounded to these limitations and may display irrational behavior as a result. The challenge for managers is to create environments and cultures, which recognize the limited cognitive resources individuals face and create guardrails, which safeguard both individuals and groups from poor decision-making. Assuming full rationality of individuals will cause a glaring oversight on the needed conditions people require to make positive decisions at work. (Fig. 3.2)

Biases	Level of influence	Example
Decision-fatigue	Individual	"I don't have time to think. I've already made so many other decisions today."
Confirmation bias	Individual	"The data and evidence are obviously flawed. I still can't see your point of view."
Cognitive dissonance	Individual	"I can't see both options as viable. It has to be on or the other."
Herding behavior	Group	"Everyone else in the market is quickly adopting this new strategy, let's try it."
Self-censoring	Group	"It is not worth the conflict. I will just keep my opinions to myself on this one."
Status quo	Individual and group	"Let's just the stay course." or "That's not how we do things around here."

FIGURE 3.2 Common limitations to rationality and knowledge creation.

3.4 ALTERNATIVE 2: PEOPLE RESPOND TO MOTIVES BESIDES MONEY, BUT THEY CAN BE EASILY CROWDED OUT

3.4.1 External Incentives Do Not Always Work

Now that we have discussed that the ability of people to act rationally is bound by cognitive biases, emotions, mindsets, and the influence of others, how should management motivate employees to strive and achieve for the elusive goal of knowledge creation at the firm? As Simon (1986) points out, economics without psychological and sociological research is simply inadequate. Without a keen understanding of what drives human decision-making apart from the extrinsic pull of maximizing one's own self-interest, leaders are left with an incomplete picture of what actually happens in reality. Consider the following examples. Rational economists have a hard time explaining the emergence of open source crowd platforms, which allow individuals to anonymously share information with no extrinsic reward attached. For example, the application WAZE, a tool generated to simply help others avoid traffic jams, roadwork construction, or police speed traps. Drivers freely provide updates for others in real-time with no extrinsic pull for doing so. Rational economic theory also has difficulty explaining the person who receives inherent pleasure from their work above and beyond monetary incentives. This has been be demonstrated in research that marveled at the hospital janitor worker who regardless of their seemingly low level in the organization, felt a strong sense of significance, and meaning in their role for being a part of the healing process for patients and contributing to the overall mission of the hospital.

To further confound the topic of motivations, the *homo economicus*, often falls short in explaining learning and creative behaviors in the workplace. In theory, individuals who are properly incentivized to create and share knowledge should do so in proportion to their earnings or extrinsic benefits received. However, this is often not the case in highly cognitive efforts. This was famously illustrated in Glucksberg's (1962) laboratory study of the candle problem. The candle problem consisted of giving participants one wax candle, a box of thumbtacks, and a matchbox filled with matches and asking them to hang the candle on the wall. This required creative thinking by using materials differently than their intended purpose.

Within the experiment, one group of students were given the opportunity to obtain a monetary incentive upon completion of the task. The other half of the students were considered the control group and were simply asked to solve the problem. Rational economic theory would presume that the group who was given the incentive should have produced better outcomes. However, the exact opposite occurred. The group of students who were offered incentives were actually less able to solve the problem and took more time to successfully complete the task compared to the control group. The presence of incentives in this case decreased the ability of the group to think insightfully.

Deci (1971) also highlighted this paradox by paying a group of people to complete a puzzle. Another group was not incentivized, but was merely asked to complete the puzzle based on the inherent reward of accomplishment. When the researchers returned and asked both groups to complete a series of puzzles again, this time with no pay to either of the groups, the first group who was originally incentivized, significantly reduced their efforts compared to the second group. The lack of incentive now made the group less motivated to engage in higher levels of thinking. A rational economic mindset took over, eliminating any sort of pleasure derived from completing the task. It can be concluded that the inherent reward one experiences from accomplishing a task can be overrode by the lack of incentive.

In this case, the presence of an extrinsic reward, crowded out the presence of intrinsic motivators to accomplish the task (Frey, 1997). Humans do indeed respond to incentives, but utilization of these tactics can unintentionally crowd out more powerful motivators. The effects of motivational crowding out were confirmed in a well-known experiment conducted in Israel. An A/B test involving a group of daycares found imposing fines on parents who pickup children late actually increased the prevalence of tardiness. It was determined that parents who once viewed picking up their children on time as a social obligation now considered it an economic transaction. If they were late they could simply pay a fine and not face the social embarrassment previously felt. Alarmingly, after the experiment was over and the fine was lifted the high level of tardiness remained (Gneezy & Rustichini, 2000).

Similar experiments have been replicated over the past 40 years with consistent results (Pink, 2007). If tasks involve high levels of cognitive performance, offering incentives usually decreases individual performance in the long run. It is hypothesized that something else must be happening, above and beyond the pull to maximize one's own interest through economic gain, when it comes to knowledge-based tasks. Many researchers suggest that learning and innovation is an inherently rewarding activity, which rational economic thought does not adequately account for.

3.4.2 Intrinsic Motivators Unlock Learning

The discussion, thus far regarding motivations has focused on external motivators and their diminishing returns, indicating that their presence can ultimately become an impediment to learning. Let's now look at the flip side and explore what motivates people to engage in learning. In doing so, we will address the necessary conditions, above and beyond extrinsic drivers, which motivate people to learn, share, and create knowledge in organizations. Having proven that the allure of extrinsic motivators can lose its influence in highly cognitive tasks, the contrary is true regarding the pull of intrinsic motivators. Specifically, an expanding body of psychology literature identifies four fundamental drivers, which cause individuals to exert effort towards learning and knowledge sharing—Autonomy with social support, growth, meaning, and belonging. These inherent human motivators are better able to sustain longer term performance in knowledge dependent environments. Self-determination theory underpins this section, by exploring the natural tendencies one has to behave in effective and healthy behaviors

(Deci& Ryan, 2000). Self-determination theory considers a much more optimistic view of the individual, believing people can inherently enjoy work and will actively seek to contribute to others, rather than succumb to maximizing their own self-interest. These four components are necessary for the development of intellectual capital within organizations and must be a primary concern for today's managers.

3.4.2.1 Autonomy With Social Support—The Need to Choose and Be Supported

Autonomy, with social support, is a necessary motivational component, which drives individual learning and performance improvement. Autonomy is defined as the degree of freedom one has when making their own decisions and choices in the workplace (Deci & Ryan, 1985; Hackman & Oldham, 1980). Autonomy is experienced when an individual believes they are able to express their own unique talent within the company without much oversight. Retailer, Nordstrom, credits their superior customer service with the level of autonomy they give employees in their stores. Nordstrom leaders simply ask their employees to "use their best judgment" when making customer service decisions. However, this is not given without the necessary support mechanisms for employees to make good decisions on behalf of the company. Nordstrom provides a rigorous training program, including scenario playing much of what a salesperson can expect on the retail floor, prior to their start. The level of autonomy given is unique within the industry and Nordstrom's performance has constantly outpaced its competitors as a result.

To further illustrate the role autonomy can have on performance outcomes, consider the classic psychological field study conducted in the late 1970s. Researchers Langer and Rodin (1976) randomly divided nursing home patients into two groups. The first group was given a considerable amount of autonomy, such as the freedom to determine their own schedule, move furniture around as they saw fit, and were even given the responsibility to care for a plant. The other group of nursing patients were told that the nursing staff was there to provide for them, make decisions and care for the plant on behalf of the patient. Thus, diffusing their sense of autonomy. The question the researcher sought to answer was, to what extent would giving patients autonomy influence their well-being. The results, while statistically marginal, are still noteworthy. The first group, who was granted autonomy, experienced not only better health outcomes, but also lived longer. The researcher concludes that providing individuals with the choice, or sense of autonomy, increases their overall satisfaction and health. However, removing the choice or sense of autonomy, could have negative effects on individual well-being.

Philosophers have long recognized that the freedom to choose is an innate human need and a necessary prerequisite for individual well-being.

Organizational behavioral researchers argue that individual autonomy directly leads to an increased sense of personal responsibility for workplace outcomes (Hackman &Oldham, 1980). Providing a sense of autonomy not only provides an individual the freedom of choice, but also a sense of ownership over outcomes. Giving people ownership over outcomes is linked to positive self-esteem and enhanced levels of pride (Weiner, 1979). Conversely, the inability to provide people ownership over the outcome deprives them of the many psychological benefits that come from success (Weiner, 1979). For example, dieters who freely chose to lose weight are much more likely to experience weight loss compared to those who are forced into a dieting program. Another study discovered that smokers who choose to stop on their own, rather than stop based on an external pressure, were much more successful in their efforts. Autonomy intrinsically motivates individuals to act and provides the psychological benefits associated with outcome ownership (Friedman, 2014).

Conversely, the removal of autonomy can lead to counterproductive behaviors. Studies show when autonomy is removed, people proactively chose to engage in reactance. Reactance refers to the active protest when one's freedom or control is threatened. Since autonomy is an essential human need, its removal actually reinforces irrational behaviors. For example, researchers at the University of Colorado found that people felt more in love with their romantic partners when their parents expressed disapproval. Another study found that therapists who tried to use persuasive techniques—Such as overtaking the patient and offering advice—were actually much less successful than those who simply listened. As Friedman, (2014) argues, the harder one tries to make a decision on behalf of another, the harder the individual resists.

This human tendency to resist being controlled is likely why Deci and Ryan (1985) found higher levels of autonomy associated with better learning and performance outcomes. Additional research linked a sense of autonomy with exploration and information seeking behaviors (Karasek & Theorell, 1990). Individuals who experience autonomy and are presented with a challenging activity, are much more likely to search out for alternative solutions, experiment, and even innovate. These types of behaviors are exactly what produces a competitive advantage in the marketplace.

An interesting question being explored within the organizational behavior literature is, can there be too much individual autonomy? New empirical research suggests the answer is yes. Autonomy alone does not result in better outcomes, but works best in an environment where the individual feels supported. Wielenga-Meijer, Taris, Wigboldus, and Kompier (2011) suggest the best learning outcomes are achieved when employees are given autonomy and also experience managerial support. Therefore, autonomy alone cannot help explain individual innovative behaviors, but one must also consider the social context in which it exists.

As a result, autonomy without the proper social infrastructure can lead to chaos. In a qualitative research study conducted at a large services firm seeking to understand the role of autonomy and managerial support, an employee remarked, "Too much autonomy leads us confused and frustrated. My manager is needed to help provide the necessary support to help navigate the organization and clarify my priorities". The point here is simple. Tell employees what to do, but not how to do it. Consequently, a new management behavior is necessary, which lessens its reliance on a command and control style, and instead finds ways to support autonomous individuals working together in complex organizations.

The advantages of providing autonomy with social support extend beyond the individual. A study by researchers at Cornell University sought to examine the impact autonomy had on small business performance. The researchers studied 320 small businesses, half of which granted their employees autonomy to make decisions, while the other organizations managed by top-down direction—Commonly referred to as a "command and control" style of leadership. The results showed that businesses who granted their workers autonomy grew at four times the rate of their command and control following counterparts. In addition, the autonomous firms experienced only one-third of the turnover as the other firms. It can be concluded that people prefer autonomous working conditions and consequently, the organization performs better. Autonomy, governed by social support, is a necessary component for firms seeking to compete in a knowledge-driven economy. Creating supportive environments for individuals to express their sense of autonomy will be an important focus for managers who are tasked with developing intellectual capital creation in the firm.

3.4.2.2 Growth—The Need to Develop and Obtain Mastery

The desire to grow is a well-documented human need within the psychology literature. Growth inherently evokes a desire to get better. Amabile's (1995) empirical study discovered that a need for growth was the single greatest motivator to employees' productivity across all levels of an organization. This, in part, may be explained by Bandura's (1997) work, who discovered that growth fuels one's sense of pride, satisfaction, and sense of accomplish. The need to grow is essential to human development.

What makes the need to grow such a powerful motivator to learn and develop? The answer lies in the neurological response growth invokes. Neuroscience studies show when one learns or acquires new information the body increases the production of dopamine (Bunzeck & Duzel, 2006). Dopamine is a neurotransmitter or chemical messenger in the brain, which motivates an individual to take action in order to obtain a reward. Dopamine is released anytime there is a perception of individual growth and learning. This chemical release provides the energy for a person to fully engage and master the task at hand. Given this neurological link, human beings are biologically wired and rewarded to pursue growth.

Csikszentmihalyi (2000) referred to the need for growth as driving individuals into a state of flow—When one engages in an activity that engages them fully, intrinsically energizing them to sustain their focus over long periods of time. When in a state of flow, the passage of time goes by unnoticed as the individual is so engrossed with the task at hand, even if it is relatively mundane. Csikszentmihalyi (2000) found that individuals experience the most flow when they are presented with a challenging opportunity. The opportunity has to be considered attainable with the right amount of individual effort or else risk frustrating the individual to the point of failure. Thus, the challenge itself becomes the reward. Amabile's (1995) research also confirmed the highest levels of creativity amongst individuals who found the activity deeply satisfying and challenging. Why? The participants believed the activity was contributing to their own growth.

Field studies confirm that the ability for employees to experience growth is key to firm innovation, and may be more influential than money. Consider the following study. Researchers studied over 11,000 US scientists and engineers seeking to determine the best predictor of knowledge worker's productivity. The study concluded that a knowledge worker's productivity was directly linked to their individual desire for growth, which came from mastering or learning something new. In addition, the same study showed that these intrinsically motivated scientists filed significantly more patents than their counterparts, who had stated money was their primary motivate for work. This once again calls into question the effectiveness of the rational economic model, which calls on using incentives for motivating highly cognitive work. Rather, behavioral research suggests a more powerful motivator may be found in fueling one's own need for growth.

Decades of psychology research has also confirmed a similar phenomenon (Dweck, 2006). A research study divided students into one of two groups—A learning-oriented group and a performance-oriented group. The learning group was given the goal to simply learn the task for the sake of acquiring new knowledge. Whereas the other group was given a goal concerned with performance. The learning goal group not only outperformed the performance goal group, but also better performed at a similar but unrelated task. Dweck (2006) recognized that individuals who apply their inherent desire to grow outperform those who simply seek after task achievement or rewards.

The need to grow may explain why high-performance athletes are able to spend a significant portion of their time and energy on mundane activities. Researchers Ericsson and Chambliss studied high-performing Olympic athletes to determine what predicted their success. The researchers conclude that the highest performers had a very different perspective on these seemingly routine and mundane activities. High-performing athletes viewed these activities as the very means necessary to increase their growth and therefore, much more effort was extended towards repetitive behaviors. As a result, these high-performing athletes spent much more time focusing and working on the repetitive activities in order to achieve greater growth in the long-run. However, the benefits reaped by engaging in repetitive activities extend beyond high-performing athletes. Employees too can develop the ability to apply their expertise in different situations through the use of practice and repetition. Simon (1957) often referred to expertise as intuition, describing it as "the situation has provided a cue; this cue has given the expert access to information stored in memory, and the information provides the answer. Intuition is nothing more and nothing less than recognition." In other words—People who have practiced enough in a certain domain, begin to recognize patterns, and are better able to provide the right information. The key here is that the practice is intentional and deliberate.

An individual's perception of their ability to grow is likely to predict their engagement at work. Environments that foster a sense of flow, growth, and development are much more likely to experience richer knowledge sharing and innovative behaviors. This is further evidenced by (Wagner & Harter, 2014), who found 12 dimensions that correlate back to employee retention, customer satisfaction, productivity, and profitability. Their multi-year research endeavor included studying over 80,000 managers throughout the world. The results showed that an employee's perceived sense of learning and development significantly predicted the firm's performance. The link between individual growth and firm performance is so correlated that a manager must foster an environment that allows individuals to experience flow in even the mundane tasks of work.

3.4.2.3 Meaning—The Need for Purpose and Significance

Whiting Williams (1957) noted "Our strongest, deepest need is our need to feel ourselves needed. Nowhere do we all seek this assurance so constantly, so zealously and so importantly, as in our daily work, on our daily job!" (p. 10). Contemporary organizational behavior researchers agree. Rosso et al. (2010) confirmed that work serves as the primary source of one's meaning and identity, simply based on the sheer number of hours spent at work. In a national study assessing Americans' most important facet of their job, meaningful work, continues to rise to the very top (Cascio, 2003). A similar study assessing Danish employees also found that meaningful work was twice as important as the next factor, which was a great manager (Zak, 2017). Meaningful work is a necessary component for individuals to engage in knowledge sharing and learning.

Meaningful work is best captured as the why behind the work, which is growing in importance in organizational studies. Its rise is likely attributed to the growing body of empirical evidence, which connects meaningful work to both individual and organizational level beneficial outcomes. For example, an empirical field study sought to determine sought to determine the influence of meaningful work on a relatively routine job—College alumni fundraising (Grant et al., 2007). Within the study, employees were randomly divided into one of three groups. The first group received information on the benefits of working at the organization. They then began their day soliciting former alumni for donations. The second group received a story about the benefits the scholarship funds had on recipients' lives before they began their phone calls. The third, and final group, was the control group and proceeded to go about their job without any sort of intervention. The question under investigation was would providing employees information about workplace benefits or customer impact make a difference on their performance? The results were somewhat surprising. The first group, who had received information on the benefits of working at the organization, had little influence over their performance. Their performance was on par with the control group, meaning the intervention did not work. However, the second group, who had been given a story which connected the employee with an end recipient, performed twice as high as the other groups. Understanding the impact, their relatively routine job had on another human being fueled meaning into their role. Other empirical studies also found meaningful work linked to increased job satisfaction (Wrzesniewski, McCauley, Rozin, & Schwartz,1997), engagement (May et al., 2004) and even individual well-being (Campbell, Converse, & Rodgers, 1976). Once again, the benefits do not stop at the individual level. Organizations also reap the benefits of meaningful work. Other research connects both employee organizational citizenship behaviors and increased customer satisfaction with meaningful work (Leiter et al., 1998).

Our understanding of meaningful work has been enriched by the spillover knowledge neuroscience is having on organizational behavior research. For example, neuroscientist Zak (2017) investigated the role of meaningful work on employee's productivity. The study measured 100 US employees working at a manufacturing facility to determine how their productivity was influenced by a perceived sense of meaning. The results? Individuals who closely connected to the organization's purpose, and found meaning in their role, were 14% more productive than their colleagues. Employees who feel a sense of purpose walking into work are much more likely to give more on the job. Not only are these employees likely to give more on the job, but they also feel better doing so. This was confirmed in another neuroscience empirical study, which sought to examine the correlations between an individual's connectedness to the purpose and people of the organization and their own job enjoyment. A resounding statistically significant correlation was found between purpose and job satisfaction ($r = 0.77$, $P < .05$). If managers are seeking to increase job engagement and satisfaction, providing a sense of meaning is essential.

The benefits of purpose also carry over onto balance sheets. Not only is purpose linked to higher individual productivity, but also firm performance. Sisodia, Wolfe, and Sheth (2007) analyses of S&P 500 company balance sheets, found companies with a well-defined purpose that extended beyond shareholders, outperformed other firms by a ratio of 8:1 from 1996 to 2006. Stengel (2011) completed similar analyses from 2001 to 2012 and found that high purpose firms generated 400% more returns than firms who did not seek a transcendent purpose. A transcendent purpose compels individuals to perform, which in turn translates to organizational success.

Consider the following. A large consulting firm found 79% of individuals who believed they were working for a high purpose-oriented organization were also highly satisfied with their jobs. Compare this to the only 19% of individuals who reported worker satisfaction when working in what was perceived as low purpose firms. Even more alarmingly, 50% of employees were unable to even identify the purpose of their firm, likely leading to the lower satisfaction scores. Can you imagine going into work every day and not knowing how your work is making a difference? This has tremendous consequences on the customers as reported by the same study. 94% of employees were rated high at customer service when working for a high purpose firm, whereas only 63% were rated high at customer service when working for a low purpose firm. This may be a way some researchers are advocating for greater adoption of the B-corporation, which seeks to not only generate a profit, but contribute to a larger purpose for its stakeholders (Kim, Karlesky, Myers, & Schifeling, 2016). Since B-corporations inherently transcend the shareholder wealth maximization model, it is of no surprise the employees are better able to find greater purpose and meaning under these incorporations. In fact, research suggests that employees are 46% more likely to be engaged and satisfied when working for a B-corporation (Kim et al., 2016).

A laboratory experiment explains why supporting and working for a cause can be a powerful motivator for action (Zak, 2017). A group of participants were exposed to a message asking the participant to lend a microloan to an entrepreneur. It was standard marketing language seeking to simply persuade the individual to take action. However, the second group was asked to extend a microloan to an entrepreneur for a very specific cause. For example, help reduce domestic violence by empowering women to become entrepreneurs. Those who were exposed to the specific cause were 45% more likely to make a loan and much more likely to give at higher rates. 28% higher rates to be exact. Why did linking an action to a specific cause compel individuals to respond in arguably irrational ways? The answer can once again be found in biology. People who were exposed to the cause message, released a higher level of oxytocin. The oxytocin hormone has been named the moral molecule, because of its link to higher levels of empathy and treating others well (Zak, 2017). Multiple studies confirm the role of oxytocin in establishing strong social bonds (Miranda et al., 2013). Just as the brain is wired to respond and reward individuals for learning, it too rewards the individual whose purpose extends beyond themselves. A sense of purpose allows individuals to feel significant and powerfully motivates them to engage in prosocial behaviors, such as knowledge sharing and development.

A question worth asking, is profit or economic gain purposeful enough for employees to engage in sustained development? Rational economic theory would assume so. However, a study completed by Deci, Ryan and Niemiec (2009) suggests not, noting the type of purpose does matter at the individual level. Within the longitudinal study, the researchers asked graduates to reflect on their purpose after commencement. What did they hope to do and accomplish over the next two years? The answers were then grouped into intrinsic purpose and extrinsic purpose goals. Two years later, the researchers followed up with each of the students to determine if they were on their way towards achieving their goals and assess their satisfaction levels. While both groups reported success towards goal obtained there was one remarkable difference. The extrinsically motivated group experienced much more anxiety post-college than those who were on their way of obtaining their intrinsic goals. The intrinsic group reported back higher levels of work satisfaction post-college and higher overall well-being. There was a notable difference in how these individuals felt pursuing their goals. The researchers probed to understand the cause of their increased satisfaction and well-being difference post-college. The answer came back to one's connection to others. It was concluded those who pursued, and met an intrinsic purpose, felt a stronger connection to others. However, those who pursued a wealth-oriented goal, reported feeling less connected and lacking the time to devote to others. A purpose that is linked to social identity, or sense of belonging, matters greatly to both individual and firm functioning. Which takes us to the next innate need necessary for individual learning and knowledge sharing—A sense of belonging.

CASE STUDY: Mayakoba Resorts: Working Towards a Larger Purpose

The hospitality industry can be difficult on the employee experience. Employees must deal with exasperated travelers and may not always have the means to meet their customer's needs. It is an industry that is marked by relatively low wages and high employee turnover rates. In addition, much of hospitality work can be classified as highly routine, and quite candidly, unappreciated. Yet, there is a region in Mexico that provides more than just a routine hospitality job, but instead provides a purpose to protect and promote a valuable ecosystem in the Mayakoba region. Employees who work at any of the luxury resorts within Mayakoba commit to protecting and maintaining a vibrant environment of flora, rainforest, mangroves, beaches, and reefs. Employees are trained and educated on the various workings of the ecosystem and empowered to take active measures to promote its sustainability. Unlike the majority of other resorts, the

(Continued)

CASE STUDY: (Continued)

Mayakoba region's resorts are dedicated to sustainability and environmental practices that go well above and beyond conversing energy. Employees work with local biologists to protect the wildlife that is now found flourishing within its properties. The resorts also actively support regional social and economic development by investing in local products and services and funding their development. As a result, the dedication of the employees of the resorts to protect over 240 acres of tropical forests and mangroves has been recognized and awarded by The Rainforest Alliance and the United Nations World Tourism Organization. This sense of purpose evokes a sense of pride, which ultimately translate into a superior customer experience.

3.4.2.4 Belonging—The Need for a Social Identity

Individual decision-making at work encompasses much more than rational cognitions, but is also influenced by the constant need to belong. In fact, rational individuals do seek to maximize their own self-esteem, which is enhanced by a strong connection with others. Remember when researchers asked participants to keep their hand in the ice bucket? Those who had resisted a temptation and were depleted prior were much less successful and unable to endure during the experiment. Another study brought back the ice bucket, but this time wanted to test the influence of a friend over the participant's ability to keep their hand in the bucket. Interestingly enough, people were able to hold their hand in the bucket much longer when a friend was by their side (Brown, Sheffield, Leary, & Robinson, 2003). The presence of a social connection allowed the individual to exert greater discipline and performance over the activity. If people are willing to keep their hand longer in a bucket based on a social connection, imagine how much more individuals would be willing to give if connected to others at others at work?

However, the impact of social dynamics has largely been ignored in rational economic theory, because individuals are viewed as actors who make private decisions based on their own preferences. Rarely, is the social context considered a predictor of one's preference or choice. However, behavioral economic theory demonstrates the impact social dynamics can exert on an individual's preference and choice. Psychologist Alfred Adler (1964) is credited for understanding that social feeling, or a sense of community, is the crucial and leading factor in healthy human development. Stated simply, people need a connection to others in order to develop healthy cognitions about themselves.

Yet, the ability to learn, transfer, and develop knowledge is enabled or constrained by the environment. Stacey (2001), while acknowledging that the individual cognitive process exists, argues it emerges not simply from within the individual, but through the relationships between people and their environment. Behavioral science argues that cognitive processes can only be understood and assessed by the environment, which holds influence over a person's choice of action. Simon (1957) also argued that the study of organizations is one in social behavior, not simply individual behavior. An organization by nature is collective and group-oriented and the individual is a social being seeking to find their place within a social group. Therefore, the ability of the individual to engage in rational cognitive reasoning is once again constrained or enabled by the social context. People do indeed often display a natural inclination to conform to social norms. As a result, the individual's preferences within the organization depend on the influence of social norms established within the firm (Simon, 1957).

As a result, an individual's behavior is closely tethered to the observed or perceived behavior of others. For example, an empirical field study sought to determine the influence of social norms on a person's behavior to conserve energy. The study randomly selected a group of gas and electric customers and placed door hangers with information on overall neighborhood energy usage while also comparing the individual's usage with those of their neighbors. The treatment group was exposed to social pressure. However, the control group received door hangers with facts regarding energy conservation, nothing relating to neighbors, or individual usage comparisons. It was a rational message describing why energy conservation is positive. The influence of social pressure worked well above and beyond the rational messages. Those selected in the treatment group, receiving the social messages, reduced their energy usage by more than 10% of the control group. The researchers concluded that invoking social norms quickly reduces the search cost for individuals who are seeking to determine what is socially acceptable in a given situation (Nolan et al., 2008). As social beings, people are constantly assessing what is deemed customary in a certain context, and simply telling participants they were more wasteful than their neighbor was enough to change behavior.

Another field study conducted sought to determine the role of social norms in reusing towels at hotels. Nearly three-quarters of all Americans believe themselves to be an environmentalist (Mackoy et al., 1995). If so, the researchers wanted to determine what would change behavior—An appeal about the environmental importance of reusing towels or a message that stated the majority of hotel guests chose to reuse their towels. Rational thinking would presume that the environmental message should work on at least the three-quarters of Americans who identify as environmentalist. However, it was the socially charged message, which caused individuals to reuse their towel at significantly higher rates (44.1%) compared to the environmental message group (35.1%). Once again, this shows our preferences for utility maximization are derailed in light of social influences.

Social norms become even more powerful to behavior when applied at a local level. For example, in the same hotel study, nearly 50% of all guests reused their towel when the message stated that the guests before them in that same room had chosen to participate in the conservation efforts. In addition, during the door hanging conservation study, showing neighborhood data compared to national energy use data had much more significant impact on behavior change. The power of social norms impacts individual decision-making the closer the person is to the group by proximity.

This of course has great impact on organizations today who rely more than ever on teams to meet changing market and consumer demands. The social influences and norms present within small communities in the organization will yield great influence over an individual's success. What explains this influence? In many cases conforming to social norms is not necessarily in the best interest of the individual. Baumeister and Leary's (1995) theory of the need to belong helps explain this deviation from rationality. Within the meta-analyses of over 300 academic articles, the authors discovered a fundamental human motivation to belong. The research concludes that individuals need frequent personal interactions with others, while also maintaining a level of stability and mutually affective concern. The need to belong is marked by a consistency of interaction with another. The theory proposes that people have a persistent drive to create and maintain significant, lasting, and positive relationships with others. This need to belong will be present anytime individuals come together to work in teams.

The need to belong may be one of the strongest needs facing people in developed societies. For example, consider one of the longest studies conducted by Harvard University, which sought to understand what drives healthy adult development. Researchers studied individuals over an 80 year time period to determine what best predicted their well-being. "The surprising finding is that our relationships and how happy we are in our relationships has a powerful influence on our health," said Robert Waldinger, Director of the study, a Psychiatrist at Massachusetts General Hospital, and a Professor of Psychiatry at Harvard Medical School. "Taking care of your body is important, but tending to your relationships is a form of self-care too. That, I think, is the revelation." This study, still forth going, concludes close relationships as the key predictor of a person's sustained happiness over time. In addition, the study found that a male's relationships at age 50 were a better predictor of their health at age 80 than their cholesterol levels. In addition, the stronger social support individuals received was also correlated with better cognitive capabilities later in life. Healthy relationships are key to one's well-being and ability to fulfill their need to belong in the workplace.

Multiple academic researchers have sought to quantify the effects of one's need to belong in the workplace. Girardi et al. (2015) hypothesized that lacking a sense of belonging in the workplace would lead to elevated stress hormones, which can impair longer term cognitive processing. To test this hypothesis, they studied 122 workers in an Italian healthcare organization. The researchers surveyed participants on their quality of relationships in the workplace and then obtained blood samples. As predicted, a lack of quality relationships was associated with elevated proinflammatory cytokines, which negatively impact one's immune system. An excessive amount of proinflammatory cytokines can lead to inflammatory diseases and has even been linked to depression and other neurological conditions. Both the Harvard and Italian healthcare study point to a noteworthy correlation—The physical and mental health of an individual is linked to the quality of their social network.

Additional experimental research conducted by Baumeister et al. (2005) shows a lack of belonging associated with irrational decision-making. Namely, participants are willing to assume longer-term costs for the sake of a short-term benefit. In addition, the studies show participants showing signs of impaired cognitive processing and logical reasoning when experiencing a lack of connection to others. More recent empirical evidence by Chen et al. (2008) demonstrate that one sensing social hurt or a lacking a social identity contributed to poorer performance on a complex cognitive task. The surprising finding was that the social hurt had much greater impact on an individual's performance when compared to other participants who had experienced a physical injury. The researchers conclude that social pain may mitigate complex cognitive processing more so than physical pain. This has tremendous consequences for managers who seek to maximize the cognitive development of individuals in hopes of generating intellectual capital. A lack of belonging within the organization may be the hidden culprit.

The good news is that the opposite is also true. A sense of belonging can lead to stronger organizational outcomes. For example, Gagne and Deci (2005) show when individuals feel a sense of belonging, they perform better in their job, display organizational citizenship behaviors, and experience overall job satisfaction. Walton and Cohen (2007, 2011) also show the positive impact a sense of belonging has on individual performance. Within the study individuals showed more effort and persistence when paired up with teams to solve a math problem rather than working individually in pursuit of their own achievement. Many universities recognizing this have turned to the cohort model to facilitate higher levels of learning. This research suggests that group learning is beneficial to adult learners and may lead to higher levels of cognitive development.

Why does the sense of belonging to a group yield such positive returns to individual performance and well-being? The answer is because relationships enhance our overall sense of self-esteem and individual worth. In a compelling longitudinal study, Deniseen, Penke, Schmitt, and Van Aken (2008) found that self-esteem levels fluctuated in relation to one's perceived sense of relationships. The greater their connection to others, the greater their sense of self-esteem. Aron, Aron, Tudor, and Nelson (1991) explain this phenomena as a result of the change in one's cognitive processing when strongly associated with others. The studies indicate that close relationships blur the boundaries between others and the self in the form of "including the other in the self" (p. 241). The brain begins to process the self in relationship to others. Managers seeking greater performance would be wise to ensure that individuals are connected and identify with others in the organization.

3.4.3 Individual Alternative Assumptions Summary

In summary, these two individual level alternatives, one's bounded rationality and the need for intrinsic motivators creates opportunities for managers to redesign the workplace to better create and develop intellectual capital through the development of a firm's talent base. The behavioral economics literature provides a pathway for doing so. For example, behavioral science studies suggest that individuals engaged in highly cognitive work actively seek out trust, reciprocity, connectedness, and transparency with their manager. In addition, while many individuals are innately motivated to apply their expertise to achieve results, they also need the right level of support and a clear path forward.

The behavioral economics literature also showcases the limitations of human thinking. Therefore, management is needed to challenge status quo performance to safeguard against the natural human tendency to avoid change, recognize the wariness that derives from repeated decision-making and understand that strongly held beliefs are hard for individuals to overcome. Furthermore, recognizing that extrinsic motivators alone are not sustainable and instead appealing to an individual's intrinsic motivations of autonomy, growth, meaning, and belonging will generate a sustainable and satisfying work experience for the employee and strong results for the firm (See Fig. 3.3).

In addition, behavioral economics reveals that a group is not simply a collection of individuals, but rather an entirely new entity emerges when people come together to form groups. Understanding the complex interactions and potential pitfalls surrounding teams will be an important challenge to overcome in the new leadership paradigm. Ensuring individuals are able to feel comfortable challenging peers and ideas with the goal of arriving at the best possible outcomes will drive the demand for knowledge sharing and result in strong intellectual capital creation. A manager's ability to overcome herding behavior, self-censoring, and groupthink within teams can prove to be the differentiating factor for organizations of the future.

We also shed light on the environmental factors and social influences that can impact an individuals' ability to perform on the job. Fitting in, social pressures, and biological responses to stress all have strong effects on an employee's ability to think and behave rationally on the job. Individual needs are met only by a healthy and functioning group. Indeed, these individual needs depend entirely on others for their fulfillment. Successfully navigating these complexities within a work context will dictate the ability for individuals to maintain strong cognitive processing on the job.

Key Managerial Impact

People respond to other motivators besides money. In particular, a sense of autonomy with social support, the need for growth, a sense of meaning and belonging are necessary components to an employee's healthy functioning in the workplace. Of course, money is still required and needed as part of an overall compensation package, however, its motivating effects on innovative behavior are more limited than what is assumed in rational economic theory. As a result, it is recommended managers consider the adverse effects from crowding out individual's intrinsic motivators can have on knowledge creation and sharing in the workplace (Fig. 3.3).

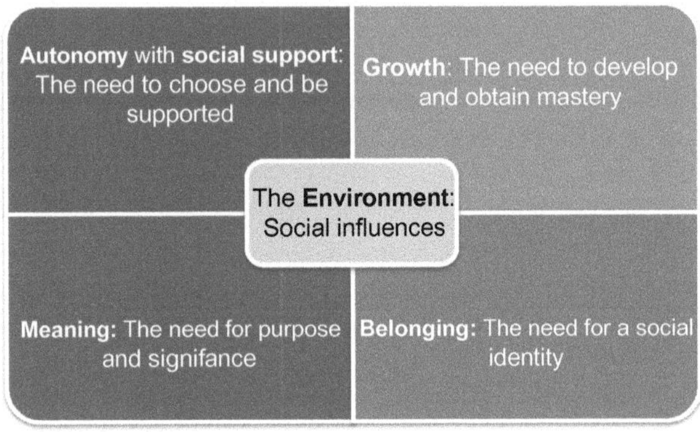

FIGURE 3.3 Common intrinsic motivators to unlock learning and rationality in the workplace.

3.5 ALTERNATIVE 3: A FIRM SHOULD SEEK TO MAXIMIZE COLLECTIVE VALUE WITH AN EMPHASIS ON MUTUALITY AND THE LONG-TERM

The first two alternatives consider the opportunities and limitations to human decision-making. We now turn our attention to a firm level alternative, which behavioral economists have been considering since Herbert Simon questioned the ability for both individuals and organizations to maximize one goal, through his development of the construct of satisfying. If we take the behavioral assumption of satisfying across multiple goals, rather than simply pursuing the maximization of profit, what new alternatives would arise? Exploring these alternatives evolves the role of the manager from one seeking to control and command through the mitigation of agency costs to one who coaches, adapts, empowers, and connects to align stakeholder interests towards collective value.

3.5.1 A Triple Bottom Line: The Economics of Mutuality

In a rational economic view of the firm, the primary purpose is defined as the pursuit of financial profits and gain. All other forms of capital are simply seen as a means to a financial end. However, these other forms of capital, as well as society at large, can incur either negative or positive *externalities* as a result of this ideology. These externalities become the unaccounted costs or benefits of doing business. A common negative externality is the resulting pollution that is created during the production of a firm's goods or services. This negatively impacts the communities, societies, and the planet at large. However, all too often, this cost is simply seen as a means to a greater end—Profits. Externalities can pose a major problem within communities and societies as the differences between those who gain or lose as a result of business production widens. In addition, the current narrow focus on profits as the bottom line can create a misallocation of resources focused almost exclusively on efficiencies leading to unintended consequences. For example, shareholders may profit from loosening pollution controls or by closing a local production facility, however, the downstream impact on the planet and people in that community are often unaccounted for. Roche and Jakub (2017) emphasize that the current singularity focus on profits, "rewards the holders of financial capital at the expense of the people (the many) – unless they are shareholders (the few) – and at the expense of the planet" (p. 9).

Therefore, there is a growing call within the business management literature to expand the bottom line to include not just profits, which are still key, but also to consider the collective and reduce the number of negative externalities produced by business operations. The call to widen the purpose of the firm to include more than profits is built upon the *economics of mutuality*. Mutuality is the process of creating shared value for stakeholders by using the principles of capitalism and responsible business practices to create win–win experiences. Mutuality ensures that the rewards of business is appropriately shared amongst those who contribute to it (Mayer, 2014). As a result, the economics of mutuality transition the focus of the firm from profit maximization to holistic value optimization (Roche & Jakub, 2017). Accomplishing mutuality requires an emphasis on, "the planet that provides, the people who transform and the capital that ensures the liquidity in the system" (p. 6). These three areas—People, the planet, and profits must mutually exist for the sustainability of business. Businesses then do not exist simply for shareholders, but also for the benefits of customers and communities they serve (Mayer, 2014). Organizations operating under the principles of mutuality seek to measure, manage, and value stakeholder interests, which include considerations of profits, people, and the planet.

Interestingly enough, numerous studies have confirmed that this emphasis on the broader scope of business has resulted in greater shareholder returns. For example, a study by Harvard researchers classified 90 companies as "high sustainability" and another 90 as "low sustainability". The difference in sustainability was marked by the focus on long-term performance and a clear alignment of executive compensation to measures of sustainability. The study found that $1 invested in the shares of the high sustainability firms was worth $23 in 2010, compared to $15 in the low sustainability firms—Resulting in a 50% difference in share performance. Firms that committed to pursuing more than just short-term shareholder returns, produced better financial metrics in the long-run.

CASE STUDY: Mars, Inc Pursues More Than the Maximization of Share Price

Mars, Inc, one of the world's largest food manufacturers, was founded upon the notion of shared benefits. Founder, Forrest E. Mars Sr. wrote a letter to all of his staff in 1947, emphasizing that the purpose of the organization was to establish "a mutuality of service and benefits across the entire range of stakeholders—From consumers, distributors, competitors, suppliers, governmental bodies, employees, and shareholders—Through the manufacturing and distribution of our products." The founder went on to say that "the company can only be successful if everyone else around it is successful."

Mars continues to consider what mutuality looks like in the 21st century economy. Their current leadership recently asked, what is the right level of profit? In order to help answer this question, they entered into a multiyear partnership with the University of Oxford's Said Business School to reconsider management practices, metrics, and governance built upon the principles of mutuality. How could the business operate by the economics of mutuality that would allow not just shareholders, but also suppliers, employees, customers, and even future generations benefit from the output of the firm? Their approach was quite simple, leadership recognized that what gets measured gets done. So, the company expanded their success metrics to encompass more than share price. These new metrics focused on their company's talent well-being, natural capital, social capital, and shared financial capital. These metrics allow business decisions to consider more than just shareholder metrics as final determents for a decision, but also bring in a variety of stakeholder concerns that would typically have been passed over as an externality of business.

3.5.2 Additional Global Perspectives on the Purpose of the Firm

The shareholder and stakeholder ideologies often stand in contrast to one another and are furiously debated within the global academic literature. One pursues short-term profits, while the other seeks longer-term sustainability. One considers individual wealth, the other collective value. One considers share price as the ultimate end, while the other perceives financial gain as means to a broader end. One emphasizes markets and competition, the other partnerships and collaboration (*See* Fig. 3.4: *Comparing and contrasting*

	Shareholder Theory	Stakeholder Theory
Time Horizon	Short-term	Long-term
Seeks to Increase	Profits	Sustained value
Capital Decision Making	Financial	Profits, People, Planet
Firm Behavior	Competitive	Cooperative
View of Employee	Divergent interest, agency costs	Key stakeholder to develop

FIGURE 3.4 Comparing and contrasting shareholder and stakeholder theory.

shareholder and stakeholder theory). However, for the 21st century manager, expanding the scope of the firm to maximize collective value in the long-term may be better aligned in knowledge-driven economies. This certainly does not exclude the importance of financial gain or shareholder wealth as part of a business outcome, but building entire strategies around this sole pursuit may limit the ability of the manager to generate wealth in the long-run given the new market realities. Therefore, alternatives around the purpose of the firm are highlighted, which promote greater worker involvement, a longer-term focus, and an emphasis on connecting various members of an ecosystem towards shared value on the principles of trust and transparency. While the shareholder primacy model may have been appropriate in financially scarce markets and caused a temporary productivity gain in short-term efficiencies, it is time to reconsider its effectiveness in knowledge-driven economies where talent coordination and development becomes paramount to a firm's ultimate success.

The shareholder maximization model has primarily been observed by the United States, United Kingdom, Canada, and Australia (Allen, Carletti, & Marquez, 2009). However, alternative perspectives of the firm emerge as one begins to broaden the lens to include other global perspectives as well as additional stakeholder considerations. It will be revealed that shareholder value is perceived by other countries as an outcome, rather than a sole purpose. Alternatively, many other cultures and scholars encourage a broader stakeholder focus of the firm rather than a strict shareholder view.

Company leaders, such as the CEO of Unilever, are already speaking out against the dominant shareholder model and, instead, are actively pursuing broader stakeholder interests (see sidebar: *Unilever goes against the dominant discourse*).

Unilever Goes Against the Dominant Discourse

Unilever CEO, Paul Polman, was highlighted in *Bloomberg Businessweek*, as a company leader going against the dominant discourse of his time. Polman states, "Too many companies are running their business into the ground, I would argue, by being myopically short-term focused on the shareholder" (p. 48). Polman,

(*Continued*)

(Continued)

instead, ascribes to a stakeholder theory of the firm, seeking to meet broader needs across the business ecosystem. Unilever actively seeks to engage in partners and friends within the ecosystem who want to make each other better and stronger. As a result, Polman engages in activities that will make the entire ecosystem better such as decoupling business growth from environmental impact, tackling gender inequality in the workplace, creating sustainable development goals, and even combating deforestation. Polman openly prioritizes customer needs over shareholder growth, stating, "I do not work for the shareholder, to be honest. I work for the customer" (p. 49). Unilever requires their executives to engage in annual weeklong stays with poor rural families to experience firsthand an often-overlooked stakeholder—Consumers and suppliers in developing economies. The company also no longer reports on quarterly earnings in order to pursue longer-term goals. The results? Polman's tenure has already significantly outlasted the average tenure of similar CEOs of a company his size. And, excluding dividends, share prices have more than doubled in the past 5 years. Polman attributes the success back to Adam Smith's guidance in *The Theory of Moral Sentiments*, "you cannot get wealth if you don't have morality" (p. 50). In the end, Polman advises that each organizational leader has a decision to make as it relates to the firm's purpose, "Do we choose to serve a few billionaires, or do we choose to serve the billons? Over time, I think the billions will win" (p. 51).

While the United States and United Kingdom have come to dominant much of management theory discourse, a wider perspective of the firm emerges if one considers alternative ideologies from other cultures. These differences once again go to show that business management is one of social science inquiry, not one that is built upon natural laws. It is a study of people and how they interact to pursue a goal, with a variety of purposes and methods at their disposal for coordinating such activities. The methods they use, however, hinge largely on the cultural norms established for business within that country. For example, research conducted by Yoshimori (1995), found that 97% of Japanese firm leaders and 83% of German firm leaders believe the firm is owned by stakeholders, compared to only 24% of US and 29% of UK business leaders who ascribe ownership of the firm to stakeholders. Instead, the majority of business leaders in the United States and United Kingdom assigned firm ownership to shareholders. This research further found that the majority of Japanese (97%) and German (59%) business leaders would prioritize job security over paying dividends when making a business decision, contrasted to only 11% of US and UK business leaders who prioritized job security over dividends.

In a different study, researchers surveyed over 15,000 managers in various countries assessing whether they thought the majority of their fellow colleagues and citizens believe it was a company's only goal to pursue profits, or if the company was also responsible for the well-being of additional stakeholders. To no surprise, the highest scoring in favor of profit pursuits came from the United States, Australia, and Canada (Hampden-Turner & Trompenaars, 1993). However, exploring alternative cultural perspectives of the firm outside of the American shareholder model may help inform today's leaders to pursue innovative business models as knowledge and a talent become key differentiators in global markets.

For example, Nordic countries (Sweden, Denmark, Finland, Norway, and Iceland) are seeing increases in productivity and innovation as the economy shifts from industrial- to knowledge-based work. Notable organizations such as IKEA, H&M, Spotify, Lego, Carlsberg, and Skype originated from this area of the world. According to the *2017 Bloomberg Fifty Most Innovative Economies*, which assess R&D intensity, productivity, researcher concentration, high technology density, and patent activity, Sweden (ranked 2), Finland (ranked 5), and Denmark (ranked 8) all outrank the United States (ranked 9). In addition, the code for Linux, which operates the world's top supercomputers was invented in Finland. Not only are these organizations within these countries increasing in productivity and growth, but the *2013 UN World Happiness Report* noted that Nordic countries ranked highest on real GDP per capita, healthy life expectancy, and perception of individual freedom to make life decisions. Noble Prize-winning economist, Joseph Staglitz, has also shown how these Nordic countries have greater social mobility compared to the United States, and even remarked Scandinavia as the land of opportunity for today's markets. Some researchers have attributed this growth as a natural alignment to the longer-term perspective inherent within many of their firms. Since the 1960s, *stakeholder theory*, which takes into account multiple considerations when assessing corporate performance, not just shareholder value, has been the leading discourse within Nordic universities and practice (Kakabadse et al., 2005). As a result, the Scandinavian cultural norms and institutional structures actively encourage relationships between a company and a diverse set of stakeholders (Gjolberg, 2010). The leading management practice is one of participation, collaboration, and performance-oriented, with much less emphasis on formal hierarchies (Grenness, 2003). It is assumed within these countries that an organizational purpose combines economic interests with broader societal interests. As a result, the corporate governance is entirely stakeholder-oriented (Strand & Freeman, 2013). Trust is remarkably much higher between employees and the corporation as result of a stakeholder perspective in these Scandinavian cultures. This is important, because trust is paramount in the role of the 21st century manager towards the development of knowledge in the firm. This long-term focus is also achieved by corporate ownership that is highly concentrated. For example, many of the firms within these countries are controlled by families who hold onto the firm throughout many generations. An example would be the Wallenberg's in Sweden who at one time employed nearly 40% of the industrial workforce in the 1970s. The way these Nordic countries think about the corporation places a much greater interest in the long-run as their primary shareholders are actively engaged to think about passing on the company to future generations. Preub (2017) summarized the purpose of the Nordic firm as one that is future focused, human-centric, and promotes individual employee freedom and ambition. Shareholders are certainly considered but only as part of a broader narrative, which seeks to create collective value for a wide range of stakeholders.

Germany also considers a broader stakeholder theory of the firm, with a greater emphasis on worker involvement. Within their country, they developed a legal system, which encourages *codetermination* rather than single minded pursuit of shareholder wealth. Codetermination in Germany provides workers the right to actively participate in the management of the companies they work for. Known as *Mitbestimmung*, this modern-day law passed in 1976, allows employees to elect representatives for nearly half of the supervisory board of directors. Allowing workers a voice on the management of the firm broadens the firm's purpose from solely maximizing the interests of shareholders. Instead, employee needs and the community at large is also represented in business decision-making. However, some have argued it is not just the workers who benefit from codetermination. Rather, organizations can use this as an instrument to align worker and capital interests for long-term productivity increases. In addition, management compensation within many German firms is not as closely tied to short-term profitability, as historically advocated for by agency cost theorist within the shareholder maximization model.

The Japanese also have a different perspective of the firm, which has helped fuel significant growth in the past decades as firms have focused on stakeholder interests and the purposeful integration of workers across levels in organizational learning efforts (see sidebar: *Toyota adopts a new perspective of the firm and employee*). The Japanese value strong interconnected relationships that cooperate towards shared objectives. Every level of worker is seen as instrumental to a firm's learning and ultimate success, so stable employment is upheld as a primary focus of the firm. The legal obligation of a board within Japan is that they do not grossly neglect their performance of their duties and it is widely accepted that their performance be towards the interests of a variety of stakeholders (Allen & Gale, 2000). In fact, a leading Japanese CEO has even remarked that it would be, "irresponsible to run Japanese companies primarily in the interests of shareholders" (Allen & Zhao, 2007). Executive compensation within Japan is among the lowest paid in the world with relatively little tied back to the stock price of the organization they serve (Brealey, Myers, &Allen, 2006). Ironically, the emphasis on stakeholders has worked well for shareholders in many Japanese firms. Allen and Zhao (2007) compare automotive stock prices of Toyota, Ford, and General Motors from 1972 to 2006 and found Toyota not only consistently beating these automakers in a buy-and-hold investing strategy, but the overall S&P500 as well. The longer-term emphasis on meeting stakeholder needs, rather than short-term quarterly gains has proven to be an effective way to increase share price in the long run.

CASE STUDY: Toyota Adopts a New Perspective of the Firm and Employee

Rather than adopt the command and control style of management practices coming out of the American auto industries, Toyota decided to go in a different direction. Instead of relying on the use of fear, pressure, and incentives to motivate unskilled factory workers, they began investing heavily in the creation of shared common beliefs and empowering employees, even those considered unskilled on the front lines, to self-diagnose strain in the process (Doshi& McGregor, 2015). Toyota relied on teams to increase the sense of community and did not adopt the commonly held practices of dividing managers and workers. For example, all employees parked in the same lot, ate in the same cafeterias, and worked right alongside one another. Even frontline factory workers completing routine production work were encouraged to problem solve and actively seek learning and improvement, wherever possible. The entire culture at Toyota promoted relentless reflection, continuous improvement, a "see for yourself" practice, and encourages employees to work like the tortoise, not like the hare. This stood in stark contrast to the practices of their competitive automakers.

In the 1980s, Toyota took over a closed GM plant that was historically plagued with "poor productivity, poor quality, and history of extensive labor troubles, including strikes, high levels of absenteeism and turnover" (Pfeffer, 1998). However, Toyota believed with a different people management approach they could turn the plant around using the same employees GM had previously employed. Toyota's leadership decided to send the American factory workers over to Japan to learn the culture and Toyota way of doing business. After experiencing the Japanese way of doing business, an American employee remarked, "I can't remember any time in my working life where anybody asked for my ideas to solve a problem. And they literally want to know, and when I tell them, they listen" (Doshi & McGregor, 2015, p. 282). The takeover was a monumental success. A 49% productivity gain was achieved and it was largely attributed to the way the firm brought people back front and center to its purpose (Pfeffer, 1998).

A key differentiation was Toyota's emphasis on the integration of teams, encouragement to think for oneself, collaboration with others, and working towards a larger purpose. The broader perspective of the firm to include stakeholders, including employees, freed capacity to invest in research and development, promote employee learning, and ultimately, produce higher quality products. In 2001, the Toyota CEO is quoted as saying, "To be sustainable, children are told, corporations must nurture relationships with stakeholders such as suppliers, employees and the local community. In Japan's case, it is not enough to serve shareholders." And yet, even today, share prices continue to outperform the majority of Toyota's competitors. What do you think—Does a broader stakeholder view of the firm produce great shareholder returns?

Key Managerial Impact

Expanding the scope of concern beyond the shareholder to include stakeholders, enlarges the role of the manager within the firm to consider an ecosystem of business relationships—Not just shareholders. This shift in perspective brings renewed interest in connecting the purpose of the firm with larger societal concerns and wellbeing. It also causes the manager's focus to move beyond simply pursuing financial capital, but also consider both the people and planet. This lessens the role of agency costs and provides a positive view of the role of the manager in aligning stakeholder interests with alternative tools to create shared value from businesses.

3.6 CONCLUSION

What type of management theory would emerge if we grounded leadership on these behavioral alternatives, which enlarge our understanding of the limitations of rationality at work? How would managers lead differently under the assumption that people inherently seek meaning and belonging and utilize work as a means to accomplish these desires? Is there an alternative way of leveraging behavioral principles to tap into an employee's sense of purpose and pride, which transcends mere shareholder wealth maximization as way to manage agency costs? What other levers besides agency costs would managers have to better align *stakeholder* interests? Once we are able to free ourselves from historical dominant rational assumptions, we can leverage newfound studies of how to best manage organizations in knowledge-driven economies. We are then able to see more clearly a behavioral theory of management, which seeks to sustain shared organizational value and leverage the intrinsic drive of workers to create and provide value for customers and society more broadly. We will now consider how these alternative assumptions about people at work lend themselves to a new style of management, which instead of utilizing command and control principles, seeks to leverage the building blocks of social capital to increase individual performance within today's organizations.

REFERENCES

Adler, A. *Social interest*: A challenge to mankind (1938, 1964).

Allen, F., Carletti, E., &Marquez, R. (2009). *Stakeholder capitalism, corporate governance and firm value*. Retrieved from http://citeseerx.ist.psu.edu/viewdoc/download?doi=10.1.1.546.5425&rep=rep1&type=pdf.

Allen, F., & Gale, D. (2001). *Comparing financial systems*. Cambridge: MIT Press.

Allen, F., Zhao, M. (2007). *The corporate governance model of Japan: Shareholders are not rulers*. Retrieved from http://finance.wharton.upenn.edu/~allenf/download/Vita/Japan-Corporate-Governance.pdf.

Amabile, T. M. (1995). *Keys: Assessing the climate for creativity*. Greensboro, NC: Center for Creative Leadership.

Aron, A., Aron, E. N., Tudor, M., & Nelson, G. (1991). Close relationships as including other in the self. *Journal of Personality and Social Psychology, 60*(2), 241–253. Available from https://doi.org/10.1037/0022-3514.60.2.241.

Asch, S. E. (1940). Studies in the principles of judgments and attitudes: II. Determination of judgments by group and by ego-standards. *Journal of Social Psychology, 12*(2), 433–465.

Ashkanasy, N. M., & Jordan, P. J. (2008). A multi-level view of leadership and emotion. In R. H. Rumphrey (Ed.), *Affect and emotion: new directions in management theory and research* (pp. 17–39). Charlotte, NC: Information Age Publishing.

Bandura, A. (1997). *Self-efficacy: The exercise of control*. New York, NY: Freeman.

Baumeister, R. F., & Leary, M. R. (1995). The need to belong: Desire for interpersonal attachments as a fundamental human motivation. *Psychological Bulletin, 117*, 497–529.

Baumeister, Roy F., Bratslavsky, Ellen, Muraven, Mark, & Tice, Dianne M. (1998). Ego Depletion: Is the active self a limited resource? *Journal of Personality and Social Psychology, 74*(May), 1252–1265.

Baumeister, R. F., DeWall, C. N., Ciarocco, N., & Twenge, J. (2005). Social exclusion impairs self-regulation. *Journal of Personality and Social Psychology., 88*, 589–604. Available from 10.1037/0022-3514.88.4.589.

Black, S. (2005). Test anxiety. *American School Board Journal, 192*(6), 42–44.

Bougheas, S., Nieboer, J., & Sefton, M. (2015). Risk taking and information aggregation in groups. *Journal of Economic Psychology, 51*, 34–47.

Brealey, R. A., Myers, S. C., & Allen, F. (2006). *Principles of corporate finance*. New York, NY: McGraw-Hill.

Brown, J. L., Sheffield, D., Leary, M. R., & Robinson, M. E. (2003). Social support and experimental pain. *Psychosomatic Medicine, 65*(2), 276–283.

Bunzeck, N., & Duzel, E. (2006). Absolut coding of stimulus novelty in the human substantia nigra/VTA. *Neuron, 51*(3), 369–379.

Cabanac, M. (2002). What is emotion. *Behavioural Processes, 60*, 69–84.

Campbell, A., Converse, P., & Rodgers, W. (1976). *The quality of American life: Perceptions, evaluations, and satisfactions*. New York, NY: Russell Sage.

Cascio, W. F. (2003). Changes in workers, work, and organizations. *Handbook of Psychology, 16*, 399–422, Part 3.

Chen, Z., Williams, K. D., Fitness, J., & Newton, N. C. (2008). When hurt will not heal: Exploring the capacity to relive social and physical pain. *Psychological Science, 19*, 789–795.

Csikszentmihalyi, M. (2000). *Beyond boredom and anxiety*. San Francisco, CA: Jossey-Bass. (Original work published 1975).

Cyert, R. M., & March, J. G. (1963). *A* behavioral theory of the firm. Englewood Cliffs, NJ: Prentice-Hall, Inc.

Damasio, A. (1994). *Descartes' error: Emotion, reason, and the human brain*. New York: Putnam Publishing.

Danziger, S., Levav, J., & Avnaim-Pesso, L. (2011). Extraneous factors in judicial decisions. *Proceedings of the National Academy of Sciences of the United States of America, 108*(17), 6889–6892.

De Bono, E. (1970). *Lateral thinking: Creativity step by step*. New York, NY: Harper & Row Publishers.

Dechawatanapaisal, D., & Siengthai, S. (2006). The impact of cognitive dissonance on learning work behavior. *Journal of Workplace Learning*, *18*(1), 42–54. Available from https://doi.org/10.1108/13665620610641300.

Deci, E. L. (1971). Effects of externally mediated rewards on intrinsic motivation. *Journal of Personality and Social Psychology*, *18*, 105–115.

Deci, E. L., & Ryan, R. M. (1985). *Intrinsic motivation and self-determination in human behavior*. New York, NY: Plenum.

Deci, E. L., & Ryan, R. M. (2000). Self-determination theory and the facilitation of intrinsic motivation, social development and well-being. *American Psychologist*, *55*(1), 68–78.

Delton, A. W., Krasnow, M. M., Cosmides, L., & Tooby, J. (2011). The evolution of direct reciprocity under uncertainty can explain human generosity in one-shot encounters. *Proceedings of the National Academy of Sciences*. Retrieved from http://www.cep.ucsb.edu/topics/HumanGenerosity.htm.

Denissen, J. J., Penke, L., Schmitt, D. P., & van Aken, M. A. (2008). Self-esteem reactions to social interactions: Evidence for sociometer mechanisms across days, people, and nations. *Journal of Personality and Social Psychology*. *95*(1), 181–196. Available from https://doi.org/10.1037/0022-3514.95.1.181.

Doshi, N., & McGregor, L. (2015). *Primed to perform: How to build the highest performing cultures through the science of total motivation*. New York: Harper Collins.

Dweck, C. (2006). *Mindset: The new psychology of success*. New York, NY: Ballantine Books.

Festinger, L. (1957). *A theory of cognitive dissonance*. Stanford, CA: Stanford University Press.

Frederick, S. (2005). Cognitive reflection and decision making. *Journal of Economic Perspectives*, *19*, 25–42.

Friedman, R. (2014). *The best place to work: The art and science of creating an extraordinary workplace*. New YorK, NY: TarcherPerigee.

Frey, B. S. (1997). *Not just for the money: An economic theory of personal motivation*. Cheltenham: Edward Elgar.

Gagné, M., & Deci, E. L. (2005). Self-determination theory and work motivation. *The Journal of Organizational Behavior*, *26*, 331–362. Available from https://doi.org/10.1002/job.322.

Girardi, D., Falco, A., De Carlo, A., Benevene, P., Comar, M., Tongiorgi, E., & Bartolucci, G. B. (2015). The mediating role of interpersonal conflict at work in the relationship between negative affectivity and biomarkers of stress. *The Journal of Behavioral Medicine*, *38*(6), 922–931. Available from https://doi.org/10.1007/s10865-015-9658-x, Epub2015 Jul 18.

Gjolberg, M. (2010). Varieties of corporate social responsibility (CSR): CSR meets the "Nordic Model". *Regulation & Governance*, *4*(2), 203–229.

Glucksberg, S. (1962). The influence of strength of drive on functional fixedness and perceptual recognition. *Journal of Experimental Psychology*, *63*, 36–41.

Gneezy, U., & Rustichini, A. (2000). A fine is a price. *Journal of Legal Studies*, *29*.

Goleman, Daniel (1997). *Emotional intelligence*. New York, NY: Bantam Books.

Grant, A., Campbell, E. M., Chen, G., Cottone, K., Lapedis, D., & Lee, K. (2007). Impact and the art of motivation maintenance: The effects of contact with beneficiaries on persistence behavior. *Organizational Behavior and Human Decision Processes*, *103*(1), 53–67, ISSN 0749-5978.

Grenness, T. (2003). Scandinavian managers on Scandinavian management. *International Journal of Value-Based Management*, *16*, 9. Available from https://doi.org/10.1023/A:1021977514976.

Hackman, J. R., & Oldham, G. R. (1980). *Work redesign*. Reading, MA: Addison-Wesley.

Hampden-Turner, C., & Trompenaars, A. (1993). *The Seven Cultures of Capitalism: Value Systems for Creating Wealth in the United States, Japan, Germany, France, Britain, Sweden and the Netherlands*. New York, NY: Doubleday.

Hannaford, C. (2005). *Smart Moves,* Why Learning Is Not All In Your Head. Salt Lake City, UT: Great River Books, Revised Edition.

Hardiman, M. M. (2012). The brain-targeted teaching model for 21st century schools. Thousand Oaks, CA: Sage Publishing.

Harvey, J. B. (1974). The Abilene paradox: the management of agreement. *Organizational Dynamics*, *3*, 63–80.

Hess, E. (2014). *Learn or die*. New York, NY: Columbia University Press.

Jourden, F. J., Bandura, A., & Banfield, J. T. (1991). The impact of conceptions of ability on self-regulatory factors and motor skill acquisition. *Journal of Sport & Exercise Psychology*, *13*(3), 213–226.

Kahneman, D. (2011). *Thinking, fast and slow*. New York, NY;: Farrar, Straus and Giroux.

Kakabadse, N.K., Rozuel, C., Lee-Davies,L. Corporate social responsibility and stakeholder approach: A conceptual review, International Journal of Business Governance and Ethics, Available from https://doi.org/10.1504/IJBGE.2005.006733.

Karasek, R., & Theorell, T. (1990). *Healthy work: Stress, productivity and the reconstruction of working life*. New York, NY: Basic Books.

Kavanagh, D. J., & Bower, G. H. (1985). *Cognitive Therapy and Research*, *9*, 507. Available from https://doi.org/10.1007/BF01173005.

Kim, S., Karlesky, M. J., Myers, C. G., & Schifeling, T. (2016). Why companies are becoming B corporations. *Harvard Business Review*.

Kotter, J. (2008). *A sense of urgency*. Cambridge, MA: Harvard Business Press.

Langer, E. J., & Rodin, J. (1976). The effects of choice and enhance personal responsibility for the aged: a field experiment in an institutional setting. *Journal of Personal Social Psychology*, *34*(2), 191–198.

Leiter, M. P., Harvie, P., & Frizzel, C. (1998). The correspondence of patient satisfaction and nurse burnout. *Social Science and Medicine*, *47*, 1611–1617.

Lord, C. G., Ross, L., & Lepper, M. R. (1979). Biased assimilation and attitude polarization: The effects of prior theories on subsequently considered evidence. *Journal of Personality and Social Psychology*, *37*(11), 2089–2109.

Mackoy, R. D., Calantone, R., & Droge, C. (1995). Environmental marketing: Bridging the divide between the consumption culture and environmentalism. In M. J. Polonsky, & A. T. Mintu-Wimsatt (Eds.), *Environmental marketing* (pp. 37–54). Binghamton, NY: Haworth.

Maslow, A. H. (1972). Defense and growth. In M. L. Silbermman, et al. (Eds.), *The Psychology of Open Teaching and Learning* (p. 50). Boston, MA: Little, Brown.

May, D. R., Gilson, L., & Harter, L. M. (2004). The psychological conditions of meaningfulness, safety and availability and the engagement of the human spirit at work. *Journal of Occupational and Organizational Psychology*, *77*, 11–37.

Mayer, C. (2014). Mutuality and morality in business. *Exploring Mutuality*, *1*, 7–9.

Muchnik, L., Arai, S., & Taylor, S. J. (2013). Social influence bias: A randomized experiment. *Science*, *9*(341), 647–651.

Mullainathan, S., & Shafir, E. (2013). *Scarcity: Why having too little means so much*. New York, NY: Henry Holt and Co.

Niemiec, C. P., Ryan, R. M., & Deci, E. L. (2009). The path taken: Consequences of attaining intrinsic and extrinsic aspirations in post-college life. *Journal of Research in Personality*, *43*, 291–306.

Nolan, J., Schultz, P. W., Cialdini, R., Goldstein, N., & Griskevicius, V. (2008). Normative social influence is underdetected. *Personality and Social Psychology Bulletin, 34*(7), 913–923.

Olff, M., Frijling, J. L., Kubzansky, L. D., Bradley, B., Ellenbogen, M. A., Cardoso, C., Bartz, J. A., Yee, J. R., & van Zuiden, M. (2013). The role of oxytocin in social bonding, stress regulation and mental health: An update on the moderating effects of context and interindividual differences. *Psychoneuroendocrinology*, *38*(9), 1883–1894, ISSN 0306-4530.

Pfeffer, J. (1998). *The human equation: Building profits by putting people first.* Cambridge, MA: Harvard Business Press.

Pink, D. (2007). *Drive: The surprising truth of what motivates us.* New York, NY: Riverhead Books.

Porter, M., & Stern, S. (2015). Social progress index 2015 executive summary. *Social Progress Imperative.* retrieved from http://www.socialprogressimperative.org/wp-content/uploads/2016/05/SPI-2015-EXEC-SUMMARY.pdf.

Preub, B. (2017). Nordic management and sustainable business. *Journal of Business and Financial Affairs*, *6*(2), 1–9.

Roche, B., & Jakub, J. (2017). *Completing capitalism: Heal business to heal the world.* Oakland, CA: Berrett-Koehler Publishers.

Rosso, B. D., Dekas, K. H., & Wrzesniewski, A. (2010). On the meaning of work: A theoretical integration and review. *Research in Organizational Behavior*, *30*, 91–127.

Simon, H. (1957). *A behavioral model of rational choice. Models of man, social and rational: Mathematical essays on rational human behavior in a social setting.* New York: Wiley.

Simon, H. (1986). Rationality in psychology and economics. *The Journal of Business*, *59*(4), 209–224.

Sisodia, R., Wolfe, D., & Sheth, J. (2007). *Firms of endearment: How world-class companies profit from passion and purpose.* Upper Saddle River, NJ: Wharton School Publishing.

Sorensen, T. C. (1965). *Kennedy* (p. 306) New York, NY: Harper & Row.

Stacey, R. (2001). *Complex responsive processes in organizations: Learning and knowledge creation.* London: Routledge.

Stanovich, K. E., & West, R. F. (2000). Individual differences in reasoning: implications for the rationality debate? *Behavioral Brain Science*, *23*(5), 645–665.

Stengel, J. (2011). *Grow: How ideals power growth and profit at the world's greatest companies.* New York, NY: Crown Business.

Strand, R., & Freeman, R. E. (2013). Scandinavian cooperative advantage: theory and practice of stakeholder engagement in Scandinavia. *Journal of Business.*

Sunstein, C., & Hastie, R. (2014). *Wiser: Getting beyond groupthink to make groups smarter.* Cambridge, MA: Harvard Business Review Press.

Sweller, J. (1988). Cognitive load during problem solving: Effects on learning. *Cognitive Science*, *12*(2), 257–285.

Thaler, R. (2015). *Misbehaving: The making of behavioral economics.* New York, NY: W. W. Norton & Company.

Wagner, R., & Harter, J. (2014). *The elements of great managing.* New York: Gallup Press.

Walton, G. M., & Cohen, G. L. (2007). A question of belonging: Race, social fit, and achievement. *Journal of Personality and Social Psychology*, *92*, 82–96.

Walton, G. M., & Cohen, G. L. (2011). A brief social-belonging intervention improves academic and health outcomes among minority students. *Science*, *331*, 1447–1451.

Weiner, B. (1979). A theory of motivation for some classroom experiences. *Journal of Educational Psychology*, *7*, 3–25.

Wielenga-Meijer, Etty G. A., Taris, Toon W., Wigboldus, Daniël H. J., & Kompier, Michiel A. J. (2011). Costs and benefits of autonomy when learning a task: An experimental approach. *The Journal of Social Psychology*, *151*(3), 292–313.

Williams, W. (1957). How can management motivate the work-force? *Summary of Lecture*, 2.

Wolfe, J. M., Butcher, S. J., Lee, C., & Hyle, M. (2003). Changing your mind: On the contributions of top-down and bottom-up guidance in visual search for feature singletons. *Journal of Experimental Psychology: Human Perception and Performance*, *29*(2), 483–502.

Wood, R., & Bandura, A. (1989). Social cognitive theory of organizational management. *Academy of Management Review*, *14*(3), 361–384.

Wrzesniewski, A., McCauley, C., Rozin, P., & Schwartz, B. (1997). Jobs, careers, and callings: People's relations to their work. *Journal of Research in Personality*, *31*, 21–33.

Yoshimori, M. (1995). Whose company is it? The concept of the corporation in Japan and the West. *Long Range Planning*, *28*(4), 33–44.

Zak, P. (2017). *Trust factor: The science of creating high-performance companies*. New York, NY: AMACOM.

FURTHER READING

Buckley, T., Campbell, T., & Chung, J. (2017). The fresh scent of success. *Bloomberg Businessweek*.

Chambliss, D. F. (1989). The mundanity of excellence: An ethno-graphic report on stratification and Olympic swimmers. *Sociological Theory*, *7*, 70–86.

Eccles, R. G., Ioannou, I., & Serafeim, G. (2011). The Impact of Corporate Sustainability on Organizational Processes and Performance. *Harvard Business School Working Paper Series*, 12 035.

Chapter 4

The Manager's Evolving Role

4.1 SOCIAL CAPITAL: RELATIONSHIPS MATTER AND HELP LOWER THE COSTS OF WORKING TOGETHER

Ask anyone who has ever left an organization what they miss and you will likely hear a response alluding to the people they worked with. For the majority of workers, it is the relationships which make work more meaningful and worthwhile. It is often the impromptu water cooler talks, team lunches, and overall comradery that keep individuals going throughout the day. In Sweden, many firms mandate this type of collective restoration through what is called a *fika*—a time for colleagues to step away from the work to connect with one another over coffee. Relationships matter, because without them work quickly becomes meaningless, detached, and void of value (Hodson, 2005). The inherent drive that we all share to belong and connect with one another can infuse even the most repetitive tasks with meaning. Whiting Williams noted this back in the industrial era when he went undercover, remarking that it was the small organic teams, which formed within manual labor firms, that allowed many laborers to find meaning and satisfaction from an otherwise disagreeable job. Therefore organizations who are able to harness the power of relationships through the creation of social capital creates newfound opportunities to align diverse interests of stakeholders toward sustainable firm value.

Social capital is defined as the quality and quantity of connections between individuals, which lowers the costs of working together. Social capital emphasizes the interpersonal process and relational components of work, which enables the organic sharing of knowledge. This is in contrast to the one-way rational economic view of transactional relationships, which often marked associations at work during the industrial era. Nahapiet and Ghoshal (1998) described social capital as the knowledge that is embodied within individuals and then utilized through interactions. Stark and Jeffries (2011) would later add that in order for one's knowledge and interactions to be considered capital, the interaction would have to provide a resource for the firm above and beyond that of routine exchange based relationships. In other words, for interactions to generate social capital, the relational affection or goodwill toward two individuals must produce an advantage otherwise not experienced in a purely transactional relationship. This perspective considers

How Behavioral Economics Influences Management Decision-Making.
DOI: https://doi.org/10.1016/B978-0-12-813531-0.00004-2

social capital as distinctively different than other forms of capital as it is embedded within the relational interaction itself and cannot be traded in an open market. As a result, social capital is highly contextual and depends on both individual and organizational dynamics. The complexities social capital presents are less about the construct itself, but found in the activities and requirements necessary to generate value from relationships. Compelling empirical research conducted by Roche and Jakub (2017) found that 75% or more of the variations across social capital can be attributed to three things: the level of social cohesion within the organization, the amount of trust between people, and the individual's capacity and attitudes toward collective actions (see Fig. 4.1). These three variables emerged amongst 60 other variables tested with 7500 participants across six countries to describe social capital. While defining and measuring social capital is more readily accessible, the concept is still marked by the complexity of sustaining these contextual key components. Cohesion, trust, and capacity for the collective are bounded by both capacity for rational thinking as well as the cognitive limitations in individual decision-making discussed earlier in Chapter 3, Exploring Management Alternatives With a Behavioral Economics Lens. The pliability of individual decision-making exists at the relational level as well. Wheatley (2006) remarks, "In each relationship we are different, new in some way" (p. 35).

To illustrate this point, consider one of the most basic elements found in nature, water also known as H_2O. It is through the bonding of individual atoms, two hydrogen and one oxygen, that an entirely new element emerges to produce water. When the individual atoms are bonded together they do not simply just produce the aggregate of individual properties, but rather form a new emergent property entirely, which do not exist at the individual atom level. Similarly, in organizations, it is the joining together of

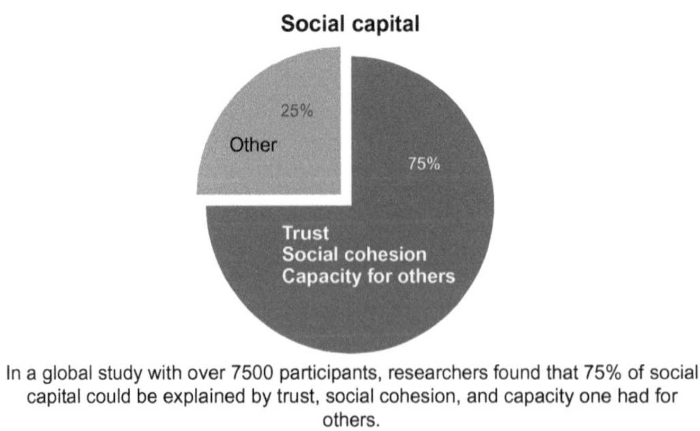

FIGURE 4.1 Social capital diagram.

individuals which cocreates new behaviors and attributes at the group level. The individual choice is hinged, in part, by the emergent group properties. The individual is a social being whose actions emerge depending on the context they are in. As one considers this truth, it becomes evident that social bonds in organizations are instrumental to new knowledge creation and development. Likewise, within organizations, it is rarely the individual efforts alone that explain learning and knowledge creation, but the strength of the bonds between two individuals that transmit ideas and energy otherwise unobservable at the individual level. It is the process of humans relating through complex social bonds and networks, which explain how companies create and distribute knowledge throughout the firm.

Even Coleman (1990), who was strong supporter of individualism, acknowledges that, "the interaction among individuals is seen to result in emergent phenomena at the system level" (p. 5). He later criticized, "the fiction that society consists of a set of independent individuals, each of whom acts to achieve goals that are independently arrived at, and that the functioning of society consists of the combination of these actions of independent individuals" (p. 300). Therefore he urged, "the correct path for social theory is to maintain a single conception of what individuals are like and to generate the varying systemic functioning not from different kinds of creatures, but from different structures of relations within which these creatures find themselves" (p. 197).

By examining the psychological and social limitations of the dominant and individualistic focused *homo economicus*, a new type of capital arises in knowledge-based markets, which further differentiates firm performance—*social capital*. Opportunities to create social capital within the firm are more readily accessible by expanding leadership's perspective of how people think and relate in organizations. Rather than assume individuals are motivated to learn and share knowledge based on utility maximization, we now understand that the story is much more complicated. Individuals are in a fluid state of relating to each other as embedded social beings, influenced by their own cognitive states and environment. Therefore social capital is a dynamic emergence of interactions that change depending on the context. It is marked by complexity rather than pure cause and effect linearity.

Truly, the broader process of work is marked less by certainty and more by ambiguity. A quote from Marlin Eller, software developer and innovation leader within Microsoft during the 1980s and 1990s, sums up the reality of complexity during the decision-making process quite well:

> *They lend the impression that the captains of industry chart strategic courses, steering their tanker carefully and gracefully through the straits. The view from the inside more closely resembles white-water rafting. "Oh my gosh! Huge rock ahead. Everyone to the left! No! No! The other left!"*

The utter volatility that accompanies many decisions in today's firms disregards the orderly application of the rational calculation of economic theory during the decision-making process. As a result, this causes decisions to be accomplished outside of the traditional organizational chart and people find ways to work around the system. It may not be the most rational approach, but it often works. Social capital is likely a causal explanation of how work is actually accomplished within organizations. Therefore a wide gap exists between what traditional management theorist often focuses on and the realities facing the 21st century manager. While traditional administrative management would advocate for planning, controlling, and organizing human capital, we know that people and work are simply too multifaceted to manage in such a linear and predictable fashion.

However, many current management theorists continue to focus on the development of individual human capital to create knowledge in the firm, drawing heavily from an individualist point of view. Offering a different perspective, Abhayawansa and Abeysekewa's (2008) extensive literature review on human capital concludes that individual talent alone does not create value for the firm, but that individual talent is most valuable within an effectively strong social context. Some other researchers go as far to argue that the concept of individualism in organizations is simply a myth. They contend developing individual talent without also developing the necessary social infrastructure and relationships to create value will do little good. Individuals are inherently social beings who rely on others to bring out the best within themselves. As a result, social capital is one of the most valuable and differentiating forms of capital a firm can create, and yet one of the hardest to manage and sustain. The bonds that are essential to form between individuals are in part determined by the amount of time, emotional intensity, trust, and reciprocation that exists between individuals (Granovetter, 1973). Of course, these dynamics can be hard to maintain and measure in any type of relationship—especially those that we form at work.

4.1.1 Complexity Marks Relationships: Interwoven Feelings, Experiences, Thoughts, Personalities, and Environments Define Human Relating at Work

Stacey (2003) refers to social dynamics as the complex adaptive responsive process of communicating and relating to each other in the workplace. Human relating occurs as an emergent process that is marked by complexity, adaption, and responses between individuals. Therefore the ability for an individual to learn and create new knowledge at work depends on the strength of the relationships within their network. To better understand the process of human relating in the creation of new knowledge, consider the following scenario. Three colleagues get together to have dinner and discuss their latest work projects. Person A makes a comment about their current work experience, which elicits a response from Person B. This then provokes an idea for Person A, who feels a sense of trust amongst this group to dialogue about this newly generated idea. Person A's new idea resonates with Person C, who has been mulling over a similar project idea for the past couple of weeks, but wasn't able to connect the dots until this conversation. So, Person C jumps into the conversation, and on and on, the conversation goes. It was this open interaction between these three colleagues, which caused novelty to emerge within each individual's thinking. It is during these types of conversations with others, which spark the capacity for new knowledge development. To understand novelty, we must begin to understand relationships and the way people communicate and interact with each other in the workplace. It is the process of effective human relating to one another through emergent interactions that create new ideas, which in turn helps create sustainable value for a firm.

However, since such complexity often accompanies these interactions, it renders them less formulaic. Complex responsive processes can best be described as an interwoven tapestry of feelings, thoughts, experiences, personalities, patterns, and environmental cues, which manifest themselves in the process of relating to one another (Suchman, 2002). Given this complexity of relating to one another, social capital becomes an effective way to more quickly find common meaning and generate knowledge sharing in the workplace. The process of individual's relating is woven by both intention as well as happenstance, consistency as well as novelty, and order as well as chaos. These paradoxes are tensions that remarkably describe the very essence of human beings relating at work. There are times innovation occurs with some luck and preparation. There are times consistency marks success, and yet other incidences where diversity is the key to unlocking higher performance. There is no doubt that on any given day the majority of workplace decision-making more likely resembles unpredictable white-water rapids as described earlier, rather than those of coherent order found within many of today's management textbooks. As a result, the emphasis moves away from the qualities found in hard science, such as analysis, prediction, and control, and instead on the configurations of relationships among the systems components and an understanding of what creates patterns of order and behavior among them. Human relating at work is not something managers should seek to control, however, they can and should facilitate appropriate conditions necessary for dynamic and healthy relationships to form.

There are two conditions identified that are necessary to create more recognizable tapestries that will then translate into shared patterns and meaning embedded throughout an organization's culture: capacity and diversity (Stacey, 2003). Capacity is defined as the ability of an individual to observe and become aware of others. The stronger the bond that exists between individuals, the more likely one will tune into another's opinion moving the individual from an "I" and "me" mentality to one that includes "we" and "us" in the decision-making process. Furthermore, the less cognitive load one carries, the more likely they will be able to be open to others and create shared experiences. The cognitive capacity an individual possesses greatly influences their ability to relate to others and identify with others in a group. Secondly, the most effective tapestries are those interwoven with diversity. Diversity can encompass the obvious, such as race, gender, and age, or more subtle forms such as previous experiences, workstyle preferences, and personality differences. Without a diversity of thought novelty cannot emerge as sameness produces echo chambers simply reinforcing existing knowledge. Therefore increasing the skills of others in the workplace can only be accomplished by having the capacity to see and respond to others, while actively seeking out diversity. Capacity and diversity are the hallmarks of humans relating to one another at work in such a way as to create new knowledge. The role of the manager becomes of upmost importance in being attune to relationships and the patterns of communication that arise within their teams and among the broader organizational culture. By embracing this approach, it frees the manager from trying to reduce agency cost by controlling people, and instead focuses attention on improving relational processes between individuals. By bringing context into focus, emphasizing relationships and encouraging openness to change, managers are much more likely to increase the likelihood of a firm's flexibility, adaptability, and innovation—which are all hallmarks that have allowed not just organizations, but animal species to survive (Suchman, 2002). Let's explore surprising insights from the field of biology to help unpack how relationships form in group settings.

4.1.2 Biology Offers Surprising Lessons in Group Behavior

Biology research suggests that how species interact with each other in groups ultimately affects their chance of survival. The most effective species do this not by forming competitive interaction rules, but rather through cooperative and collective efforts over time. Groups who align themselves within a localized order experience the largest range of movement and protection from outside predators. However, the ability of the collective to effectively synchronize is largely dependent on the amount of time and strength of the social interactions between individual members of the group. A lack of social interaction has been observed to reduce the speed and response of information sharing within the group leading to communal confusion. Furthermore, erratic patterns of group behavior are marked by a lack of efficient food signaling or as a reactionary response to external threats. As a result, group behavior may end up resembling more of a disorderly swarm, moving in a circular motion, rather than fluid movement driving the collective forward and evading potential dangers.

Lesson 1: Individuals need groups to survive. Some species are so well coordinated that they work together in ways that supersedes any one individual's effort alone. For example, some groups of flocking birds or schooling fish can move faster than any individual within the species. These observed movements are so brilliantly coordinated that early biologists in the 20th century actually believed that these species directly transferred thoughts to one another through a form of telepathy. It was presumed that these animals must share a collective mind in order to create the speed and accuracy of their emergent movements. However, today's biologists are able to more accurately measure behaviors and brain activity in ways that 20th century biologists could not. As a result, today's biology research showcases that these animals are exhibiting emergent complex adaptive behaviors in response to one another's movement.

One of the most studied species to exhibit these behaviors are golden shiners—a type of fish that travels a long distance in a remarkable coordinated fashion. Like most species, golden shiners are comprised with stronger fish within their schools. These fish swim faster and acquire information from their environment more quickly than others. Some biologist even speculate that these are the hungriest and most motivated to act within the group. They will often reside at the front of the pack or out to the sides, most able to see the environment and pass along information and cues to the broader group. These fish also exhibit the most influence over the school based on their highly interconnected local network. Their relationships are marked by a strong few close connections, but they also maintain and connect with longer range connections, which exposes them to novel information within their network (Tunstrom et al., 2013). These networks are much more efficient for movement and coordination compared to other species who quickly form swarms or milling patterns in response to dangers and are unable to obtain new knowledge quickly (see Fig. 4.2).

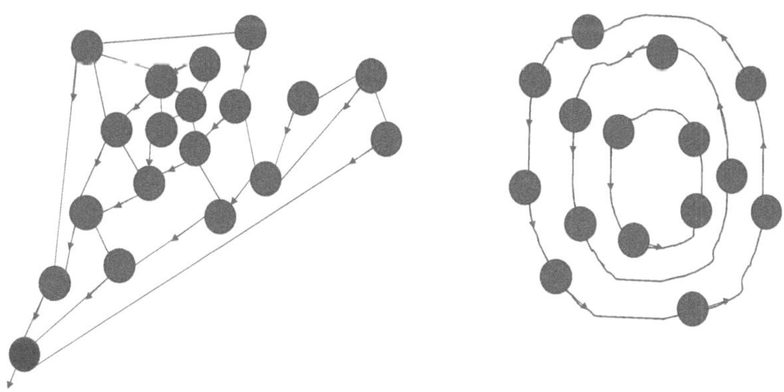

Example of collective coordinated movements that utilizes information from the entire network to determine individual behavior

Example of as warm, which creates circular motion and is often ineffective for moving the group forward

FIGURE 4.2 Patterns of movement.

Lesson 2: Groups need leadership. As a result, these leading fish are the most aware of the social and environmental dynamics occurring around them. Yet, these fish choose to stay within the group and actively participate in its collective movement. Biologists have contemplated this behavior inquiring, if these individual fish are so in tune with their environment, why don't they seek out their own interests instead of reporting back to the group formation? It was concluded that the cost of information necessary for survival was simply too high on one's own. Leaving the school to feed on their own while steering clear of predators proves too risky and decreases the chance of survival. Instead of swimming independently, the leading golden shiner chooses to stay within the collective. However, these more socially aware fish do take on a leadership position within the group—signaling the collective toward new sources of food and warning the school of potential threats. They actively participate in social interactions to ensure better information sharing, which lowers the cost of finding food and ultimately surviving. Likewise, members of the group quickly align to the expert's movement knowing it is for their own benefit. Researchers conclude that, "This analysis [of shiner fish movement] demonstrates that a precise and quantitative understanding of collective behavior in large, self-organized animal groups can be achieved if the hidden pathways of communication are effectively revealed" (Rosenthal, Twomey, Hartnett, Wu, & Couzin, 2015). It is the shiners ability to effectively communicate and interact with each other, which allows the group to achieve the goals of each individual member—which in this case is simply survival. The shiners are a remarkable social species whose existence depends on the ability of the collective to navigate through strong emergent leaders. As a result, they operate from a "we" mindset rather than an "I," which is much needed in many of our organizations who rely on the processes of human relating to create newfound value.

Lesson 3: Groups need individuals to depend on each other. Additional learnings from studying the patterns of movement within the species found that the probability of one's response to another's movement was completely predicated by the strength of connectivity between individuals within the network. Weakened connections whether from proximal distance or a lack of communication received from their neighboring members impacted the individual's ability to respond to collective movements. This biology research regarding groups holds a paradox for business leaders to consider. While it is important to have a few strong central connections in the form of close advisors, much research has shown that having a diverse set of weaker connections is more beneficial for obtaining new knowledge (Granovetter, 1973). Future organizations depend upon the strength of the collective moving forward, and this can only be accomplished through highly communicative relating individuals. Here we understand the need of the individual as well as the group to recognize how to build social capital among peers. If individual needs are not met nor satisfied by the group, their connection will likely become weak and their corresponding behaviors less responsive to environmental cues. Over time, behaviors can become in opposition to the overall group's movements, either creating collision points or by simply drifting off on their own. Gleaning from biology research, this type of individuality actually lessens the chance of one's survival as well as the ability to meet individual needs. Berg and Smith (1995) spend much time within their work reflecting on the paradox of individuals in groups. They note,

> *A group functions only if members are able, at times, to be dependent on each other...To deny this dependency, or try to make it into something other than what it is, diminishes the group's capacity to come together as a whole. The metaphor for the paradox of dependency is ecological. For any part of a system to be able to act interpedently it must accept its dependency on the other parts together with which it makes up a whole (p. 144).*

Often the biggest barrier keeping individuals from experiencing strong connections with one another ultimately stems from a lack of trustworthiness. As Diamond and Allcorn (1987) express, "The central dilemma for the individual in the work group rests in his or her ability to maintain individuality (personal identity and self-esteem) and group membership (a sense of belongingness and affiliation) without becoming overly distressed" (p. 526). Therefore, since groups are simply networks of connected individuals, it is of no surprise then that the same elements, which hold together networks, are those that also meet the individual's intrinsic needs. The group functions only as well as the individual bonds which hold it together. Therefore new behavioral assumptions of management are needed which address both individual as well as collective needs to effectively relate to each other in the workplace.

Lesson 4: Groups thrive on collaboration, not competition. Contrast the aforementioned golden shiner research with an empirical study reviewing chicken behavior that revealed the challenge species face when forming groups centered around competitive interaction rules rather than cooperation (Muir, 2013). A group of identified super chickens were selected to live together to maximize their productivity based on their individual performance. These were the highest producing chickens, as measured by eggs laid. What would happen if you put them all together? Would they be able to produce a greater level of output? Unfortunately, this group of super chickens worked not as team, but as individuals, fiercely competing with one another. Their behaviors were marked with aggression, dysfunction, and even were observed to have pecked one another to death. In fact, by the end of the experiment only three chickens were alive. Competition nearly destroyed not only their performance, but their chances of survival. The story of the super chickens is a lesson in which managers would be wise to heed. Cooperation mechanisms allow for forward productive movement of the collective, while competition often leaves the majority behind allowing for only the survival of the fittest. Without the right social capital dynamics in place for humans to effectively relate to one another and coordinate efforts in order to move the collective forward, they are bound to simply compete and eventually destroy each other in the workplace.

It is found in biological studies that the strength of social interactions increases with age, learning, and growth. The same can likely be said of humans in the workplace as well. The more experienced we become at relating to one another—tuning into another's informational signals and needs, the more likely we are able to better relate and collectively move forward in the workplace. Conversely, the less we relate and depend on each other, the more likely our organizations will resemble disorderly swarms, marked by competition and lacking the necessary information sharing required to advance.

Leaving the majority behind, as found in the super chicken study is not a formula for success, nor is holding back high potential individuals who are able to effectively lead the group as noted by the golden shiners. The fluidity and informality of power dynamics within the gold shiner behavior study, where leading fish choose to remain intermingled within the group, even when possessing enough individual strength to forge alone, can hold unexpected lessons for today's leaders. The tension and challenge for managers today is creating the right building blocks for people to more effectively coordinate their movements together, while also ensuring people are moving in the right direction. You certainly don't want your super chickens pecking each other to death nor do you want swarms of chaos ensuing from a lack of coordination and leadership. Rather, you want to find that aligned and coordinated effort, which seeks movement for the benefit of the collective with different individual roles emerging depending on the expertise required. Managers are both blessed and burdened to remain within the collective and seek out new knowledge and opportunities for their teams, while ensuring individuals within the group stay aligned and continue to move forward. Management's choice of action to achieve this end is what can make or break the employee experience; managers can choose to accomplish this through the mechanisms of competition between individuals, emphasizing strong individuality and performance, or through the power of cooperation—finding the right people to lead at the right time to ensure the success of the collective at work.

4.2 THE GENERAL BUILDING BLOCKS OF SOCIAL CAPITAL

Today's organizations are manifestations of interdependent relationships and networks that form between individuals to meet larger collective goals. The most basic of these needs is economic in nature, however, as discussed, higher performing organizations are those that are also able to leverage the interdependency of individuals to meet higher order intrinsic desires—such as

Social capital building block	Definition	Type	Fuels individual
Trust	Willingness to be vulnerable and openly share	Relational	Need for autonomy
Shared objectives	A purpose for action, the "why" for group formation	Structural	Need for meaning and belonging
Reciprocity	Mutual give and take found in relationships	Relational	Need to belong and feel valued
Expertise	Specialized knowledge transmitted to others	Cognitive	Need for growth

FIGURE 4.3 The building blocks of social capital within networks.

making a difference or experiencing a sense of belonging to others. The general building blocks of strong social networks consist of trust, reciprocity, shared objectives, norms, and expertise development, which are shown in Fig. 4.3. It is these building blocks which generate the development of social capital that ultimately fuels the fulfillment of intrinsic needs. These building blocks allow for greater social cohesion and create individual capacity for the collective.

The building blocks of social capital contain cognitive, relational, and structural components. Arguably one of the most important relational facets is a sense of trust between others. If there is any sense of mistrust or unethical behavior, members will quickly resort back to competitive and self-seeking ways. Social capital hinges on trust in the system—without it, relationships will not provide the means to lower transaction costs in the firm. If group members are unable to trust each other within their networks they are much less likely to grant other members genuine autonomy, and rather seek to control their actions. An atmosphere of trust permits individuals to experience genuine autonomy and more easily assume positive intent in the workplace. One of the ways relational trust can be established is through the acceptance of shared objectives and norms, which is the structural component of social capital. Without the right structure of shared goals and norms, it would be all too easy for the sway of individuals to pursue their own ends and revert back to viewing others as a means for doing so. In addition, defining clear and compelling shared objectives and norms provides a sense of meaning toward individual efforts. Without a clear sense of "the why" behind one's work will likely result in rational self-interest at best, and myopic self-interest at worst.

Furthermore, reciprocity, a relational component of social capital, helps individuals feel a sense of belonging by contributing to and receiving from others' efforts. Reciprocity helps bring balance to the relationship of divergent individuals relating to each other in the workplace. A sense of belonging is an outcome of reciprocity rather than egotism, which derives from individual self-interest efforts. Lastly, the development of one's cognitive growth wholly depends on the strength of networks as well as establishing connections with firm experts. This effort leads to the obtainment of growth and mastery which propels organizations forward. When these critical elements are established among individuals it becomes embedded within the collective network.

4.2.1 Trust

Trust is defined as, "the willingness to be vulnerable to another party when that part cannot be controlled or monitored" (Mayer, Davis, & Schoorman, 1995, p. 712). The more that trust exists between individuals the more likely knowledge and cooperation will ensue. Trust limits the probability of opportunism and lowers the costs of sharing between individuals and groups. Szulanski's (1996) empirical study found that a lack of trust was the most notable obstacle in knowledge sharing.

There are key attributes that must exist in an individual's behaviors before trust can fully form. These are honesty, authenticity, a perceived sense of fairness and concern for others, as well as displaying consistency in decision-making. We will explore each of these attributes of trust and consider ways managers can leverage them in the workplace. The first is honesty and authenticity. No one likes to feel like they are being lied to nor spoken to in a calculated manner, which is a direct violation to forming trust between individuals. Rather, individuals in the workplace thrive on transparency and authenticity. In a qualitative field study research conducted by Jochims (2016), employees criticized the majority of corporate communications remarking, "Communication is too tactical instead of open, honest and authentic...Too often, communication happens based on management-handbooks...Management is afraid to tell us the truth...We are adults, we can handle the truth". These primary insights into employees' reactions to common day communications reveal a startling truth. The lack of authenticity that marks so much communications in the workplace hinders the creation of social capital, further increasing the costs of working together. Trust is built on authentic communications.

The second condition for the formation of trust is fairness. There is nothing more harmful to the creation of social capital than a perception of inequity in the workplace. There is also nothing more likely to bring out irrational decision-making in an individual than feeling a sense of injustice. Economist Bewley (2004) has conducted a series of experiments to gauge how participants make decisions in regards to fairness. Within the workplace study fairness in decision-making was perceived when managers set impartial rules for handling conflict and had set structures and parameters around decisions regarding promotions and pay increases. In particular, employees perceived fairness in wages and promotions when pay differentials were based on education and trainings, tenure, experiences, and productivity. The perception of fairness is created in transparent and clearly set processes that help guide decision-makers.

Thirdly, trust hinges on the perception of one's concern for others. In order for trust to form, one has to believe that the other actor will not simply act in their own interest, but also consider the welfare of others. Simon (1991) describes that trust can form once one is able to demonstrate their transcendence of self-interest, because the individual is able to think in terms of consequences of their own actions on others. As a result, the other person is able to trust that their preferences will at least be accounted for in the actor's decision-making process.

Lastly, a key factor in building trust is stability and consistency in decision-making. Effective relationships need to have a since of predictability that lessens stress and promotes trust. As much as complexity is marked by emergent properties, in order for the system to sustain itself, core principles and values must remain intact for trust to form. Even though complexity theory often postulates unpredictability, the system itself is still constrained to order generating rules. Emergent order and patterns begin to arise over time in complex systems. Likewise, for trust to form, chaos cannot continually abound. Rather, consistent rules must guide the emergence of new properties and behaviors in the workplace. With consistency and time, trust forms and allows the flow of information to more easily pass between participants.

4.2.2 Shared Objectives and Norms

One of the necessary structural components required in the building of social capital is clearly defined shared objectives and norms. If objectives create a purpose, which provide the why behind the formation of a group, then the norms provide the behavioral code, or the how, for achieving the objectives. Without either of these two facets intentionally defined, individual members are less likely to align to the collective. Shared objectives also enable an interdependent network, rather than a functional silo approach to work. It is clearly defined shared objectives, which provides unity to the purpose of diverse individual members within the organization. A shared purpose also creates the willingness of individual members to weather storms, keeping their eye on a longer term objective that is worth the temporary bumps in the road. In addition, a shared purpose creates a collective identity that produces partnership rather than competitive independent silos throughout the organization's networks. By creating a connection between individuals and an organizational purpose, socialized dynamics emerge, making individual efforts more meaningful by connecting them to something bigger than themselves (Weick, 1995; Allen & Meyer, 1990). This may be why Spence (2009) state that, "the secret ingredient of extraordinary companies is purpose" (p. 10).

Organizations, and even groups, who lack a shared purpose and objective are bound to use money and extrinsic values to motivate their individual members—which are far less effective. As Henderson (2012) states, "money is a weak glue" (p. 1). In fact, some organizations' deviant behavior has been directly linked to a lack of a common purpose and shared goals. Without an overarching purpose, individuals will likely revert back to rational self-interest. As a result, it is all too easy to make profits the binding glue rather than take the emotional and psychological investment required in pursuing shared and collective objectives that transcend extrinsic ends. As Doshi and McGregor (2015) suggests, the value of directly connecting individuals to others through shared values results in much higher performing organizations. Money is simply a means to a much deeper end and connecting to that deeper end is what drives higher performance within organizations and groups.

Shared objectives, the why, and the norms of operating, the behavioral code, provides the necessary guardrails to keep self-interest in check. John Seely Brown, who led one of the most respected communities of practice in business, the Palo Alto Research Center, noted the success as a direct result of a shared purpose. "What holds them [diverse group of engineers and scientists] together is a common sense of purpose and a real need to know what each other knows" (p. 232). Knowledge sharing and learning became commonplace as individuals were motivated to keep information flowing throughout the network for the benefit of both the individual as well as the research center as a whole.

The question is, whether a shared value exists that transcends cultures and binds individuals together in such a way as to mitigate myopic self-seeking behaviors. Research suggests that there is a core value that at least 13 nations ascribe as the most important in guiding human behavior—benevolence (Schwartz & Bardi, 2001). Benevolence can be defined as the act of kindness and goodwill toward others. Ironically, even when exposed to economic research that prescribes rational self-interest, a majority of individuals unprompted still state that goodwill and kindness toward others is the ultimate value people should strive after. This finding was also supported by researchers who found that job choice and satisfaction hinged not on pay or promotion, but rather a sense of fairness and the ability to help others. Doshi and McGregor (2015) conclude that the best way to create a shared purpose is to create, "an objective that is so plainly and obviously helpful to others" (p. 153). Ultimately, managers should inspire a vision that supersedes a reliance on a select few and recognize and reward the efforts of the collective group.

4.2.3 Reciprocity

Reciprocity helps balance the required "give and take" during the formation of social capital within firms. It allows for both pursuit of one's own good as well as that of another. As a result, the economics of self-interest maximization do not apply within this construct. Rather than assuming individuals make rational calculations, reciprocity assumes people will sense moral obligation to act on behalf of the interests of others. Those who are assumed or have proven to only act in their own interest are not suited for reciprocal relationships, which ultimately harms the firm. Jochims (2016) shows that individual performance within the organization is highly dependent on reciprocal relationships and norms. Employees assess whether or not their efforts will lead to longer term benefits for both themselves and other stakeholders in which their efforts impact. This leads to another reason why the shareholder profit maximization model leaves no room for reciprocal relationship building with employees in the workplace. As Jochims (2016) asks, "Are the employees only assisting to maximize the company's profit or does the employer voluntarily take care of the employees' well-being without expecting a direct service in return?" (p. 193). The answer to this question dramatically influences employee behavior in the workplace. For example, a large metaanalysis of over 70 studies shows that employees who perceived their organization as caring and supporting their well-being were much more likely to increase their commitment to the organizations goals, increase their individual performance, and reduce withdrawal behaviors (Rhoades & Eisenberger, 2002). There is an undisputable connection with the organizational behavioral literature on the perceived organizational support and an employee's satisfaction and performance in the workplace.

Conversely, the lack of reciprocity within a relationship ultimately leads to one feeling undervalued and unappreciated. These are two strong components that lead to disengaged and deviant workplace behaviors. And unfortunately, when many firms turn to extrinsic means to showcase the value of employees' efforts, employees are often looking for something different. Consider the following case study as an example of the power of reciprocity. A manufacturing organization was facing a mounting problem—increasingly dissatisfied employees. A new CEO had recently taken over the firm and was not personally engaging with the general employee population. However, the former leader, who had recently retired, had worked alongside employees, especially during weekends, and was famous for bringing in schnitzel—an all-time favorite of this German-based firm. During the former leaders tenure, employees felt heard and valued, even though the work was often laborious and demanding. Yet, the new CEO took an entirely different approach, turning instead to incentives to motivate the workforce. The new leader did not make the time to work alongside the employees as his job was to go out and secure additional funding of the firm's operations. Rather than directly coming alongside the employees to hear their concerns and interests, this CEO preferred material gifts. The new CEO thought that employees would much rather see increases in their pay rather than experience face-time with their leader. Hence, the new leader was utterly dismayed when the general satisfaction of employees was not turning around—referring to them as simply "ungrateful." A researcher was brought in to help determine the root cause of this growing dilemma as production was slowing. It was eye-opening what employees had to say in response to the extrinsic rewards being leveraged as reciprocity. For example, one employee remarked, "We're nothing to him [the new CEO], the main issue is profit" (Jochims, 2016, p. 201). The researcher concluded that, "instead of engaging with his employees during shifts on the weekend, the boss tries to appease his employees with materials gifts" (p. 202), which were not nearly as effective as building social capital with his staff.

An important aspect to note at this point is that the argument for creating social capital should not be used as a replacement for good wages and monetary recognition. Extrinsic means are still necessary for a worker's overall experience. Rather, social capital is complementary and even more effective when combined with fair pay. Consequently, social capital does not excuse poor wages or justify the growing inequity between CEO and the average employee's pay. However, social capital does provide a compelling reason to come to work each day above and beyond a paycheck for the majority of workers. As a result, it's benefits far outweigh the costs required to build and maintain social capital in the firm. Today's managers should seek to leverage both fair wages alongside the creation of social capital to promote better relationships in the workplace.

4.2.4 Expertise

While social connections can provide great communal support for an individual, it is the connection points to internal experts, which can generate greater value within organizations. After all, social capital becomes valuable to a firm when it lowers the transaction costs of working together—which experts can frequently do. Expertise is defined as specialized knowledge that represents a highly developed skillset or technique within a given domain that is not ordinarily known (Gerver & Bensman, 1954). In addition, for expertise to be considered a form of social capital, it must be transmittable to others. Yet, as knowledge becomes more specialized, it becomes more unavailable to the public at large, which makes expertise that much more valuable to a firm (Gerver & Bensman, 1954). In addition, expertise embedded in one's social network leads to better decision-making. For example, empirical research found that business owners who surround themselves with a core set of advisors make higher quality business decisions (Renzulli & Aldrich, 2005). Similarly, individuals who depend on a small homogeneous network to draw their conclusions make suboptimal decisions often leading to inaccurate judgments (Ross, 1977). Experts are able to provide a perspective that otherwise would not have been accessible to the decision-maker. As a result, they provide a host of benefits to their social networks. For example, a social connection to an expert has been linked to increased labor market success (Granovetter, 1973), greater socioeconomic gain and the promotion of both individual and societal well-being (La Puma, Stocking, Lavoie, & Darling, 1991).

When is the connection to an expert most valuable to both parities involved in the relationship? Quietly simply, when it extends beyond a transactional relationship. For example, Mead and Bower (2000) found that medical expertise was most valuable when the expert also possessed an informal relationship with the patient. The combination of personal and professional connection is referred to as *multiplexity*, which allows the passage of information to become more fluid and frequent translating to more effective treatment. Multiplexity benefits both the expert and receiver of the information.

Experts are also able to apply their knowledge in a new context more rapidly, which allows their expertise to strengthen. Cohen and Levinthal (1990) found that learning and expertise is cumulative—it is in the application of expertise, which allows it to further grow. Simon (1956) went further to describe expertise as nothing more than deliberate practice and repetition, which slowly becomes part of one's intuition. Simon (1956) described it as such, "the situation has provided a cue; this cue has given the expert access to information stored in memory, and the information provides the answer. Intuition is nothing more and nothing less than recognition." In other words—people who have practiced enough in a certain domain, begin to recognize patterns and better connect to the right answer in a particular situation. Expertise often begets more expertise when applied.

The best way for experts to apply their knowledge is through the establishment of strong informal connections within their network. Access to informal relationships allows expertise to be transferred more cheaply, easily, rapidly, and more frequently. Informal expert relationships lower the transaction costs of working with others on a team. Why is this the case? Informal relationships with embedded expertise allows knowledge to be perceived as relevant, novel, credible, and comprehensible within the network. The move beyond a pure transactional relationship with an expert allows for the fluid nature of information and ease by which it travels throughout the expert's network. In addition, Thomas-Hunt & Phillips, (2004) found that experts more readily participate in problem solving across their network as they possess greater self-confidence in their ability to acquire and transmit valuable information.

In knowledge driven environments, Hodson (2005) found that a baseline of technical competency and expertise is required to create social capital in the firm—especially at the management level. If managers are perceived to lack expertise within the necessary domain, employees are much less likely to share information and remain engaged in the task. Choi's (2015) empirical research on knowledge sharing between government employees found that information flow in the organization was predicted almost entirely based on the perception of expertise. A sense of expertise was linked to others actively pursuing networks and more readily sharing information. If a person saw themselves as an expert, they were more willing to share information out into their network. Expertise lowered the costs of knowledge transfer between others and was positively related to proactively engaging in knowledge sharing behaviors.

Expertise is key to establishing the mechanisms by which to create social capital within the firm. However, this alone is not enough to ensure knowledge is readily transferable to others throughout the firm. Rather, expertise coupled with strong social components is most effective for generating intellectual capital in the firm. These social components are marked by the level of trust, shared objectives, and reciprocity between individuals. The building blocks of social capital are key to help lower the costs of working together. However, we will now turn our attention to the binding agent, which keeps all the building blocks of social capital together.

4.3 TRANSCENDING SELF-INTEREST: THE BINDING AGENT THAT KEEPS GROUPS TOGETHER

While it may be easy to fixate on the singular components that build social capital—it is more worthwhile to contemplate the binding agent which holds these types of relationship together. To illustrate, as much as one would marvel and remark on an architectural structure of a beautiful building, noting the fine materials used—few would give note to the mortar holding the precious materials together. However, the value of these materials increases when they become perfectly molded together to form something truly great. Similarly, the dialogue around business management is often focused on the tangible components that can be easily assessed and measured at the individual level, while neglecting the binding agent or the transcendence of self-interest, which ultimately makes the individual components valuable. It is the ability for individuals to transcend self-interest, that forms and sustains strong social capital in relationships, similar to the mortar or binding agent found in buildings. The binding agent for the creation of social capital comes from the desire and ability of individuals to transcend their individual self-interests for the benefit of the collective. Transcending the climb of self-interest is a day-by-day journey that requires much intentionality and support. However, firms who are able to create the conditions for individuals to more easily do so will also reap the benefits associated with organizational citizenship behaviors, such as innovation, knowledge sharing, and higher levels of performance (Nahapiet & Ghoshal, 1998).

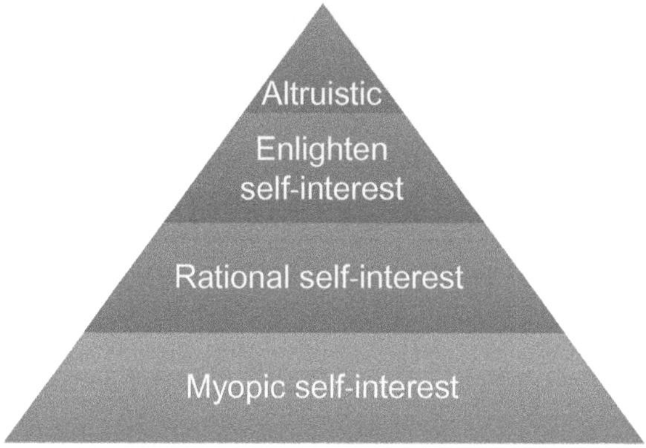

The optimal decisions often occur at the enlighten self-interest level, when people make decisions that consider the benefit of others, without losing sight of their own needs.

FIGURE 4.4 The levels of self-interest in decision-making.

Intentional decision-making can be assessed at four basic levels of an individual choice framework (see Fig. 4.4). At the most basic level is one's own myopic interests, which pursues goals at the expense of others. The next level of decision-making is rational self-interest, which most economic theories assume, by which people act only in regard to their own interest, but believe an invisible hand will ultimately cause individual actions to benefit the collective. These individuals intend no harm by pursuing their own self-interests, but also do not internalize or regard the preferences of others. Moving further up the decision-making framework is reciprocal or enlighten self-interest, which considers the preferences of others, and believes that by doing good and considering collective interests will benefit all. This is the most sustainable and effective decision-making stage for individuals and organizations seeking to create knowledge. Lastly, is altruistic decision-making, where one actually sacrifices their own good for the well-being of others. While this is admirable and at times even considered heroic, it is often not sustainable over the long term as individuals nor organizations can continually forgo their own interests.

Transcending self-interest, which Simon (1983) defined as fully internalizing another's preference, requires a move away from viewing others as a means to an end and rather to a, "behavioral paradigm that considers both the individual's and other people's interests" (Pastoriza, Ariño, & Ricart, 2009, p. 334). It is engaging in the process of pausing to consider how one's own actions will ultimately influence others before deciding to act. It moves the person from "I" to "we" in the decision-making process. Rational self-interest simply takes into account one's own utility and does not bring others into their consideration set. However, just as people are not always fully rational and seek after their own interest, likewise, people are not always fully altruistic simply seeking after others well-being. There is a complex, and yet, orderly interconnection between one's own interest and those of others in the enlighten self-interest decision-making phase. One who is able to transcend beyond their own interests and consider how the consequences of their decisions influence the well-being of others are both rational and benevolent at the same time. As much literature suggests, this is where the power of collective networks can be harnessed to achieve superior results. The individual retains a sense of their own individual preference, while also considering how it will impact others. The sense of others orients the individual toward the pursuit of other's well-being by leveraging their own strengths and skillsets. Satisfaction is ultimately achieved when one's skills are able to solve the problems of someone else (Pastoriza et al., 2009).

In many of today's leading organizations a deficit can be detected between employees and their ability to have intrinsic needs met in stage three of the individual choice framework. Gallop research continues to point to some of the lowest employee engagement levels on record, yet work place conditions have only improved over history. If you compare jobs in the modern era versus the industrial revolution you will find there really is no comparison. Gone are the days of hard labor and potential personal risk due to lax rules protecting employee safety. The majority of job settings today now ensure workers have appropriate breaks, lunch hours, suitable working conditions, and a host of other environmental comforts. So, with the increase in worker rights and accommodations, why are so many employees left feeling disenfranchised and less fulfilled than ever before? It is argued that too many firms have lost their emphasis on the collective well-being of their employees, and as a result, lack the necessary environments where individuals can form the networks required to achieve greater productivity and engagement. By organizations remaining in stage two of rational self-interest, decision-making does not allow nor even consider the formation of social capital as a necessary mandate for both individual and firm wide collective well-being.

While social capital can create the guardrails for lowering agency costs, many traditional firms continue to rely on individualistic command and control techniques to align behavior to the firm's interests. While the traditional self-interested firm may still achieve economic success, more often than not, Jochims (2016) warns, "they are limited in their potential due to rather dissatisfied employees ("soulless workhouses"). In these relationships shaped by instrumentalization, there is often mutual lack of trust amongst the parties involved" (p. 191). When considering these realities, social capital can help bring "the soul" back into an organization and inherently constrains the pursuit of unbridled self-interest within the firm. This in part is driven by a necessary change of perspective moving away from viewing people as merely cogs in a wheel and a means to an end, but instead as relating human beings who coorient toward the collective well-being of all individuals within the firm.

There may be no more powerful example of individuals transcending self-interest or even altruistic decision-making, then when an entire country came together to transcend their own interests in the way Americans did during World War II. Today economists, sociologists, and management theories marvel at the social and economic prosperity that was gained during this time (Gordon, 2016). While this was a complex time in history with multiple underpinnings to explain the prosperity experienced, one thing is certain—there was incredible cooperation across businesses, communities, and governments to propel the country forward. The entire motivation for doing so was for the benefit and protection of the collective society. The individual was asked and even called upon to transcend their own self-interest and do good by serving in whatever capacity they could. And many, especially minorities such as people of color and women, began entering into the workforce for the very first time. Industries experienced a sense of unprecedented diversity as many of the men left their occupations to fight in the war. Organizations, with support from Eleanor Roosevelt, placed greater emphasis on employee morale, forming sporting leagues, picnics, and other work sponsored events to create a sense of community in the midst of growing workplace diversity. Restaurants even got involved helping prepare warm meals for the many dual-working parents to pick up on their way home. In addition, and maybe most profound to workers, was the frequent visits from soldiers who directly linked the workers tasks back to the efforts being made on the frontlines. Many military leaders would remark that without the production and role of businesses, the soldiers could not effectively do their jobs. Recent behavioral research suggests that directly linking workers efforts to the end customer greatly enhances productivity (Grant et al., 2007). All of these newfound pressures elevated the level of worker productivity across industries, in part on the, "patriotism and the sense of purpose, which bonded workers and management together, and workers were more eager to raise their efficiency (often in ways that made their lives easier) than before" (Gordon, 2016, p. 550).

While social capital cannot be solely credited for the economic boom that was experienced, it was indeed a compelling facet toward its creation. Can you imagine going to work everyday believing your efforts directly impacted the well-being of an entire nation? Imagine the response if your customers walked throughout your offices explaining firsthand the impact your work was having on their welfare? This level of cooperation did not eliminate the need for competitiveness either—the President encouraged healthy competition between firms so that the collective could win. Competition was not leveraged as a way to cut down or beat out others, but rather as a motivator toward higher levels of performance. It is a remarkable narrative of a time that emphasized the collective, which led to an entire nation banding together in solidarity developing a fabric of social capital among the masses.

The pressing questions facing today's organizational leaders is, how can the same level of social capital be created around a collective narrative?

It is not just looming war that can band a group of individuals together to sacrifice for the well-being of others. Yet another remarkable example occurred during the 2008 financial crisis at a large chemical manufacturing organization. The company was in the midst of a cultural transformation emphasizing unity and the people of its organization after many years of profit decline. A new CEO stepped in and began building relationships across the firm and the organization began to experience a great economic turnaround. However, the CEO had a decision to make as the financial crisis persisted. The option was to either do what the majority of his peers in the industry were doing—laying off workers—or, he could ask all employees to forgo a few week's pay so everyone could keep their job over the long term. After declining his $4 million bonus that year, he decided on the latter asking employees to forgo their salary for a period of time to which they agreed. In fact, many economists may believe this was truly the most rational decision to make. As the recession began to rebound the company was able to regain its footing in the market and restore full-time employment to all employees. While this resulted in short-term individual sacrifice, it shows that business leaders can transcend self-interest, calling on their organizations to do the same, ultimately benefiting the majority over the long-run. The key is creating a compelling purpose or reason to transcend one's interest. All too often organizational leaders wait until a crisis has occurred. However, good management in the 21st century will strive to provide the "why" or shared objective proactively, well before a crisis occurs. Doing so will help others in the organization transcend their rational interest and make decisions based on enlighten self-interest, benefiting a wider range of stakeholders in the decision-making process.

4.4 WHY SOCIAL CAPITAL WORKS IN TODAY'S FIRMS

In historical industrial economies knowledge often resided within the organization—whether on the factory line, in process documents, or within the top ranks of management. Employees could come and go and the effectiveness of the organization would continue on. As a result, many managers began to see labor as easily replaceable. It was not the employee's knowledge they were hiring for after all, but their hands and ability to repeat low cognitive work that made them valuable. In fact, in many cases management would prefer workers not utilize their creativity or cognitions as the industrial process was built upon predictable repetition and quality control. However, today's value creation process is very different as the economy shifts from products and services to knowledge. Managers now hire for a person's unique set of "know-how" that will challenge existing paradigms and generate new ideas. Courageous firms actively seek out a diversity of thought in today's labor markets and encourage a culture of radical candor to further develop intellectual capital in the firm. However, intellectual capital, while protected by patents and noncompetes, still originates and permanently resides with the person. Today, knowledge is embodied within a firm's talent base, and when a person leaves the organization, so does that knowledge. Mason (2015) notes, "With information, part of the product remains with the worker in a way it did not during the industrial era" (p. 135). The cost of losing employees is no longer only accounted for by the efforts required to acquire new talent. Rather, a hidden intangible cost in the form of lost knowledge occurs as that employee leaves the organization. This poses difficulty for today's managers, seeking to retain and grow knowledge within teams and ultimately the firm. There are two distinct approaches the manager can utilize to mitigate the risk of knowledge loss. The first is through traditional coercion techniques that leverage fear. Managers can actively create controls and policies that restrict knowledge from leaving the organization through noncompeting contracts and other policies that restrict the individual's ability to own the intellectual property created while employed with the organization. However, we know from Chapter 3, Exploring Management Alternatives With a Behavioral Economics Lens, that fear-based tactics actually restrict the creation of new knowledge. Or alternatively, managers can utilize a greater alternative by leveraging the development of social capital within teams. We will now unpack why social capital is an effective and efficient way to leverage and grow knowledge within today's organizations.

4.4.1 Nonmarket Mechanisms Need to be Leveraged

Firm success depends less on establishing predictable controls that ensure a stability of output and more on creating dynamic connections with others throughout an emergent ecosystem of partners. As a result, managers can no longer rely on the administrative theory to guide them through knowledge creation and development as social capital in particular can only be sustained through trust, shared objectives, reciprocity, and expertise. The question becomes if agency costs were once mitigated through aligning interests through incentives, which have proven to be questionable in the new market dynamics, is there a better way managers can evolve to align interests across a variety of stakeholders to create sustained value for the firm? To answer this, we have to consider nonmarket mechanisms for behavior coordination. Rather than rely on an invisible hand that weaves through rational self-interested people that compete with one another toward the collective good, it is suggested that a visible hand of intentional decentralization, cooperation, and mutuality are pursued in order to lower the transaction costs of exchanging information. Economic inquiry still is needed to understand how and why people come together, but behavioral alternatives provide a greater currency of exchange that lessen the value of incentives and increase the value of relationships and networks. In reality, extrinsic levers work not simply because of the tangible good exchanged, but rather its symbolism toward something more intangible—such as pride, happiness, or benevolence.

Of course, managers will continue to be presented with the tension that people still act toward their own interest and not those of the collective network. Chaos and disorder are an ever-present concern without the proper guardrails, or as Adam Smith would refer to—*moral sentiments* that guide people toward the collective good. Moral sentiment is the inherent drive of humans, which seeks to empathize with others, ultimately keeping the rational self-interested person in check. His or her interest will be pursued only as far as his or her sense of others. Smith (1776) argued that while individuals are autonomous agents, they are social beings inherently tied to the desire of others. The need to be connected to a larger identity and purpose must be met to fuel the intrinsic desire of humanity to collaborate toward something bigger than any individual could achieve on their own. Therefore the evolving role of the manager considers an intentional and disciplined approach to lowering the cost of producing and sharing information—namely, through the development of social capital.

As discussed, the rise of intangible assets causes an inquiry into the rational economics model that is built upon incentives, rationality, and competition. In scarce and competitive markets these assumptions are applied and often work very well to predict supply and demand for goods and services. In fact, rational economics are very useful in scarce and perfectly competitive markets, where self-interested individuals must compete toward the lowering of costs and spreading the purchasing power of the collective. However, the knowledge-driven markets are much less likely to respond to competition and self-interest to benefit the collective value of a firm. Rather, the current economic system is set up to underutilize information, because in the midst of abundance, competitive and self-interested firms are trying at all costs to lessen its information flow into the greater ecosystem. As a result, asymmetry quickly occurs with monopolies rising to dominate a market.

Hart (2017) recently raised concern around the growing asymmetrical market that data and information cause. For example, her research notes that Google's market cap is larger than the GDP of Chicago, while Amazon's market cap is larger than the GDP of Washington DC. E-marketer reported that Google owned 40.7% of the US digital ad revenues in 2017, while Facebook reportedly owned 39.1% of the display ad market. Indeed, there is a concentrated data market rising as firms seek to control information and utilize that toward markets dominance. However, others argue that these tech giants of today—Google, Amazon, and Facebook—were simply yesterday's startups, which disrupted the market through innovation. For example, it was less than a decade ago that *Fortune* named Yahoo! the undisputed winner in the search engine space. MySpace just a few years ago was the leading social media platform. Other argue that while each of these technology companies offer different products and solutions, they are all in competition for the same thing—consumer attention. This drive toward capturing attention drives a greater desire to find value through obtaining customer data. Firms who are able to effectively gather this data and convert it into valuable insights are winning in today's market—even outperforming cities with millions of workers. As a result, the economic conditions are exhibiting different behaviors that lend itself more to information asymmetry, complexity, and even toward monopolistic tendencies.

Therefore current market conditions no longer represent perfection information or competitive markets with many players competing for scarce goods. As Warsh (2007) summarized, "The fundamental categories of economic analysis ceased to be, as they had been for two hundred-year, land, labor and capital. This most elementary classification was supplanted by people, ideas and things. . .the familiar principle of scarcity had been augmented by the important principle of abundance." Another way of saying it is that markets have come to differentiate firms who produce information first and then things (Mason, 2015). Value is no longer inherent to tangible products, however, found in the social construction of ideas and solutions that flow throughout a firm. Firms who are able to harness the power of social capital are much more likely to find success in today's markets, where non-market mechanisms, such as relationships and attention, come to the forefront of firm value.

4.5 OUTCOMES OF SOCIAL CAPITAL

There is much empirical evidence to support the rise of social capital differentiating firms in today's knowledge-driven environments. For example, research suggests that business units' success or failure depends on how well the internal network shares expertise, learning, and resources (Ghoshal and Bartlett, 1990). A group of researchers studied multiple teams in a highly interdependent task environment, which sought to develop new product and services in a research and development lab. The research found that one of the most predictive factors to innovation was the strength of the identification team members had with one another (Drazin et al., 1999). The researchers urged managers to employ strategies related to social bonds to complement task-related connections. Far too often managers focus on connecting the right people with the right task, without also considering connecting the right people with each other.

Outcome 1: Social capital allows for more efficient and effective information sharing. Many researchers argue that knowledge is inherently relational, requiring social interaction for its formation (Tsoukas & Mylonopoulos, 2004). Social bonds allow information, knowledge, and resources to more easily transmit between individuals, thus lowering the costs of information sharing and development within firms. For example, consider the following study by Tsai and Kilduff (2002), which sought to understand the flow of information between family and nonfamily units within an organization. The organization under investigation consisted of 36 business units, with 14 business units led by members of the family that founded the company. The researchers hypothesized that units run by family members were more likely to share information than units with nonfamily leadership. Their results found strong support for their hypothesis, which discovered that these 14 family-led business units were much more favorable to each in knowledge sharing. They shared much more information with each other in an efficient manner. The researchers conclude that, "Knowledge transfer was, in fact, embedded in kinship relationships rather than following purely economic logic" (p. 26).

Outcome 2: Social capital is linked to increased team performance. Team performance is another notable outcome of strong social capital between individuals. A study conducted by MIT researchers on high-performing teams found that teams perform best when individuals have a social sensitivity to each other as well as allowing equal time for everyone, regardless of status, to voice their opinions (Woolley, Chabris, Pentland, Hashmi, & Malone, 2010). This speaks clearly to the power of capacity and diversity within organizations, which allow individuals the freedom to relate to each other in authentic ways in order to create new knowledge and meaning at work. Without social capital, team performance will begin to suffer simply because individuals are unable to bring their best. They will self-censor, exhibit herding behaviors or remain trapped in the status quo. Yet, with social capital, teams can reach remarkably higher levels of performance and overcome the many biases that get in the way.

Outcome 3: Social capital leads to greater level of well-being. Benefits exist at the individual level as well. Kawachi and Berkman (2001) found strong social ties related to one's own well-being and cognitive health. Christakis and Fowler (2007) also found brain health linked to one's social network. The stronger the network, the stronger is the intellectual capabilities of the individuals who share the bond. The role of the manager is necessary to ensure that levels of trust, reciprocity, norms, and connectedness are formed amongst individuals to lower the costs of intellectual capital creation.

4.5.1 Historical Examples: Social Capital Has Always Been Necessary

While the construct of social capital may be fairly new, its existence has been fundamental to business success throughout history. Even today's most technical roles depend on social dynamics to work. By looking back into history, we can learn from the previous challenges management has faced in the wake of technology disruption. With the introduction of the telegraph, invented in the early 1800s, it forever changed the way long distance communication could transpire. Telegraph operators were highly skilled workers, analogous to software developers today. Ironically, it was not the worker's willingness to adopt the technology or skills required to operate the technology, but rather the navigation of social dynamics that determined the actual benefit of leveraging this new capability. However, examining the memoirs and writings of telegraph operators highlight the difficulties the social nature of technology brought to a technical role (Mason, 2015). The telegraph could only work as fast as the person on the receiving end could accept it as it was built on a network that required sharing of communication lines. As a result, receiving information was a much more complex task because the room was filled with both senders and receivers that would have to negotiate with each other for line capacity. Some of these negotiations were done with far distant operators in other cities. One of the biggest challenges to effectively operating the new technology was the lack of social capital caused by poor interpersonal dynamics. A telling memoir of a lead telegraph operator notes, "Handling egos was as much a part of an operator's work as handling a telegraph key. Considerate, helpful operators made work easier; domineering, cavalier, or self-righteous ones made work more difficult" (Tillotson, 1991).

As history reveals, intellectual capital without the necessary supportive social capital leads to a lack of value capture, even in the midst of technology gains. Shifting market dynamics place an emphasis on the development of the intellectual power of the workers (Mason, 2015). Without strong social capital, firm differentiation is hard to achieve as the costs of knowledge transfer becomes too high. Therefore it is argued that managers within firms must have a holistic view of their employees, team dynamics, and social environments in order to shepherd employees toward successfully creation of intellectual capital through the development of high-exchange relationships. Because social capital lowers the costs of intellectual capital creation and development, it becomes a powerful mechanism for a firm looking to collaborate broadly across an ecosystem, while also navigating the challenges of market information asymmetry and the rise of monopolies. This evolution hinges upon the notion that individuals are social creatures and that organizations are inherently social constructs dependent upon the amount of social capital present. This progression directly impacts the role of managers from simply seeking to plan, control, direct, and organize tangible resources, to one that must pursue effective coaching, empowerment, adapting, and connecting behaviors.

4.6 AN ALTERNATIVE TO AGENCY COSTS: THE ROLE OF SOCIAL CAPITAL IN MANAGEMENT

Bringing together a diverse group of people with conflicting interest is and will continue to be a leading challenge for the 21st century manager. As much as business has evolved—the markets, organizations, products, and services—the nature of people remains the same throughout history. The sum of rational economic assumptions has led to a concentration of management efforts which artificially drive employee behavior through command and control processes. With the integration of new perspectives including behavioral science, it becomes central to consider alternatives outside of merely managing agency costs and establishing incentives in order to achieve the purpose of an organization. While group dynamics can be leveraged to help create cooperative environments, divergent interests will still need to be aligned in order to accomplish the firm goals. Rather than overly rely on inducements that influence behavior, there can be a different, and perhaps even more compelling lever a manager should consider to effectively lead talent today. It is a lever that Adam Smith wrote and talked about nearly two decades before writing the *Wealth of Nations*. Smith writes that rather than assume people are fully rational self-interested beings, he suggests that people have a pull toward a more alluring desire, which is to connect and belong with others. Smith (1759) begins his theory of moral sentiments with, "No matter how selfish you think man is, it's obvious that there are some principles in his nature that give him an interest in the welfare of others, and make their happiness necessary to him, even if he gets nothing from it but the pleasure of seeing it" (p. 1). This innate drive of mankind—to see himself in relationship with others—limits the ability to pursue full rationality. As Mason (2015) remarks, "Nothing has changed about humanity. It's just that our human desire to make friends, build relationships based on mutual trust and obligation, fulfilling emotional and psychological needs, has spilled over into economic life" (p. 130). If this is accurate, rather than designing environments and talent management practices that promote competitive and self-seeking behaviors, what would happen if we designed and managed talent as if people inherently desired to cooperate and be in good standing with one another? Could we design environments where the cooperation with others was a primary concentration for individuals? Could an alternative *alignment lever*—in the form of social capital—be employed in lieu of attempting to manipulate behavior through external means?

4.6.1 Managers Drive Social Capital Through High-Exchange Relationships

Managers are instrumental and essential for the formation of social capital to form within teams and organizations. While the design of human resource policies, processes, and practices can help promote social capital, so too can the everyday personal interaction of managers with the employees of all levels within the organization. Some organizational behavior research suggests that the highest responsibility of a manager is to influence the well-being of others and encourage others to also transcend their own self-interests in decision-making to further promote the creation of social capital throughout the firm. Sison and Fontrodona (2013) remark that it is the manager's duty to emphasize and value the consequences an individual's actions have on others in the workplace. The manager is most influential in this case by modeling self-transcendent behaviors and taking time to coach and develop others. Ghoshal and Moran (1996) note "people developer" as the primary role of the manager (p. 16). To this end, Pastoriza et al. (2009) summarize the role of the manager in creating social capital as follows:

> *If management wants to move to a position where goodwill in social relations is the norm, managers should be the meditating figures with whom employees identify, and that facilitate the process through which employees transcend their self-interest, and develop associability and identification-based trust with the firm (p. 338).*

However, we know this means shedding the burden of assuming self-interested agents who need to be controlled to mitigate agency costs. McCollom (1995) warns, "Teaching M.B.A.'s or anyone else to manage group formation by exerting strong control of the task process alone is courting disaster" (p. 48). How then does the manager create the conditions necessary to generate strong social networks throughout the firm? The leadership literature helps provide a rather simple roadmap. Start moving from purely economic transactions with employees to the development of social relationships. Transactional relationships or low-exchange relationships, which solely focus on the work to be done, are less likely to generate additional efforts beyond the task at hand. The lack of social capital within these interactions does not provide any value for either the individuals or the firm above and beyond the exchange. Contrast this to high-exchange relationships, which are built on trust, transparency, and frequent interactions apart from the task at hand. High-exchange relationships are built on the notion that there is no such thing as "it's just business, not personal." Rather high exchanges are built on the mantra that accomplishment of business objectives is highly personal. Leaders who engage in high exchanges take time to get to know their teammates, spend time honing their interests, and provide opportunities for these members to further develop their own unique talents. These high exchanges are marked with tremendous benefits at both the individual and organizational level. Research shows that high-level exchanges fuel additional creativity, effort, and satisfaction throughout the workforce (Graen & Uhl-Bien, 1995). This is because a higher effective state results in greater transmission of resources between individuals. Individuals are compelled to respond to high exchanges by exerting more effort toward shared goals.

What is the hallmark of a high-exchange relationship? Sincere concern for the other person's needs. Consider the following large metaanalysis, which spanned over 85 years. One of the most significant predictors of a leader's effectiveness was their level of agreeableness and greater concern for others (Judge, Bono, Ilies, & Gerhardt, 2002). Another group of researchers, which measured leadership in 14 samples across 200 organizations, found that agreeableness was the most consistent variable related to effective leadership (Judge & Bono, 2000). Likewise, Bass and Bass (2008) summarized empirical evidence that groups are more likely to prosper with collectively minded leaders and fail more often with self-interested leaders. Further evidence shows that agreeableness is closely linked to the success of a group because individual members perceive their workplace to be more fair, just, and ethical (Schoorman et al., 2007). The researchers conclude that, "due to their concern for others, agreeable leaders may be more successful in communicating respect, avoiding impropriety, and providing candid justifications for decisions that were tailored to employees' needs" (p. 951). Moerschell and Lao's (2012) research on the characteristics of emergent leadership found that a person's motivation to act, compassion for others, and a sense of responsibility toward others were all predictive of effective leadership traits. One of the most effective styles of leadership in team settings is when the manager played a role of facilitator, which implies a helpful attitude to others. These research examples point to the fact that leaders who are most in tune with individual needs on the team generate not only social capital, but greater team performance. Yet, all too often managers lead not by thoughtful concern for others in the workplace, but rather by authority and through control. This style may have worked in environments of scarce resources, low connectivity, and limited labor skills; however, today's markets demand the distribution of control for more optimal decision-making. Managers who establish strong social capital through the development of high exchanges will be much more likely to distribute control to the experts within the networks.

The goal of generating social capital within a firm is challenging and redefining the role of management. Rather than following a management model based on resource command and control, social capital allows managers to foster and negotiate based on the principles of trust and reciprocity, which are much more cost effective in today's markets. Social capital allows the firm to go from anomic and alienating to one that is defined by normative values and integration (Hodson, 2005).

4.6.2 A Behavioral Shift for the 21st Century Manager

As people, ideas, and things become at the forefront of economic prosperity, how does a manager today seek to maximize, or at least in the words of Simon (1956), satisfy the creation and development of these factors in the firm? It was discovered that social capital is an effective means of lowering the transaction costs of working together in a firm to create and capture value from information and knowledge. However, this perspective poses a behavioral shift for today's managers. While the activities within talent management do not necessarily change—such as hiring and performance management—the way that managers go about those activities certainly does. In particular, managers must now consider a longer term perspective of value creation, while also balancing the complexity managing people in dynamic organizations brings.

4.6.2.1 Long Distance View

If social capital is such a powerful mechanism for mitigating agency costs, why is it so rarely leveraged? The answer more often than not resides in the fact that social capital and reciprocal decision-making takes time to build. In order to truly consider the interests of others, it requires more often than not, a connection and sense of trust within the relationship. This of course takes time and a longer distance perspective than next quarters return. And so, freeing oneself from the dominant rational assumptions, which currently bind management theory allows greater freedom to pursue longer term gains. Letting go of commonly held pessimistic views that people simply want to work for money or will often deviate from a company's interest allows the manager to explore intrinsic and social levers that may better enrich the employee experience at work. Encompassing a broader group of stakeholders also allows the manager greater opportunity to connect individuals both inside and outside the firm to strengthen the firm's purpose. These changes evolve the role of the manager as an administrator of resources to one who guides the creation and flow of information through the development of social capital in the firm (see Fig. 4.5 for a comparison of traditional and behavioral management). Stated simply, managers guide the inner life of the firm and help develop the individuals who work there. To effectively do this, it requires a new management language behind the traditional skills of planning, controlling, directing, and organizing resources. Instead, today's managers need to connect, coach, empower, and adapt. These new management behaviors are critical in order to navigate the role of people, information, and decisions in a knowledge-driven firm.

A critical management mindset shift that will be key when leading teams in longer term focused organizations is the ability for leaders to adjust the pace of which work is expected to be achieved. To illustrate this need, the example of a runner's pace-setter is ideal. Pace-setters are frequently hired by leading marathon runners who require a strong level of expertise to successfully compete in challenging long-distance races and reach higher levels of performance. Pace-setters must also possess deep expertise and knowledge of the course to accurately guide others toward goal obtainment. Similarly, in the quest to build social capital, managers should consider the full scope of the journey ahead and ultimately guide individuals to achieving success. Too many times in hurried workplaces teams are plagued with last minute

Assumptions	Rational economic view	Behavioral view
Market conditions	Perfect, competitive, and complete information	Imperfect, irrational, and asymmetrical access to information
Purpose of the firm	Pursue the maximization of shareholder wealth	To generate collective value across stakeholders
Resource allocation	Solely concerned with efficiently distributing financial capital to maximize share price	Includes a variety of resource allocation capital decisions including financial, social, talent, and environmental and focus is on satisfying
Individual worker	Actively seeks to restrict output	Inherently engages in work within the right conditions
Incentives	Must provide extrinsic rewards to motivate workers	Be careful not to misuse extrinsic incentives as a way to crowd out intrinsic motivators
Role of manager	A fiduciary duty to minimize agency costs to maximize share price of firm	Actively develop internal talent and facilitate the conditions necessary for social capital to generate long-term value for the firm
Management activities	Planning, controlling, organizing, and directing	Connecting, coaching, empowering, and adapting

FIGURE 4.5 Comparing traditional and behavioral perspectives on management.

"fire drills" and leadership tends to get swept up in the race and become focused on getting the job down quickly rather than holistically. Using this example, rather than management being the sprinter in the workplace, a more consistent and long-distance pace-setter approach will be more effective when leading teams toward longer term goals. In addition, managers who seek to build social capital must adopt this pace-setter mentality as a way to transcend their own rational self-interest decision-making. This means not going too fast and burning your employees out too soon, while at the same time avoiding going too slow and not reaching the final performance outcome. The purpose of the pace-setter is to help provide the context of the course ahead and to do so in a way that assists those behind them with the ability to navigate obstacles that could impede their performance. These individuals set the expectations for speed, note the boundaries and limitations ahead, and encourage higher levels of performance as their role becomes primarily for the benefit and enablement of others.

One of the most compelling behaviors of the pace-setter once runners are considered set for the race, usually around the half-way point, they exit the race. Their role shifts yet again and they then become the runners biggest advocate on the sidelines, cheering them on toward success. All too often, managers today, try to stay too long in the race, managing rather than empowering people to run on their own. Managers should empower and come alongside rather than remain in front once social capital has been established within relationships. However, this will require a new set of management behaviors and skills, which allow managers to become the long-distance pace-setters of their organizations.

4.7 TALENT MANAGEMENT FRAMEWORK

Rather than following a management model based on compliance and monitoring, social capital allows managers to foster and develop talent based on the principles of trust and reciprocity, which are much more cost effective in today's knowledge-driven markets. The question is, how can managers effectively leverage the newfound alternatives afforded in behavioral economics to navigate talent decision-making in firms? The type of management activities surprisingly remains unchanged. For example, managers still must make decisions around talent acquisition, goals, performance management, engagement, and change management. However, how they can go about it, does dramatically change applying a behavioral lens. For example, the key activities of the manager shift from planning, controlling, directing, and organizing resources to one of connecting, coaching, empowering, and adapting.

Fig. 4.6 provides a cohesive management framework to better understand the role of the 21st century manager in knowledge-driven economics. The *y*-axis shows the type of social capital required to effectively complete the necessary management activities in an employee's lifecycle at the firm. Social capital, requiring time, trust, and transparency, grows in importance to lower the transaction costs of knowledge transfer as the employee progresses

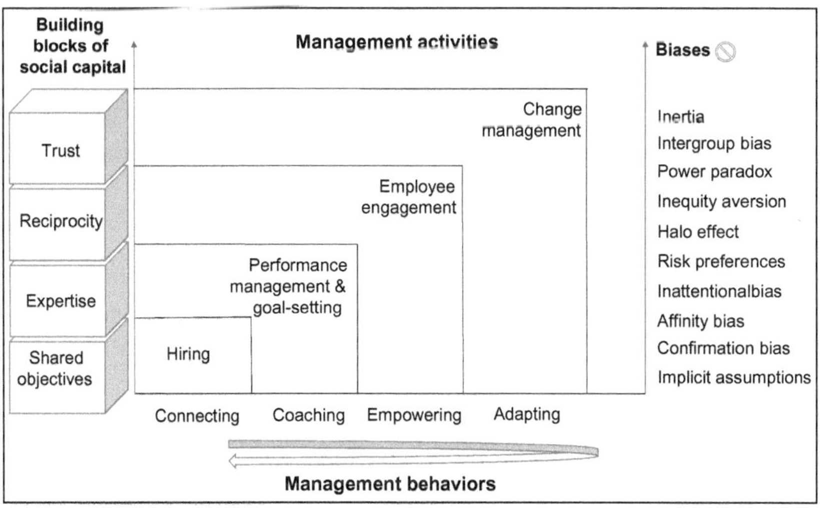

FIGURE 4.6 Management framework.

throughout the talent lifecycle at the firm. For example, as the manager moves from hiring and resource allocation decisions to engagement and change management decisions, a higher level of social capital is needed to efficiently complete the task at hand.

The *x*-axis indicates the type of management skillset and behaviors required throughout each of the core talent decision-making stages. The manager will have to engage in connecting behaviors to adequately acquire the right talent needed to grow the firm's intellectual capital. Whereas to navigate the process of change management, a manager's focus will be more on adapting behaviors. However, each of these core management behaviors—connecting, coaching, empowering, and adapting—are cyclical and not necessarily linear in nature. It is likely that as a manager adapts to change there will be new resource considerations, which require connecting behaviors. Therefore at any given time, depending on the size of the team and the type of firm, a manager is likely to be weaving in and out of each of these behaviors on any given day. The complexity of talent management poses newfound opportunities and challenges for the 21st century manager. In addition, a behavioral lens provides us with the cautionary biases, or heuristics, which are likely to emerge throughout the decision-making process, which are found on the right-hand side of the framework. For activities that rely less on social capital, individual biases such as confirmation bias or planning fallacy are likely to be of concern. As social capital increases throughout the employee lifecycle, it is more likely that group biases and social influences may be of management concern—such as social inequity aversion or intergroup biases. As a result, managers must consider opportunities to either leverage or guard against the biases that might derail the talent lifecycle and thus disrupt the ability of a firm to capture value from intellectual capital development.

4.8 SUMMARY

The role of the manager must still grapple with the possibility of agency costs when managing individuals within today's organizations. However, the building blocks of social capital help provide the tools necessary for individuals to transcend their own rational interest and consider others in the form of enlightened self-interest, which considers others before acting. Managers have the ability to use social capital as a way to align divergent interests of individuals toward organizational goals. To do so, they must abandon the administrative theory behaviors of planning, directing, controlling, and organizing resources to one who connects, coaches, empowers, and adapts to others in the workplace. Relationships define and mark the role of managers in knowledge-driven environments. The rest of the book will spend time examining each of these core behaviors, while also exploring the various biases that impeded the ability of the manager to effectively engage in these behaviors and their corresponding activities.

REFERENCES

Abhayawansa, S., & Abeysekera, I. (2008). An explanation of human capital disclosure from the resource-based perspective. *Journal of Human Resource Costing & Accounting, 12*(1), 51–64. Available from https://doi.org/10.1108/14013380810872752.

Allen, N. J., & Meyer, J. P. (1990). The measurement and antecedents of affective, continuance and normative commitment to the organization. *Journal of Occupational Psychology, 63*, 1–18.

Bass, B. M., & Bass, R. (2008). *Handbook of leadership: Theory, research, and application.* New York: Free Press.

Berg, D. N., & Smith, K. K. (1995). Paradox and groups. In J. Gillette, & M. McCollom (Eds.), *Groups in context: A new perspective on group dynamics*. Lanham: University Press of America, Inc. (1995).

Bewley, T., Fairness, reciprocity, and wage rigidity (May 2004). IZA Discussion Paper No. 1137; Cowles Foundation Discussion Paper No. 1383.

Choi, Y. (2015). Employees' knowledge-sharing behavior: An empirical analysis of U.S. federal agencies. *Public Performance & Management Review, 39*, 381–405.

Christakis, N. A., & Fowler, J. H. (2007). The spread of obesity in a large social network over 32 years. *New England Journal of Medicine, 357*, 370–379.

Cohen, W. M., & Levinthal, D. A. (1990). Absorptive capacity: A new perspective on learning and innovation. *Administrative Science Quarterly, 35*(1), 128–152.

Coleman, J. (1990). *Foundations of social theory*. Cambridge: Harvard University Press.

Diamond, M., & Allcorn, S. (1987). The psychodynamics of regression in work groups. *Human Relations, 40*(8), 525–543.

Doshi, N., & McGregor, L. (2015). Primed to perform: How to build the highest performing cultures through the science of total motivation. New York, NY: Harper Business.

Drazin, R., Glynn, M. A., & Kazanjian, R. K. (1999). Multilevel theorizing about creativity in organizations: A sensemaking perspective. *Academy of Management Review, 24*(2), 286–307.

Gerver, I., & Bensman, J. (1954). Towards a sociology of expertness. *Social Forces, 32*(3), 226–235.

Ghoshal, S., & Bartlett, C. A. (1990). *The Academy of Management Review, 15*(4), 603–625.

Ghoshal, S., & Moran, P. (1996). Bad for practice: A critique of the transaction cost theory. *Academy of Management Review, 21*, 13–47.

Gordon, R. J. (2016). *The rise and fall of American growth: The U.S. standard of living since the Civil War.* Princeton, NJ: Princeton University Press.

Graen, G. B., & Uhl-Bien, M. (1995). The relationship-based approach to leadership: Development of LMX theory of leadership over 25 years: Applying a multi-level, multi-domain perspective. *Leadership Quarterly, 6*(2), 219–247.

Granovetter, M. S. (1973). The strength of weak ties. *The American Journal of Sociology, 78*, 1360–1380.

Grant, A., et al. (2007). Impact and the art of motivation maintenance: The effects of contact with beneficiaries on persistence behavior. *Organizational Behavior and Human Decision Processes, 103*, 53–67.

Hart, K. (2017). Policing the power of tech giants. *Axios*. <https://www.axios.com/the-growing-antitrust-concerns-about-u-s-tech-giants-2433870013.html>.

Henderson, W. (2012). In Lattman, P. Dewey & LeBoeuf files for bankruptcy. *The New York Times*. Retrieved from <https://dealbook.nytimes.com/2012/05/28/dewey-leboeuf-files-for-bankruptcy/>.

Hodson, R. (2005). Management behavior as social capital: A systematic analysis of organizational ethnographies. *British Journal of Industrial Relations*, *43*(1), 41–65.

Jochims, T. (2016). Social reciprocity as a critical success factor for small and mid-size enterprises: Work relationships as reflections of social exchange structures. *Management Revue*, *27*.

Judge, T. A., & Bono, J. E. (2000). Five-factor model of personality and transformational leadership. *Journal of Applied Psychology*, *85*, 751–765.

Judge, T. A., Bono, J. E., Ilies, R., & Gerhardt, M. W. (2002). Personality and leadership: A qualitative and quantitative review. *Journal of Applied Psychology*, *87*(4), 765–780.

Kawachi, I., & Berkman, L. (2001). Social ties and mental health. *Journal of Urban Health*, *78* (3), 458–467.

La Puma, J., Stocking, C. B., Lavoie, D., & Darling, C. A. (1991). When physicians treat members of their own families: Practices in a community-hospital. *New England Journal of Medicine*, *325*, 1290–1294.

Mason, P. (2015). *Postcapitalism: A guide to our future*. New York: Farrar, Straus and Giroux.

Mayer, R. C., Davis, J. H., & Schoorman, F. D. (1995). An integrative model of organizational trust. *Academy of Management Review*, *20*, 709–734.

McCollom, M. (1995). Group formation: Boundaries, leadership and culture. In J. Gillette, & M. McCollom (Eds.), *Groups in context: A new perspective on group dynamics* (pp. 34–48). Lanham, MD: University Press of America, Inc.

Mead, N., & Bower, P. (2000). Patient-centredness: A conceptual framework and review of the empirical literature. *Social Science & Medicine*, *51*(7), 1087–1110.

Moerschell, L., & Lao, T. M. (2012). Igniting the leadership spark: An exploration of decision making and punctuated change. Emergence: Complexity & organization — An international transdisciplinary. *Journal of Complex Social Systems*, *14*, 54–67.

Muir, W. M. (2013). Genetics and the behaviour of chickens: Welfare and productivity. In *Genetics and the behaviour of domestic animals* (2nd ed.) (Vol. 2, pp. 1–30), Cambridge, MA: Academic Press.

Nahapiet, J., & Ghoshal, S. (1998). Social capital, intellectual capital, and the organizational advantage. *The Academy of Management Review*, *23*(2), 242–266.

Pastoriza, D., Ariño, M. A., & Ricart, J. E. (2009). Ethical managerial behavior as antecedent of organizational social capital. *Journal of Business Ethics*, *78*(3), 329–341.

Renzulli, L. A., & Aldrich, H. (2005). Who can you turn to? Tie activation within core business discussion networks. *Social Forces*, *84*, 323–341.

Rhoades, L., & Eisenberger, R. (2002). Perceived organizational support: A review of the literature. *Journal of Applied Psychology*, *87*, 698–714.

Roche, B., & Jakub, J. (2017). *Completing capitalism: Heal business to heal the world*. Oakland, CA: Berrett-Koehler Publishers, Inc.

Ross, L. D. (1977). Social roles, social control, and biases in. social-perception processes. *Journal of Personality and Social Psychology.*, *35*(7), 485–494.

Rosenthal, S. B., Twomey, C. R., Hartnett, A. T., Wu, H. S., & Couzin, I. D. (2015). Revealing the hidden networks of interaction in mobile animal groups allows prediction of complex behavioral contagion. *Proceedings of the National Academy of Sciences of the United States of America*, *112*(15), 4690–4695.

Schoorman, D. F., Mayer, R. C., & Davis, J. H. (2007). An integrative model of organizational trust: Past, present and future. *Academy of Management Review, 32*(2), 344–354.

Schwartz, S. H., & Bardi, A. (2001). Value hierarchies across cultures: Taking a similarities perspective. *Journal of Cross Cultural Psychology, 32*, 268–290.

Simon, H. A. (1956). Rational choice and the structure of the environment. *Psychological Review, 63*(2), 129–138.

Simon, H. (1983). *Reason in human affairs*. Stanford University Press.

Simon, H. A. (1991). Bounded rationality and organizational learning. *Organization Science, 2* (1), 125–134.

Sison, A. J. G., & Fontrodona, J. (2013). Participating in the common good of the firm. *Journal of Business Ethics, 113*, pp. 611–625.

Smith, A. (1759). The theory of moral sentiments.

Smith, A. (1776). An inquiry into the nature and causes of the wealth of nations.

Spence, R. (2009). *It's not what you sell, it's what you stand for: Why every extraordinary business is driven by purpose*. New York, NY: Penguin.

Stacey, R. (2003). *Complexity and group processes: A radically social understanding of individuals*. New York: Brunner-Routledge.

Stark, E. E., & Jeffries, F. L. (2011). Social capital via leader-member exchanges: An avenue to human capital? *Current Topics in Management, 15*, 117–136.

Suchman, A. L. (2002). *An introduction to complex responsive process: Theory and implications for organizational change initiatives*. Retrieved from <http://www.rchcweb.com/Portals/0/Files/Intro_to_CRP_and_implications_for_org_change.pdf>.

Szulanski, G. (1996). Exploring internal stickiness: Impediments to the transfer of best practice within the firm. *Strategic Management Journal, 17*, 27–43. Available from https://doi.org/10.1002/smj.4250171105.

Thomas-Hunt, M. C., & Phillips, K. W. (2004). When what you know is not enough: Expertise and gender dynamics in task groups. *Personality and Social Psychology Bulletin, 30*(12), 1585–1598.

Tillotson, S. (1991). We may all soon be first-class men: Gender and skill in Canada's early twentieth century urban telegraph industry. *Labor/Le Travail, 27*, 97–123.

Tsai, W., & Kilduff, M. (2002). *A structural approach to knowledge transfer: Cross-block ties and business unit performance*. Working paper, Smeal College of Business Administration, Pennsylvania State University.

Tsoukas, H., & Mylonopoulos, N. (2004). Introduction: Knowledge construction and creation in organizations. *British Journal of Management, 15*(Special Issue), S1–S8.

Tunstrom, K., Katz, Y., Ioannou, C. C., Huepe, C., Lutz, M. J., & Couzin, I. D. (2013). Collective states, multi-stability and transitional behavior in schooling fish. *PLoS Computer Biology, 9*(2), pp. 1–11.

Warsh, D. (2007). *Knowledge and the wealth of nations: A story of economic discovery*. New York: W.W. Norton & Company.

Weick, K. E. (1995). *Sensemaking in organizations*. Thousand Oaks: Sage Publications.

Wheatley, M. (2006). Leadership lessons from the real world. *Leader to Leader, 2006*, 16–20. Available from https://doi.org/10.1002/ltl.185.

Woolley, A. W., Chabris, C. F., Pentland, A., Hashmi, N., & Malone, T. W. (2010). Evidence for a collective intelligence factor in the performance of human groups. *Science, 330*(6004), 686–688.

FURTHER READING

Jung Young, L., Swink, M., & Pandejpong, T. (2011). The roles of worker expertise, information sharing quality, and psychological safety in manufacturing process innovation: An intellectual capital perspective. *Production & Operations Management, 20*(4), 556–557.

Kilduff, M., & Tsai, W. (2011). *Social networks and organizations.* Los Angeles, CA: Sage Publications.

Chapter 5

Connecting: Bridging Across Networks to Attract New Talent Under Shared Objectives

5.1 CONNECTING BEHAVIORS: A BEHAVIORAL LENS NEEDED

> I am convinced that nothing we do is more important than hiring and developing people. At the end of the day you bet on people, not on strategies.
>
> *Lawrence Bossidy, GE.*

The role of the 21st century manager moves from passively planning and administrating resources to one who proactively leverages and creates networks across ecosystems to attract a pipeline of talent through the development of shared objectives. This can be a challenge as a known scarce resource in the knowledge-driven economy is highly skilled and socially proficient talent. In addition, the traditional administrative theory of management offers little insight into the management behaviors required to successfully bring new talent into the organization. Rather, many leading MBA program textbooks presume that the resources or talent already exists within the firm and instructs managers on best practices for organizing rather than connecting to new resources. However, this presents a missed opportunity as today's organizations fiercely compete to attract the right individuals at the right time to the right role. As a result, it is argued that one of the hardest tasks of management today is hiring, otherwise known as talent acquisition. While the human resource function has traditionally played a large role in shaping the recruiting and hiring process, today's managers now play a much more active role. Indeed, one of the most important decision managers make in the workplace is who they will introduce into their team. This decision changes everything—from the ability of the individual to perform to the way the team responds and relates to one another as a group.

The end goal of hiring is to bring in the needed diverse talent to continue to expand a team's capabilities for creating intellectual capital, thus providing a greater chance of firm survival in complex environments. As noted in Fig. 5.1 this can be accomplished by practicing connecting behaviors through

How Behavioral Economics Influences Management Decision-Making.
DOI: https://doi.org/10.1016/B978-0-12-813531-0.00005-4

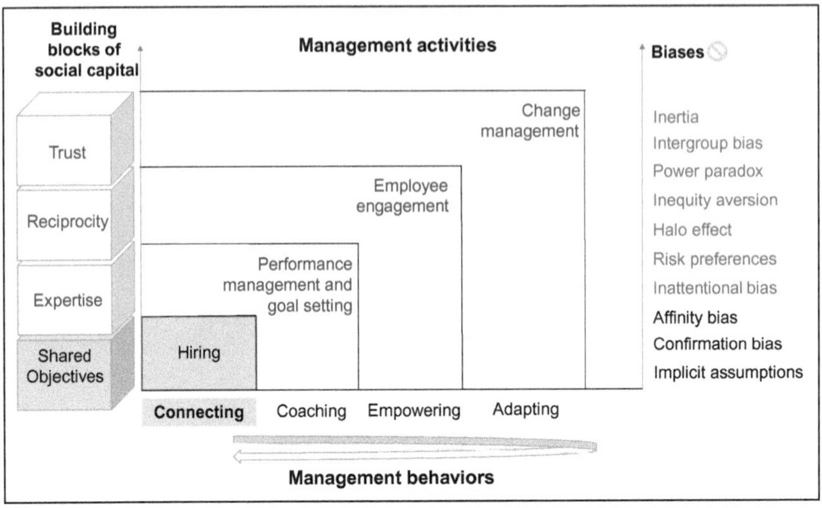

FIGURE 5.1 Management framework—Connecting behaviors.

the development of shared objectives. However, biases, or heuristics can get in the way, as noted on the right-hand side of Fig. 5.1. The most notable barriers to the practice of connecting behaviors that lead to diverse networks are implicit assumptions, confirmation biases, and the affinity bias. To combat the presence of these biases requires managers to establish guardrails during the hiring processes, which connecting behaviors on the building block of shared objectives help do.

Yet, complexity and heuristics arise in the hiring process when predicting how well an individual will perform in a new role. This can be one of the hardest challenges as past performance does not always predict future success, as noted by the *Peter Principle*. The *Peter Principle* describes a strong tendency and temptation for people to use what worked before in a prior context, even though it may not be appropriate for the current or future circumstances (Peter & Hull, 1969). This tendency to rely on past performance data, rather than assessing fit for future needs, often occurs when making hiring or promotion decisions. Therefore a behavioral lens must be considered to determine how to best mitigate the biases that quickly arise when making talent judgments, especially as it relates to the prediction of future performance. In addition, most managers are not just simply seeking to predict individual performance, but also how well the person will fit within the team dynamics and overall culture of the firm. This too brings a host of challenges with today's current methodologies, which all too often rely on unstructured interviews that lead to a host of unconscious biases. By applying a behavioral lens we are able to redefine the way managers make decisions to better assess individual fit. This includes finding the most effective ways to establish fair and transparent hiring guidelines as well as actively connecting into a larger and more diverse ecosystem.

There are two primary ways managers can seek to acquire talent. The first is through the traditional and formal method of recruiting. Managers typically work closely with their human resource partners to craft job descriptions and post job openings broadly across social networks to find qualified candidates. Candidates are screened and selected for interviews through a formalized acquisition process. However, this process has increasingly been called into question by leading behavioral economists who argue that this process is not only expensive for a firm, but riddled with biases that mitigate long-term value from their hires (Sunstein, 2016). For example, some researchers argue that unstructured interviews lead to inferior decision-making as many unconscious biases override rationality during the talent acquisition process (Dana, Dawes, & Peterson, 2013). Assistant Professor of Management at Yale School of Management, Jason Dana, described today's job interviews as "utter uselessness," noting they hold no predictive value of an individual's success at work (2017). As will be discovered, much of the lengthy interview process only seeks to confirm what a manager assesses within the first 10-seconds of meeting someone new. Yet, nearly 50% of new hires enter an organization through a formalized recruiting process with no prior connection to the firm (Montgomery, 1991). Therefore establishing behavioral guardrails to help protect against the unintentional biases are necessary for the 21st century manager seeking to bring in the right talent into the firm.

The other half of talent acquisition occurs through more informal mechanisms, which includes the acquisition of talent through one's social networks, including personal and professional connections. Much research has confirmed that candidates who come in through employee referrals tend to find more satisfaction, perform better, and stay longer (iCIMS, 2015). In addition, strong networks throughout a firm's talent base also increases the likelihood of finding higher quality talent (Fernandez, Castilla, & Moore, 2000). However, while leveraging social networks can significantly reduce the costs of talent acquisition and increase the likelihood of employee satisfaction, it too, creates challenges. For example, networks that are highly connected through strong homogenous bonds can exhibit a high level of sameness and favoritism, actually reducing the opportunity for new information and higher quality talent. However, as will be discovered, social networks that leverage bridging behaviors across diverse connections, which connect two unrelated or distance networks, are much more likely to create value for a firm during the hiring process.

5.2 CONNECTING THROUGH FORMAL MECHANISMS: OPPORTUNITIES AND CHALLENGES

Formal mechanisms for attracting and hiring talent are necessary to establish a strong pipeline of qualified talent. Formal mechanisms, when structured and used appropriately, can be perceived as fair and transparent to both perspective and current employees. In addition, formal mechanisms take out much of the guess work on how someone comes into the firm. Today, many firms are even relying on sophisticated algorithms and software tools to help initially screen for an applicant's fit and the current talent needs of the firm. While in theory this process should be relatively straightforward and fair, in reality, the formal process tends to unintentionally create roadblocks for certain individuals depending on the language used in the job description, biases that arise in the interview process, and the tendency for the decision maker to fall victim to the confirmation bias by seeking to confirm existing implicit assumptions.

5.2.1 Crafting Job Descriptions: Language Matters

Managers often scramble to quickly assemble together a job description when they are faced with a role vacancy. They may either be faced with updating an older version of the job description or face the challenge of crafting a new one. Either way the language used to describe the role can change the type of applicants one receives for a position. The language used to describe a position can be surprisingly biased towards a particular gender. For example, research finds that words such as "competitive" or "determined" may actually turnoff female applicants, further perpetuating gender inequity in currently male-dominated employment areas (Gaucher, Friesen, & Kay, 2011). This is because females are less likely to find jobs that contained masculine traits as appealing, due to fear of being excluded on the job as a female. Humans are hard wired to avoid loss and alienation based on the need to belong, and so behavioral economist Iris Bohnet (Bohnet, 2016) recommends that a first step in de-biasing an organization is to "start with job ads" as they are "super-low-hanging fruit".

The language used in the job description can be a gateway or barrier to finding the best possible talent. Another academic study suggests the power of language and one's biases. Within the study the researchers found that female gender positions such as "chairwomen" were perceived by men to be significantly less warm and even marginally less competent as women who retained a masculine job title such as "chairman" (Budiziszewka, Hansen, & Bilewicz, 2014). One of the most alarming finding from this study was that men reported to be less likely to hire candidates with a female position on their resumes. Language matters greatly to human relating. Unfortunately, a host of biases have been shown to exclude well-qualified candidates before they even walk into the door for an interview.

As a manager seeking to attract the most qualified and skilled candidates, it is necessary for the job role to appeal to as diverse a set of candidates as possible. To do so requires that nearly all who look at the job opening feel a sense of belonging rather than potential for exclusion. Therefore, a sense of belonging is likely to be a key contributor to whether or not an applicant finds an open position appealing. And the words used to describe the job may be an unintentional roadblock for minorities who may sense fear of not fitting in. For example, Walton and Cohen (2007) found that Blacks and Latinos who felt a sense of belonging in academia by normalizing their fears about not fitting in were much more engaged, increased their grades, and were less likely to drop out. Academia held a stronger appeal once their fears were mitigated and a sense of belonging was experienced. To do so in a job description requires removing unneeded words that imply implicit gender or racial traits and keeping the required qualifications of the role to only essentials. A laundry list of must have's is likely to negate a sense of belonging and further exclude diverse and qualified candidates. See the *Do Now Exercise* for practice on crafting job descriptions that help de-bias the first step of acquiring new talent.

Do Now Exercise

Think through any current openings within your organization. Pick one opening and write down a list of words that you would use to describe a successful candidate. Now put together a brief summary of the role's duties and expectations or if the job is posted review the written job description. Close your eyes and imagine the type of person who would likely fill this role. What type of person first came to your mind? Was there a particular race or gender that quickly appeared? For example, if the job description was for a nursing position are you likely to imagine a female? Or if a job opening was for a software engineer you were more likely to imagine a male? If so, that is okay. We all make these types of implicit associations, however, it is not okay to continue to act on them once we are aware. Rather, use this opportunity to reflect on why a particular person or skills set would best suit the open role. Now, revisit your list of successful word attributes and job duties to determine if any need to be rewritten. Also, be aware as you go to recruit for this open role that you may be unintentionally screening out a highly qualified candidate because of an unintentional bias. The more you can practice reflective thinking and awareness around your own implicit associations and certain types of jobs, the better able you will identify their existence.

5.2.2 Screening Potential Candidates: The Hidden Influence of Implication Associations

In the 1960s and 1970s the top orchestras in the United States were facing a wide gender gap. While there was nearly an equal number of female graduates' coming out of universities with music degrees, less than 5% of the top five ensembles were comprised of female musicians. As a result the orchestra knew it had to fundamentally change the way it was recruiting and hiring talent. Previously the leader of the ensemble would handpick his or her top candidates from a pool of about 20 musicians to audition. These candidates usually came from particular universities or had a connection with the orchestra's leader. This recruiting approach narrowed the selection of candidates well before many others even a chance to audition.

To change the hiring process the first thing the orchestra did was expand its reach and networks. They broadly advertised open positions and actively sought to expand their network. This brought in nearly 100 applicants each time a position was posted. This was an immediate 133% increase in candidates' auditions for open positions. However, the orchestra knew that it would take more than just expanding their candidate pool to overcome the glaring gender bias facing their orchestras. To combat this bias the orchestras conducted blind auditions with only the performance being evaluated as the candidate's identity was hidden behind a large drape or screen. As a result an individual's talent was able to be evaluated in a rational manner without an unconscious bias overriding their judgement. Researchers were astonished to learn that that the blind auditions dramatically increased the number of female participants in the orchestra, concluding that 30%–55% of an increase in female orchestra members was a direct result of the blind auditions. By the 1990s female representation had grown from 5% to 25% in the top five orchestras. The Philadelphia orchestra experienced the greatest increase moving from nearly 0% of females to 35% by the 1990s (Goldin & Rouse, 1997).

Implicit biases, also known as implicit social cognitions, can derail the best of intentions for those seeking to recruit and hire quality candidates. Implicit biases are the unconscious stereotypes or associations we make, which impact our understanding, actions, and decisions. The most common implicit biases are those that are associated with ethnicity, gender, age, and appearance. For example, one may quickly associate teaching as a female profession. Or take another startling finding from research. When asking people to reflect on immigrant workers, most participants immediately stereotyped them into minimally productive and low wage–paying jobs. However, the fact remains that 46% of immigrant workers work in white collar roles. Yet, many individuals initially did not make that connection, and instead quickly responded based on an implicit assumption. These implicit biases reside within the subconscious and develop over the course of one's lifetime. As a result, implicit biases are pervasive, yet malleable. Unless managers take proactive measures to combat against their emergence, as the orchestra did, they are hard to overcome. It can be all too easy to quickly assess and judge the person rather than their work or performance. Consider the following research studies, which note the unintentional predominance of implicit biases impact hiring decisions.

Many organizations today actively recruit from top tier universities under the assumption that students who go to these types of colleges will outperform those who went to a public or community-based college. This was true for Google who actively recruited from only 100 top ranked universities. However, the student population from these universities reflected a much higher homogenous makeup than other types of colleges. Additionally, Google was facing an alarming diversity gap with few minorities holding leadership positions. Google's Head of People Operations, Laszlo Block, remarked that they had the "wrong" hiring strategy, which was built on flawed assumptions rather than data. After much statistical analyses, it was determined that the type of university one went to or even their grades held little predictive value of their success at Google. Rather, their ability to solve problems, work in teams and possess intellectual humility were some of the strongest indicators of one's ability to be successful at Google. In 2014 Google changed their recruitment strategy, doubling the number of universities they actively recruited from. By expanding their networks and candidate outreach they are taking the first step the orchestra did to combat biases in the talent selection process. All too often organizations fail to obtain the best talent possible because a false assumption causes them to initially narrow down the pool of qualified candidates.

While one may believe that they will not fall victim to implicit biases during talent selection processes, many research studies note their irresistible pull in our decision-making. For example, in 2012, researchers designed a double-blind study of 127 participants to determine the influence implicit biases had on hiring a scientific lab manager within an academic sciences department. The researchers randomly assigned science faculty identical applications with one small difference. One resume had a female name, while the other had a male name. The results were startling. Male resumes were given significantly higher competency ratings during their application reviews compared to the *exact same* application with a female name. Not only that, but the male applicants were offered higher salaries and identified for more opportunities for career mentoring compared to their identical female counterparts (Moss-Racusin et al., 2012). There was an undisputable implicit gender bias that arose from these evaluators that was not intentional or malicious, but simply existed based on implicit assumptions, which in this case more closely associated science professions with men. As DeHouwer, Thomas and Baegens (2001) note, people make these types of biased decisions without any conscious intent. Without the proper guardrails in place implicit biases are bound to override rational talent decision-making.

In another classic academic study, researchers found that an implicit bias towards Caucasian or nondiversity sounding names arose in the candidate selection process. In a field experiment where researchers randomly responded to job postings with the exact same resume except the name was either "White sounding" such as Greg Smith or "Black sounding", such as Lakisha Jones (Bertrand & Mullainathan, 2004). The results revealed another startling revelation. Resumes with the associated White names received 50%

more callbacks from interviews than their Black sounding counterparts. It took a White sounding name resume approximately 10 resumes to receive a callback, while a Black sounding name took nearly 15 resumes. The researchers conclude that White sounding names were given an approximate 8-year experience advantage simply due to the sound of the name itself.

Organizations would be wise to heed the lessons learned from these studies around implicit biases to help broaden their talent pools and ultimately influence social capital both inside and outside the firm. It is unlikely that managers will be able to rely on their own awareness to guard against implicit assumptions, however, organizations can take steps to help safeguard against gender and racial bias by simply removing identifying information during resume reviews (See the *Do Now Exercise* to discover your own implicit biases). Much like the orchestra, which now relies on blind auditions to improve their talent selection process, managers should also review blind resumes to evaluate talent in a rational manner knowing they are prone to a quick judgment as soon as identifying information is available.

Do Now Exercise

It is nearly impossible to identify your own implicit biases without the help of data to guide you on where your unconscious stereotypes exist. Researchers from Harvard University developed an assessment called the Implicit Association Test, which assess an individual's unconscious biases (Greenwald, McGhee, & Schwartz, 1998). These tests help bring to light some of the subtle and often hidden associations that may be impairing your decision-making. You can find the various implicit association tests here: https://implicit.harvard.edu/implicit/. Once you complete the various tests meet with a trusted friend or advisor to share your results and how your decision-making may be influenced by these stereotypes in the workplace.

In addition, work on developing guardrails, such as seeking out diverse associations to broaden your scope of understanding. The more you can actively seek out examples that go against stereotypes the most likely you are to relearn and form new associations. However, seeking out diversity is not commonplace. A 2013 study conducted by the Public Religion Research Institute sought to quantify how diverse individual's circles of influence and trust are. They asked participants to identify up to seven people whom they have discussed "important matters" within the past 6 months. Go ahead, and make your own list of up to seven people. Now fill in their demographics—race, gender, age. It may not be surprising that the majority of participants in their study reflected zero diversity within their own social networks. Most lists reflected up to 91% homogeneity. To help overcome biased implicit associations, actively seek to broaden your network and intentionally expose yourself to diverse situations.

5.2.3 The Interview Process: The First 10 Seconds, Confirmation Bias and Affinity Bias

What is the most important part of an interview? Research suggests it is what happens in the first 10 seconds (Prickett, Gada-Jain, & Bernieri, 2000). Consider the following research study. Researchers showed participants clips of actual interviews conducted. These clips began as soon as the interviewee knocked on the door and ended 10-seconds after the interviewee took a seat. The participants observing the interview rated the interviewee on employability, competency, intelligence, trustworthiness, warmth, politeness, likeability, expressiveness, ambition, confidence, and nervousness. While participants only observed a small slice of the interview, 9 out of the 11 variables rated were highly correlated with the final evaluation of the real-life interviewer. The researchers conclude, "Thus, immediate impressions based on a handshake and brief introduction predicted the outcome of a structured employment interview" (Prickett et al., 2000). The reason why the first 10 seconds were so important is due to the previously discussed *confirmation bias*, where one seeks to confirm what he or she initially preconceived. For example, if a candidate walks in appearing nervous, the interviewer may simply keep looking for cues and responses that note the candidate's lack of confidence. The rest of the time interviewing is simply confirming what one initially thought rather than actively listening and acquiring new information.

One of the most commonly used tools to determine talent fit for an open position is the unstructured interview. While managers may go in with a set of questions, most often than not, they engage in informal conversation and have different types of conversation with each candidate. Research suggests that managers perceive the unstructured interview as the most effective tool for assessing talent and fit within the organization. However, research shows that the unstructured interview is actually the least effective in predicting a candidate's future success at the firm (Highhouse, 2008). Yet, unstructured interviews prevail and bring a host of biases to the decision-making process. Most notably the confirmation bias and affinity bias are present during interviews, which are initiated as soon as the candidate walks into the office.

One way to help combat this bias is to rely on uniform structured interviews, where every candidate is receiving the same questions. A leading government agency uses this approach by asking each candidate the exact same questions and writing down verbatim the candidate's response. This forces the interviewee to simply focus on the responses and to not be influenced by unstructured dialogue, which may irrational sway the evaluation. The transcripts are then shared broadly during the evaluations and each candidate's response is equally compared to the others. Additional research confirms that a structured interview is better at reducing biases than unstructured dialogues as it is less susceptible to quick biases judgments on physical characteristics of the person. For example, in a ground-breaking study, researchers in the

1980s discovered that medical students were being rejected to medical programs due to nonobjective factors identified during the interview process (DeVaul et al., 1987). Applicant reviewers were unintentionally misjudging the ability of a student's potential success during the interview process as a result of bias. The researchers followed students' performance who were at first rejected from the school, but later accepted due to a mandate at the state level to increase capacity in university's medical programs. Those students who were initially rejected showed the exact same performance outcomes as those students originally allowed in the program. The researchers conclude that nearly 75% of the difference in application ratings and evaluations had to do with nonobjective factors picked up during the interview. In other words, candidates' actual responses were only 25% of the interview evaluation. Unfortunately, this shows that all too often interviews are used for assessing a person and not their work or future potential at the firm.

As a result, the problem with most interviews is that people are not assessing one's future potential within the organization, but rather how much they simply like the person sitting across from them. In another study conducted, researchers collected over 120 real-life interviews at professional service firms to see what was most important during the interview. By far the most important factors to managers interviewing was someone who shared the same leisurely pursuits, experiences and styles as the manager themselves. The managers remarked that they were simply seeking out cultural matches, which ironically were those that mirrored their own. As a result, the managers assessed candidates based on these similarities much higher during the evaluation than productivity based responses (Rivera, 2011). This bias it referred to as the *affinity bias*, which suggests we have a tendency to select others who remind us of ourselves. A sense of familiarity fuels an immediate liking to the other person. Additional research has shown during interviews that if you have some affinity with the candidate, be it attending the same college or growing up in a similar neighborhood, you actually treat them differently. For example, we tend to smile more at them and offer greater words of encouragement throughout the interview. However, if we have no affinity with the other person, we are less likely to be warm and dismiss them as a poor culture fit. It is hard to build diverse networks that create intellectual capital when the affinity bias keeps us preferring candidates who remind us of ourselves.

Formal mechanisms are important and necessary for a firm to recruit and attract a strong pipeline of talent. However, without the necessary guardrails in place they are prone to much biases that restrict a firm's long-term ability to create diverse networks and build out strong intellectual and social capital (See Fig. 5.2). As a result, it is recommended that managers actively seek to remove identifying information from candidate applications, proactively seek out diverse connections outside their network, and bring strict uniformity to the interview process. Without these guardrails, it is nearly impossible not to

Formal Mechanisms	Watch out for	Guardrails to implement
Craft job descriptions	Language that excludes or evokes a stereotype; overly long list of requirements	Rely on gender neutral words to describe position requirements; include only those that are absolutely necessary
Screen candidates	Implicit assumptions	Remove identifying information from resumes
Interview process	Confirmation bias	Utilize structured interviews

FIGURE 5.2 Formal talent acquisition mechanisms can have unintentional biases without the proper guardrails in place.

fall victim to biased decision-making. It is all too easy, and even human, to misjudge a person based on flawed assumptions, rather than allowing rational thinking to guide you to the best talent hire.

5.3 CONNECTING THROUGH INFORMAL MECHANISMS: OPPORTUNITIES AND CHALLENGES

While nearly 50% of employees enter into the organization through formal mechanisms, nearly half of all employees enter in through informal mechanisms, such as employee referrals. The power of social networks and finding employment is well documented in the literature with many extensive studies showing how different types of social networks can create and connect others to job opportunities (i.e., Granovetter, 1973, 1995; Montgomery, 1991). The ability of individuals and firms to leverage their social networks helps lower both the direct and indirect costs associated with talent acquisition (Montgomery, 1991). The Institute for Research on Labor and Employment at the University of California at Berkeley suggests that the average cost to replace an employee across all categories and levels is approximately $4000. While lower cognitive workers are estimated to cost around $2000 to recruit and train, higher cognitive roles can cost as high as $7000. However, when firms are able to leverage existing employees' networks, these costs tend to go down (Fernandez et al., 2000). Not only that, but employees who come in through a referral tend to report higher job satisfaction and stay longer at an organization compared to those who came through a formal mechanism (Jobvite Index, 2012). Therefore capturing value from informal connections can be beneficial to managers seeking to build robust pipelines of talent.

Two specific types of connections, weak ties or strong tires, often lead to an increase in job opportunities and new information, but one in particular is riddled with biases as it leads to redundant information rather than new opportunities. Strong ties are those that are formed with bonds to another person. They are marked by strong affinity and shared values and often found amongst family members and closed-knit friends and communities. Strong ties take a lot of work, energy, and effort to maintain. Weak ties, on the other hand, are those formed by infrequent contact and may better be known as acquaintances. Granovetter (1973) discovered that individuals who hold weak ties to others are actually better able to access new information. These weak, but diverse connections, allow for greater opportunities to discover something otherwise not known. While there is still important to hold strong bonds, such as in families or amongst a group of friends, novel information is likely to come in the form of a bridge rather than a bond (See Fig. 5.3). While maintaining a few close strong bonds are essential to healthy human functioning, the majority of employees may be better served forming a diverse set of weak bridges to access new information in the marketplace.

Strong close ties are connected by bonds within one's network. Bonding often occurs amongst homogenous groups and communities. These bonds are tightly held together by duty, frequency of contact, strong shared values, or affinity towards other individuals in the network. Fukuyama (1995) describes these relationships as those that seek to narrow the radius of trust. They are marked by strong in-group dynamics, which often resemble an "us" versus "them" mentality. While social bonds are an essential part of human life, their presence can pose threats to organizations and individuals seeking to create value from new information and learning. For example, strong bonding relationships can be closed off to new opportunities, preferring to protect the status quo. At a more alarming level, strong bonds can lead to favoritism in the workplace, nepotism and even unethical practices (Fukuyama, 1995) (see Do Now Exercise for an example of how strong bonds can impede team

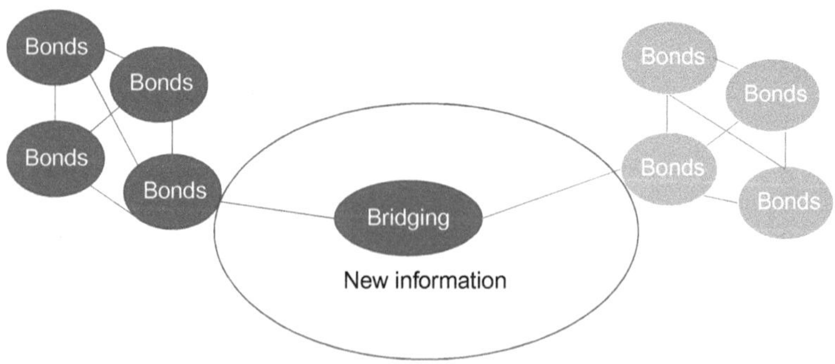

FIGURE 5.3 Bonds are formed by frequent interactions between individuals, but often contain redundant information rather than access to new information. Connecting behaviors bring together two diverse groups of individuals and forge a bridge for new information flow that otherwise may not be accessible within the closely knit community of homogenous bonds.

performance). An empirical study found that the presence of strong bonds, formed amongst family businesses, had a hard time sustaining their business during times of change as they lacked the necessary access to new resources and ideas that a more diverse network would have presented. While strong bonds are important to maintain, their presence in the workplace may best be limited due to the dangers of exclusion they pose, which will ultimately hinder the ability of diverse individuals to relate and connect to each other. Another study found that informal hiring recommendations from workers often resemble a similarity and sameness to the person who is doing the recommendation (Heneman et al., 1980). In other words the researchers found that people were much more likely to recommend a homogenous member of their network, rather than a diverse candidate. The real problem strong bonds pose to organizations competing in knowledge-driven markets is their level of sameness, which is marked by redundant rather than novel information. While strong bonds may allow for efficient coordination, they are less likely to create something new and contain diversity of thought.

Why hiring a strong bond may not be optimal for your team's performance

Joel was recently hired to form a small startup team within a larger organization. The team's mission was to focus on highly cognitive tasks that would help produce innovative solutions for the company. There were already two internal employees who transferred to help kick off the team's efforts. Joel's job was to hire three additional new employees within the course of the year. Joel quickly began leveraging his network and called on a former colleague, Ben, who worked with him at his former company. Joel and Ben shared many common interests and frequently socialized around their shared passions outside of work. Each of their families knew each other well and even shared a beach house during the summer months. Joel was thrilled when a few weeks later Ben was hired onto the team. Over the course of the next several months two new and unrelated hires would come into the team through various formal recruiting efforts. These two new employees were both diverse candidates and brought a wealth of new information that Joel knew the team needed.

However, within a few months the team did not seem to be getting along and were performing under expectations. There was an overall lack of trust, and at times, hostility emerged during team meetings. Joel, perplexed by the team's dysfunction and unsure of what to do, called on human resources to help solve this dilemma. The human resources team conducted interviews and quickly identified the root cause—the strong homogenous bond between Joel and Ben had unintentionally excluded the other team members. The other team members felt Ben was experiencing preferential treatment on the team based on his close relationship with Joel—obtaining important information about the company from Joel in informal settings that was not shared broadly amongst team members. In addition, Joel would often leverage Ben as a sounding board and often

(*Continued*)

(Continued)

prioritized his voice during team meetings. The close bond that Joel and Ben formed, while built on the principles of social capital, excluded the other team members, and as a result created much dysfunction within the team. Within a few months HR recommended that Ben transfer to another leader to alleviate the tension and perception of favoritism that was broadly experienced by the rest of the team. While social capital can be positive, during the very early stages of team formation, it can pose challenges if hiring decisions are made at the expense of others. If you were Joel, would you have hired Ben? Why or why not? Do you agree with the human resources team's recommendation to transfer Ben to another team? What could Joel have done differently as not to let his strong bond with Ben alienate the rest of the team members?

A better and more sustainable approach to build social networks is through the process of finding bridges, or what Burt (1992) referred to as structural holes and becoming the liaison between unconnected networks. Kilduff and Tsai (2003) describe it as such, "Individual actors (people, subunits, organizations) have been portrayed as seeking to increase their social capital by performing the liaison role of connecting two otherwise disconnected cliques, or by bridging from one group to which they belong to another group that they can join" (p. 28). Bridges are formed between heterogeneous groups that represent diverse interests. Bridging across networks actively seeks to increase the radius of trust amongst individuals and pass along new information that otherwise might not be received. Bridges are formed when one brokers the connection between two weak ties as shown in Fig. 5.3.

A manager should consider how to bridge individuals into the organization, while also connecting them cross-functionally once they join the organization. The manager benefits from having formed this bridge and having access to information from both parties—the individual joining the organization who brings newness and diversity as well as possessing existing organizational knowledge. The more a manager can connect two diverse networks together by creating a bridge, which still relies on the components of social capital, the more likely the manager and team will benefit. This is because bridge connectors pose a competitive advantage in their network by possessing less redundant information and enhance the capability of new knowledge to form (Burt, 1992). A 3-year longitudinal study within a publishing company showed that promotions were largely captured by individuals who spanned across structural holes and communicated broadly across the firm (Brass, 1984). Bridges may be one of the best ways to find new and diverse talent to bring into the organization. In addition, it is much less susceptible to bias, which strong bonds can present.

Bias trigger	Bias	Guardrail
Stress/Distractions	Confirmation bias: I already made my decision in the first 10 s of the interview	Make hiring a priority and create buffers between interviews to recharge
Lack of time	Implicit assumption: This person is not qualified because of their educational background	Practice reflective thinking after interviews. How did you arrive to your conclusion? List factual information and subjective inferences separately
Lack of accountability	Affinity bias: I am just going to hire a former colleague that already works well with me	Create strong accountabilities to others in the organization for the hiring decision. Allow cross function teams to engage in the hiring process

FIGURE 5.4 Biases and guardrails in hiring decision-making.

5.4 CONNECTING WITH THE RIGHT PEOPLE AT THE RIGHT TIME

Connecting across diverse networks by becoming a liaison or bridge between two unconnected parties takes both time and cognitive capacity. Therefore managers must possess both the fortitude and time to guard against both the biases and pull towards sameness and homogeneity when hiring new talent. We know from Chapter 4, that human relating occurs best under the circumstances of diversity and capacity. However, many of our current work environments, routines, and processes are set up to retain status quo and therefore fall victim to the many biases that impede rational decision-making. What are the conditions necessary for managers to solicit candidates based on logic rather than unconscious biases? There are three recommendations that various research studies confirm help safeguard managers against bias when making talent hiring decisions. These recommendations help elicit System 2 thinking during the hiring process, which allows managers to be more open to a diversity of thought and engage more fully in rational decision-making (see Fig. 5.4).

5.4.1 Limit Stress and Distractions When Making Talent Decisions

One of the environmental factors that often highjack rational during making during the talent acquisition process is stress and distractions (Gilbert, Pelham, & Krull, 1988). When a person is under a state of stress, such as responding to project "fire drills" or feeling "under the gun" for a deadline, and then try to interview a potential candidate, they are much less likely to make a rational decision-making. Rather, it is much more likely that System 1 thinking will override System 2 rationality and cause individuals to fall victim to the confirmation bias by over relying on their initial impressions. This is because one's cognitive capacity is focused on the stressor or deadline in the background causing the manager to be physically present for the interview, but mentally absent. And this poses a problem, because hiring is one of the most important decisions a manager can make, and it all too often falls behind a list of more urgent priorities. It is observed that managers often try to fit in potential candidates between meetings, and they rush through interviews in order to move on to the next thing. The message from decades of behavioral research is simple. As humans, we are not good at multitasking or practicing rational thought when stressed or rushed. Heed this lesson and take the time necessary to make hiring a priority over other tasks. If hiring falls into the "nice to have" category behind a laundry list of other to do's, the chances are much less likely that you will have the needed capacity to engage in the intentional thought required to make rational talent judgments.

5.4.2 Practice Reflective Thought

Research suggests that individuals who actively engage in practices that encourage reflective thought, such as mindfulness, are better able to identify their strengths and weaknesses in decision-making (Branch & Parajape, 2002). Reflective thinking, which is a practice of critically evaluating one's assumptions, leads to greater self-awareness and even allows individuals to recognize their own areas of potential bias and discrimination. After interviews spend time reflecting on not just the candidate themselves, but how you arrived at your judgments regarding their potential in the role. Was it based on data and facts shared or are there subtle biases that may be impairing your thinking? Without taking time to think in the workplace, especially when it comes to talent decision-making, managers are much less likely to be successful when making hiring decisions.

5.4.3 Practice Strong Accountability to Others

While practicing reflective thought and making time to clear away stressors before engaging in talent decision-making is important and even necessary, another powerful lever should also be considered, which is accountability to others. Rarely are decisions made in a social vacuum, but rather carry obligations and duties to others. The stronger those accountabilities are towards others in the organization the more likely one will engage in rational decision-making (Tetlock, 1985). Strong social norms and expectations to hire for performance, to encourage a diversity of thought and create broader connections in the marketplace will help hold managers accountable for maintaining these social dynamics. The stronger accountabilities one feels towards the success of the organization and team the more likely they will hire for the collective good and functioning of the organization rather than be swayed by a strong social bond or bias. Creating social accountabilities through the use of cross-functional and cross-team interviews are positive guardrails to ensure managers are hiring in the best interest of the organization and not swayed by the affinity bias. By engaging with other members of the organization who are assessing for broader culture fit, will help hold managers accountable during the hiring process.

5.5 BRIDGING THROUGH SHARED OBJECTIVES TO CREATE A SENSE OF BELONGING AND MEANING AT WORK

One of the most efficient ways to recruit and connect with highly skilled talent, whether through informal or formal networks, is through the creation of clear shared objectives (see REI case study). Shared objectives help build the bridge between two diverse networks, which through their collective efforts might create something new and meaningful. What makes shared objectives so powerful? Quite simply. Shared objectives help fuel one's intrinsic need to belong and find meaning, which creates capacity for greater diversity in the workplace. If people are perceived as working towards the same end goal, who they are and what they look like matter much less. Therefore without tapping into these intrinsic needs misses an opportunity at the very front end of the employee experience to engage in one's need to belong and find meaning in something greater than themselves. In fact, before asking individuals to transcend their own self-interests towards the broader collective good of the organization, it is important to provide the purpose or reason why at the onset of their employment. Too many hiring conversations center around extrinsic factors and faulty reasoning, rather than clearly and transparently determining if the person and organizational needs align under a shared objective. In addition, shared objectives can also help protect against biases as managers seek to align people with purpose, rather than form a likable homogenous team. As a result without initial alignment of shared objectives social capital is unlikely to form. The initial alignment of bringing diverse people together to accomplish something greater than themselves will help mitigate agency costs and lower the costs of working together. Strong and clear shared objectives are necessary to begin that process.

CASE STUDY: REI Engaging Potential Employees With the #optoutside Campaign

REI, a large outdoor clothing retailer, made a countercultural and bold move by closing down their retail operations for Black Friday, one of the largest shopping days of the year. Instead of asking employees to cut their holiday short to come into open stores early for Black Friday, REI requested that its 12,000 employees spend the day outdoors with friends and family. They not only created a social media campaign #optoutside that quickly went viral, but also paid their employees to take the day off. As nearly 49% of other retailers and competitors began to open their doors for business on the Thanksgiving holiday, REI doubled down even further, choosing to remain closed both days, including their online store, which would not process orders until after the holiday.

The results of this strong value statement were met with tremendous support from both customers and employees. The month after the #optoutside campaign went live, it led to an over 100% increase in job applications. The CEO of REI recognized that organizational behaviors, which supported its core values, such as closing operations on the holiday or supporting programs that preserve nature and outdoor spaces are ways to recruit and find talent who are aligned to the objectives REI is seeking to achieve.

In addition, REI is able to take a long-term perspective on their business objectives based in part on their organizational structure and governance. REI is not a publicly traded firm, but is co-op owned by nearly 6 million members, which allows them to chase after shared long-term goals, rather than quarterly profits. This strategy has not only led to an increase in their talent pool and networks, but also strong company growth. This case study teaches an important lesson. It is important not only to have a strong company objective and value statement to recruit highly skilled talent, but also to live out those values in tangible ways. By making such a countercultural decision to close operations on the largest shopping day of the year messages to both perspective employees and customers what the company is all about—"inspiring, educating and outfitting its members and the community for a lifetime of outdoor adventure and stewardship."

All too often managers and candidates put their best foot forward during the recruiting process and fail to capture the needed alignment and trust necessary to forge a successful relationship in the workplace. Too many employees find themselves misaligned due to lack of transparency during the initial conversations with their prospective employer and manager. It is important and even necessary for an organization to take steps well before the employment phase to ensure a candidate is aligned to their overall objectives and culture. This alignment fosters not only higher performance, but also satisfaction as people come together to achieve a common objective. Before a manager is given the permission and social capital to begin coaching employees in the workplace, they must first ensure they connect individuals with the organization's and team's objectives first. The best managers do this with stunning transparency and actively seek to liaison between diverse networks to their cause.

5.5.1 Case Study Netflix: Recruiting Through Transparent Shared Culture Objectives

Many times applicants may visit an organization's website or when walking into an organization's lobby see value statements. Enron was famous for espousing the values of integrity and respect. Yet, the way the company actually behaved differed dramatically from its promoted values. As a result, it can be hard for applicants to assess how a company actually operates during the recruiting phase. Netflix, an online streaming service, seeks to remove ambiguity right up front and err on the side of radical transparency.

In 2009 the CEO of Netflix, Reed Hastings, published a 125-slide deck on how Netflix actually operates. It describes in detail how the company hires, fires, and rewards talent. The purpose of this deck is to broadly recruit top talent and be up front with the type of environment Netflix seeks to create. Chief Talent Officer of Netflix, Tawni Cranz, recognizes that top talent is not just simply choosing to work for the work itself, but "for the company culture and leadership." As a result, Netflix wants to be exceedingly clear the culture and style of leadership that thrives at Netflix. The slides contain statements such as, "We're a team, not a family" noting the bridging type of networks they seek to form, rather than the strong closed-knit bonds found in families. Another slide states, "Our high-performance culture is not right for everyone," acknowledging that it will take a certain type of person to thrive at Netflix. Netflix values and seeks out individuals who are responsible and thrive with little oversight. Vacation days are not tracked and there is no official dress code for the offices. Rather an overarching statement guides behaviors, "Act in Netflix best interest." Because of this, Netflix requires all job candidates to review the culture deck and engage in honest candor during the interview process on alignment or where potential pitfalls may arise. If a candidate is used to a lot of policies, boundaries, and rules Netflix may not be the right culture for them. Cranz remarks, "It's a more honest way to start a relationship" by putting the truth of how the company actually operates out there.

As organizations increasingly rely on culture as a differentiating factor for high-performing talent it is important to engage early and often during the talent acquisition process to ensure shared alignment to core values and objectives. Authenticity and transparency during this stage of the employee journey will begin to build the necessary social capital building blocks to engage them as they progress at the firm. The recruiting process is a crucial moment to build the necessary trust required to sustain employee engagement long after they enter the firm.

5.6 SUMMARY

As noted, hiring may be one of the most important decisions facing today's managers. Who they decide to bring into their teams can make or break their entire team's performance. The goal of hiring is to bring in a diverse set of talent to help create new knowledge and intellectual capital within the firm. The most effective mangers do this by creating strong and transparent objectives and actively seek to bridge across networks to attract candidates based on shared alignment towards the end goal. As discovered, too much social capital at this stage may actually mitigate team performance as perceptions of favoritism and feelings of exclusion can quickly arise. However, managers who actively bridge across diverse networks and set up guardrails during the formal hiring processes, such as removing identifying information from resumes or establishing strong accountability to other functions in the organization, are much more likely to stay clear of the many biases that can derail even the most rational decision maker. As the quote at the beginning of this chapter noted, managers ultimately take a bet on people, not strategies when forming high-performing teams. Connecting through hiring activities is the first step in that process, and managers who recognize the stakes will take the behavioral approach needed to build a sense of belonging and meaning on day one of the employee experience.

REFERENCES

Bertrand, M., & Mullainathan, S. (2004). Are Emily and Greg more employable than Lakisha and Jamal? A field experiment on labor market discrimination. *The American Economic Review*, *94*(4), 991–1013.

Bohnet, I. (2016). *What works: gender equality be design*. Cambridge, MA: Belknap Press.

Branch, W. T., & Paranjape, A. (2002). Feedback and reflection: Teaching methods for clinical settings. *Academy of Medicine*, *77*, 1185–1188.

Brass, D. J. (1984). Being in the right place: A structural analysis of individual influence in an organization. *Administrative Science Quarterly*, *29*, 519–539.

Budiziszewka, M., Hansen, K., & Bilewicz, M. (2014). Backlash over gender-fair language: The impact of feminine job titles on men's and women's perception of women. *Journal of Language & Social Psychology*, *33*(6), 681–691.

Butt, R. S. (1992). *Structural holes*. Cambridge, MA: Harvard University Press.

De Houwer, J., Thomas, S., & Baeyens, F. (2001). Associative learning of likes and dislikes: A review of 25 years of research on human evaluative conditioning. *Psychological Bulletin*, *127*(6), 853–869.

Dana, J., Dawes, R., & Peterson, N. (2013). Belief in the unstructured interview: The persistence of an illusion. *Judgement and Decision Making*, *8*(5), 512–520.

DeVaul, R. A., Jervey, F., Chappell, J. A., Caver, P., Short, B., & O'Keefe, S. (1987). Medical school performance of initially rejected students. *The Journal of the American Medical Association*, *257*(1), 47–51.

Fernandez, R. M., Castilla, E. J., & Moore, P. (2000). Social capital at work: Networks and employment at a phone center. *American Journal of Sociology*, *105*(5), 1288–1356.

Fukuyama, F. (1995). *Trust: The social virtues and the creation of prosperity*. New York, NY: Free Press.

Gaucher, D., Friesen, J., & Kay, A. C. (2011). Evidence that gendered wording in job advertisements exists and sustains gender inequality. *Journal of Personality and Social Psychology*. Available from https://doi.org/10.1037/a0022530, Advance online publication.

Gilbert, D. T., Pelham, B. W., & Krull, D. S. (1988). On cognitive busyness: When person perceivers meet persons perceived. *Journal of Personality and Social Psychology*, *54*(5), 733–740.

Goldin, C., & Rouse, C. (1997). Orchestrating impartiality: The impact of "blind" auditions on female musicians. NBER working paper no. 5903.

Granovetter, M. S. (1973). The strength of weak ties. *American Journal of Sociology*, *78*(no. 6), 1360–1380.

Granovetter, M. (1995). *Getting a job: A study of contacts and careers*. Chicago: University of Chicago Press.

Greenwald, A., McGhee, D., & Schwartz, J. (1998). I.A.T. Measuring individual differences in implicit cognitions: The implicit association test. *Journal of Personality and Social Psychology*, *74*(6), 1464–1480.

Heneman, H. G., Ill, Schwab, D., Fossum, J., & Dyer, L. (1980). *Personnel/human resource management*. Homewood, IL: Richard D. Irwin.

Highhouse, S. (2008). Stubborn reliance on intuition and subjectivity in employee selection. *Industrial and Organizational Psychology*, *1*, 333–342.

iCIMS (2015). The impact of successful employee referral programs. Retrieved from https://www.icims.com/sites/www.icims.com/files/public/The%20Impact%20of%20Successful%20Employee%20Referral%20Programs_0.pdf.

Jobvite, 2012 Social Recruiting Survey Results. Retrieved from http://web.jobvite.com/rs/jobvite/images/Jobvite_2012_Social_Recruiting_Survey.pdf.

Kilduff, M., & Tsai, W. (2003). *Social networks and organizations*. Los Angles: Sage Publications.

Montgomery, J. (1991). Social Networks and labor-market outcomes: Towards an economic analysis. *The American Economic Review*, *81*(5), 1408–1418.

Moss-Racusin, C. A., et al. (2012). Science faculty's subtle gender biases favor male students. *Proceedings of the National Academy of Sciences of the United States*, *109*(41), 16474–16479.

Peter, L. J., & Hull, R. (1969). *The Peter Principle: Why things always go wrong*. New York: William Morrow and Company.

Prickett, T., Gada-Jain, N., & Bernieri, F.J. (2000). *The importance of first impressions in a job interview*. Paper presented at the annual meeting of the Midwestern Psychological Association, Chicago, IL.

Rivera, L. (2011). Ivies, extracurriculars, and exclusion: Elite employers' use of educational credentials. *Research in Social Stratification and Mobility*, *29*, 71–90.

Sunstein, C. (2016). Job interviews are useless. Bloomberg Business Week. Retrieved from https://www.bloomberg.com/view/articles/2016-11-04/job-interviews-are-useless.

Tetlock, P. E. (1985). Accountability: The neglected social context of judgment and choice. *Research in Organizational Behavior*, *7*, 297–332.

Walton, G. M., & Cohen, G. L. (2007). A question of belonging: Race, social fit and achievement. *Journal of Personality and Social Psychology*, *92*(1), 82–96.

FURTHER READING

Hastings, R. (2009). Netflix culture: Freedom and responsibility. LinkedIn SlideShare. Retrieved from https://www.slideshare.net/reed2001/culture-1798664/88-Exceptions_to_Context_not_Control.

Matter, G. (2017). The utter uselessness of job interviews. The New York Times. Retrieved from https://www.nytimes.com/2017/04/08/opinion/sunday/the-utter-uselessness-of-job-interviews.html.

Chapter 6

Coaching With and Toward the Development of Expertise

6.1 COACHING: SHIFTING EXPECTATIONS OF THE ROLE OF MANAGEMENT IN TALENT DEVELOPMENT

As organizations continue to evolve to meet the changing market demands that are presented by the increase in technologies and complexities that arise, the priorities of the manager shift as well. Chapter 5, Connecting: Bridging Across Networks to Attract New Talent Under Shared Objectives discussed the management behavior of connecting across diverse networks to bring people into the organization as the first part in the process of building social capital. One of the most effective ways to do this is by aligning talent to transparent and authentic shared objectives to fuel one's sense of belonging and meaning in the workplace. Shared objectives helps transcend an indivi dual's own interests and connects them to a group in order to accomplish a goal that supersedes what they might accomplish on their own. Leveraging the building block of shared objectives begins to form social capital within organizations, and is a critical element for managers to effectively engage with individuals across the organization.

However, once individuals are brought into the organization, the next behavior and potentially most time-consuming behavior managers must focus on is coaching. Rather than directing resources as noted in the theory of administration management, which implies a transactional relationship, a behavioral perspective advises management to coach and develop talent throughout the organization through high relational interactions. The goal of the manager as a coach is to guide employees into the process of self-discovery in order to capture benefits toward organizational objectives. As noted in Fig. 6.1, managers do this by leveraging the social capital build block of expertise. A manager's expertise when shared through coaching behaviors helps fuel an employee's intrinsic need for growth and mastery. As will be discovered, not only is expertise a required building block of social capital formation, but also a necessary component found in effective coaching behaviors. Expertise is fundamental to coaching behaviors and meeting an employee's need for growth.

How Behavioral Economics Influences Management Decision-Making.
DOI: https://doi.org/10.1016/B978-0-12-813531-0.00006-6

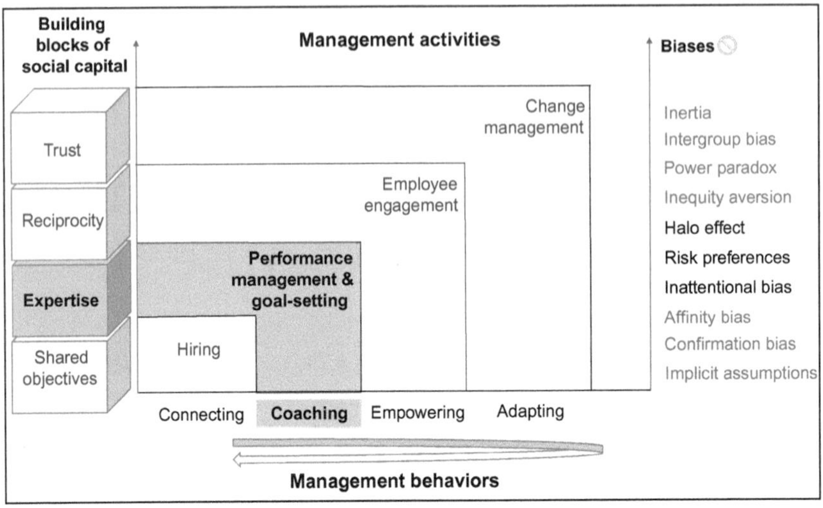

FIGURE 6.1 Management framework coaching behaviors.

Coaching brings newfound opportunities to create both intellectual and social capital throughout the organization through the activities of goal-setting and performance management. Yet, the amount of time this takes in today's organizations can be surprising to both tenured and first-time managers. Historically, managers were able to leverage the organization's top-down mechanisms to engage in performance management. Even today, many organizations use well-defined traditional command and control levers in the development of their workforce (Lips-Wiersma & Hall, 2007). As a result, managers were historically removed from the formal process and expectation of the coaching and development of employees. In addition, developed economies have led to an individualistic career management mindset in many large organizations, which places a lot of the responsibility on an employee for their own development (Baruch, 2006). In addition, management Prof. Valcour (2014) recently remarked, "Strangely, at most companies, coaching isn't part of what managers are formally expected to do" (p. 1). Rather, many employee development activities are assumed to fall under the human resources, training or learning, and development professionals. Yet, organizational research suggests that the most effective behavior, which separates highly effective managers from average ones is the behavior of coaching (Gavin, 2013). It is undisputed in the organizational behavior literature that effective coaching behaviors, within the right context, make for better employee experiences, ultimately leading to greater organizational performance.

As managers begin to realize that one of the leading aspects of their role is the development and coaching of employees, this can pose newfound challenges. A manager at a large financial firm recently remarked at a new manager training, "I was promoted because I was really good at the technical aspect of my job. I am not sure I would have taken this position if I knew how much time was required to coach and develop employees." Another newly hired manager worried about losing their technical knowledge, "If I spend all this time developing employees, how will I maintain my own expertise?" While these concerns are both practical and valid, they do show a lack of understanding around what coaching does for both the individual employee, the manager's own development as well as the organization. Effective coaching and development makes both the employee and manager stronger through their shared discovery of newfound meaning and information during conversations (Dunn, 2009). Segers, Vloeberghs, Henderickx, and Inceoglu (2011) define coaching in organizations as, "an intensive and systematic facilitation of individuals or groups by using a wide variety of behavioral techniques and methods to help them attain self-congruent goals or conscious self-change and self-development in order to improve their professional performance, personal well-being and, consequently, to improve the effectiveness of their organization" (p. 204). Coaching focuses on helping people acknowledge and identify the wide range of resources available, including their own personal strengths and contextual resources to fulfill their goals. Dunn (2009) further adds that coaching helps employees, "identify the crux of the issue and leverage point for development" (p. 25). As a result, strong coaching manifests itself in the activities of clear goal-setting and continuous performance management. However, before exploring the activities themselves, it is necessary to consider the conditions required for managers to assume coaching behaviors in the workplace.

6.1.1 The Manager as Coach

There are five considerations that allow for effective coaching behaviors between managers and their respective employees. Each of these elements are supported by various research from the psychology and organizational behavior literature and are needed in order to engage in higher exchanges with employees during coaching sessions. Even just missing one of these facets can hinder the chances of building social capital during the coaching process. However, each of these factors requires an amount of what Kim Scott, former executive at Google, refers to as "emotional labor." As Scott (2017) notes, "We undervalue the emotional labor of being the boss...Emotional labor is not just part of the job; it's the key to being a good boss" (p. 5). As a result, good bosses must invest in the emotional side of human relating. They must seek to build trust, provide guidance, listen and create healthy relationships in the workplace. Scott (2017) recommends that these activities take at least a quarter of a manager's time. While that may initially sound like a lot of time, spending this time coaching though will "save enormous lost time and headaches later" (p. 10). It is a short-term investment that reaps longer term gains as expertise is formed during the coaching process. Let's explore the five facets of coaching that effective managers do well.

6.1.1.1 Lead From a Growth Mindset

One of the fundamental components required in successful coaching at the management level begins with a manager's mindset. Dweck (2007) found that the belief in whether or not one can change holds tremendous weight and influence on our decision-making and behaviors. For example, managers who possess a growth mindset, or hold the belief that people's abilities and skillsets can change, not only make for better coaches but are also much more sensitive to improvements in their workforce. A fixed mindset, on the other hand, blinds managers to improvements in teammates' progress, as they hold tendency to think people's capabilities are innate. As a result, they are much less likely to see observable improvement once a judgment has been made on an individual's performance potential.

A forthcoming study conducted by Monahan (2018) found that a manager's mindset almost entirely explained their level of employees' engagement on the team. After further investigation, it was not necessarily the mindset itself that engaged employees, but the way that the core belief "people can change" manifested itself into more effective and frequent coaching and development behaviors. These managers who scored high on a growth mindset were much more likely to have the self-efficacy to help facilitate positive change in those around them. The study concluded that a manager's growth mindset matters to employee success, because it fuels the manager with the motivation to engage in coaching and development behaviors. Likewise, a fixed mindset may unintentionally be demotivating managers from engaging in coaching behaviors, because they are less likely believe they can even influence change or see improvements.

Consider the following real-life story taken from the frontlines of management. J.J. was a high performer on this team and quickly began leader within his department. He held very high standards and expected top performance from others. However, his expectations around performance were rigid, and he would quickly judge people as competent or not. As a result, J.J. spent little time with employee development and coaching. If he thought a person on his team was incompetent he would work around them or try to find menial work for them to do so they would not fail. This led to low engagement on the team, and an overall lack of creativity that the team desperately needed to practice if they would continue to be successful within the firm.

Recognizing something needed to change, J.J. took a mindset assessment, which revealed high fixed mindset thinking. He attended training and spent most of the time with his arms crossed across his chest, skeptical that he could change behaviors in the workplace. However, during the training, his peers who scored high on growth mindset thinking shared story after story of their own surprises in employee development after spending time coaching their workforce. J.J. began to experience his own mindset shift during this training and examined more data, which revealed that his counterparts who engaged in growth-oriented activities, such as coaching, were having much better experiences with their clients and performing at a higher level.

J.J. returned from the intensive 2-day training and decided to run his own experiment. He would start scheduling 1:1's with each member of his team twice a month for coaching sessions. He asked questions on where they needed help and the type of work that energized them. J.J. realized after these conversations that many of his team members were misaligned. In addition, he had many individuals who needed his help on how to navigate the organization. These employees weren't incompetent J.J. realized, but simply lacked the necessary experience to effectively navigate the organization. After a year of consistent coaching J.J. could not believe the progress his team made. Their overall engagement was higher than ever before, and he saw performance improvements in nearly every member of his team. J.J. was able to recognize that change is hard, but not impossible and, it begins with adopting the right mindset.

6.1.1.2 Build Expertise

Nearly as important as mindsets, is whether or not mangers are perceived as an expert within the organization or in a position to influence change. In a forthcoming study, qualitative research revealed that the number one factor employees look to in their manager is expertise (Monahan, 2018). Coaching is only effective when the coach is considered an expert in their field. A leading CFO at a large industry firm remarked that he would rather work for a jerk who knew what they were doing, than a nice person who couldn't tell you a thing about their business. While ideally, an employee works for someone who is both competent and pleasant, this statement reveals a startling truth about effective leadership. It is what you know that matters most to many employees. Employees look directly to their managers to guide their growth and help navigate their success at an organization (Monahan et al., 2017). Effectively doing this requires both declarative (knowing) and procedural (doing) knowledge of a particular work domain (Anderson, 1982). Dunn (2009) remarks that, "internal coaches offer a deep understanding of the organizational context, the culture and 'how things really work around here,' insights about organizational politics and career options, and a broad-based perspective on how the individual is viewed within the organization" (p. 26).

Management expertise is manifested by their behaviors, experiences, and strategies they set forth (Cote & Gilbert, 2009). Employees expect managers to have the specialized knowledge to help solve ill-defined problems. Many times, employees may be experiencing a problem for the first-time and lack the necessary experience to effectively solve. As a result, a manager's expertise is most valuable when applied and results in better outcomes for those around them. For example, many times in sports, a coach's expertise is judged by the performance of their team, not simply their domain knowledge of the sport. Likewise, in workplaces, a manager's expertise can best be assessed by examining the performance of their team. A manager may know a lot about the technicality of their field, but without the experience and knowledge on how to apply it in such a way as to help others, proves less useful in the workplace.

Expertise is one of the building blocks identified to create social capital in the workplace. As managers move from connecting through the building block of a shared objective, they must now spend their time focused on applying their expertise to the coaching and development of their staff. Without this key ingredient, the ability of a manager to continue to build the necessary social capital to engage in more complex transactions and activities is likely to diminish.

6.1.1.3 Lend Time to Develop Others

While expertise was the number factor to emerge in a study which sought to understand what created the most effective managers, a close second theme to emerge was time. Multiple employees remarked within a study, "I need a manager who is willing to lend their time to guide my growth" (Monahan, 2018). Time may be the largest limiting factor to managers who simply lack the capacity to coach others in the workplace. Yet, giving of their time may be the single gift that will lead to tremendous return on their investment for their workforce.

What motivates managers, who are already busy individuals striving after their own goals and development, to carve out to spend coaching others? A 2015 study published in the *Harvard Business Review* remarked, "They are not coaching their people because they are nice – they see personal involvement in the development of talent as an essential activity for business success" (p. 1). Managers who make time for coaching do not believe this is a "nice to have" activity, but an urgent "must have" activity each week. Further research suggests that managers who frequently coach have recognized that their time and involvement is necessary for retaining top talent, operating successfully in highly violate markets and creating deeper problem-solving skills to further free capacity for managers (Weintraub & Hunt, 2015). Managers who find and devote the time for coaching possess the longer term vision and rationality to recognize that the shorter term deposit of their energy will reap greater benefits, capacity, and time in the future. Coaching is one of the most rational and necessary activities today's managers can concern themselves with.

The question many managers ask is how much time should be spent coaching employees each week? While the answer ultimately is "it depends," a compelling research suggests that spending too little time leads to disengagement, while too much leads to the perception of micromanaging. In 2014, a leadership consulting and training organization Leadership I.Q., surveyed over 32,000 American and Canadian leaders and staff on the following two questions: How many hours do they spend interacting with their direct leader and how many hours *should* people in general be interacting with their direct leader? The goal of the research was to find a tangible number to help guide managers on the appropriate number of hours to spend on coaching. The results of the research reveal a startling gap in the time today's employees are spending with their direct leader. 20% of the study respondents reported that they were spending less than 1 hour per week interacting with their direct leader. The median number of hours reported on interacting with one's direct leader each week was 3 hours. Is that enough? It appears not. The researchers found that the optimal number of hours that employees need to spend with their direct leader is approximately 6 hours per week. Those who reported spending 6 hours each week interacting with their direct leader were 29% more inspired, 30% more engaged, 16% more innovative, and 15% more intrinsically motivated at work compared to those who only spent 1 hour per week with their direct leader. The benefits were not just experienced at the staff level. Executives within the study felt their highest levels of inspiration when they spent at least 7 hours interacting with their respective leaders. And the group that requires the most coaching? Middle managers, who felt their highest levels of inspiration when they spent at least 9 hours a week with their leaders.

However, can managers spend too much time trying to coach employees? It appears so. The study also found that once people reported spending upwards of 10, 15 and even 20 hours a week interacting with their leader, a corresponding drop occurred in their engagement, inspiration, motivation, and innovation. It is also important to note that this study found that not all types of time yielded the same return on investment to employee outcomes. The most effective time spent was the time spent interacting face–face with their leader. Yet, as the workforce continues to become more dispersed and digital, email communications will likely rise as a primary form of communication. It will be important for managers to spend their efforts and energies on the types of coaching communications that will yield the greatest return on investment. In most cases, managers should seek to leverage in-person opportunities or virtual video communications for remote workers when engaging in coaching activities. In most cases, coaching is best facilitated in-person, however in remote environments, coaching can also be done using immersive digital tools by utilizing video technologies.

6.1.1.4 Listen and Ask Open-Ended Questions

As discussed, managers need to lead with the right mindset, possess expertise, and make the time for coaching their employees. However, how can managers best leverage the time they actually spend with employees? One of the best uses of their time is spent listening and asking open-ended questions. Dunn (2009) notes that open-ended questions and intentional listening can lead to exploratory inquiries that result in deeper meaning and learning by both employee and manager. Open-ended questions often require the employee to engage in "System 2" or slow thinking, which activates the more rational part of the mind. In addition, the more one listens the more trust is woven throughout the relationship, which is a necessary component of creating effective social capital. Furthermore, research finds that listening has a positive effect on influencing others and building positive relationships in the workplace (Ames, Maissen, & Brockner, 2012). As managers in the 21st century rely more on interpersonal skills and relationships to create alignment to broader organizational goals, rather than command and control techniques, listening and asking opened questions becomes a leverage point to influence others at work.

How can managers practice better listening skills during their time with employees? Research suggests that they practice curiosity. Weintraub and Hunt (2015) found that managers who placed a priority on coaching were genuinely interested in problem-solving, finding opportunities for the business, and wanting to find ways to do things better. As a result, these coaching mangers asked a lot more questions with their employees and sought to engage in frequent dialogue to learn. Managers viewed coaching not only as an opportunity to develop others, but to also obtain an opportunity to learn firsthand how things were going and what could be improvemed upon. Listening and asking questions offered key inputs ultimately resulting in their own success in solving problems and finding creative solutions in their own work.

6.1.1.5 Provide Clarity and Frequent Feedback

Along with listening and asking open-ended questions, effective coaching behaviors include providing role clarity and feedback. Unlike most traditional performance management systems, which leverage an annual process to review goals and performance, today's shifting market dynamics require more frequent and agile performance feedback mechanisms. Branham (2005) notes that one of the top and often hidden reasons that employees leave organizations is based on a lack of coaching and feedback. In particular, Branham (2005) suggests that employees do not know the answer to four relatively simple yet pertinent questions that stand to motivate employee performance within the organization.

The first question is, "where are we going as a company?" In other words, what is the vision, mission, and purpose of the organization? This of course connects broadly to one's need for meaning and belonging. If managers are effectively practicing the connecting behaviors discussed in Chapter 5, Coaching: Goal-Setting and Performance Management through alignment of shared objectives, this first question should be well answered before an individual joins the organization. However, the following questions will likely be more fluid and require greater coaching throughout the employee's journey within the organization.

The second question is, "how are we going to get there?" This question begins to address the team dynamics and expands upon roles and operating norms. A once high-performing team began to experience a decline in their output over a course of a year. The team had been working together for nearly 3 years, yet something had shifted. The problem? The company began changing direction in the market and overhauled their strategy and operating model, but the team made no adjustments. They clung to goals and operating norms that while serving them well for the first couple years no longer were successful in the new operating model. Part of a manager's role as a coach is to ensure that there is clarity around how a team's operations fit broadly into alignment with the larger organizational mission. This is likely to change more frequently than in times past, as agility is cited as one of the most necessary factors for success in today's organizations. Staying current on addressing how the team will get to where it needs to go is an important consideration in today's rapidly changing contexts.

Thirdly, employees are seeking answers to how their team leader expects them to contribute to the success of the team and organization. "How will employees contribute to the success of the team?" Rather than wait for a formalized annual goal-setting process, it is important to ensure employees are frequently aware of priorities and the impact their work is anticipated to make to the broader organization. As will be discovered, Microsoft has recently shifted this conversation from the various inputs employees are expected to engage in to instead the outcomes of employee's activities. This slight shift provides greater autonomy and creativity on the employee side, while also ensuring that certain outcomes are prioritized.

Lastly, and maybe one of the most difficult for many managers, is addressing the question, "How am I doing?" Without this individual knowledge of one's performance, many employees are unable to draw the connection between their work and the need to grow and develop. In addition, without properly addressing one's feedback, poor performers may be tolerated, hindering the entire team's efforts. Consider the following scenario to illustrate this point: A team of approximately 10 employees were brought together to engage in a highly cognitive and interdependent project. The success of the project rested on how well the team worked together. After a few months into the project, Emily one of the more senior team members, began missing team meetings. Eventually she began missing deadlines and was putting the entire team's efforts in jeopardy. Yet, no one on the team was willing to give feedback based on her seniority, and the team leader ultimately decided to turn a blind eye to these mishaps. This continued on for months before the entire project imploded. Finally, the team leader decided to directly address Emily's performance and its impact it had on the project. Emily felt completely blindsided and could not believe this was the first time she was receiving negative feedback on her performance. She felt betrayed and unable to fix her behaviors in time to save the project. What started off as a strong team dynamic and much promise ended in a disaster due to an overall lack of honest feedback throughout the project. In addition, two of the highest performing team members decided to transition off the project and instead focus their efforts elsewhere in the organization.

Coaching behaviors will continue to be a priority for the 21st century who is looking to effectively develop intellectual and social capital throughout the organization. However, it will take much preparation and development on the managers part to ensure they are ready to engage in effective coaching. Consider the following: Do Now Exercise as a way to get started on developing the tools necessary to be an effective coach in today's organizations.

Do Now Exercise

Becoming a coach requires a lot of energy, time, and investment on the part of the manager. However, one of the best ways to coach others is to develop in yourself as a manager. Consider the following exercises to help assess your own coaching skillsets and identify areas of opportunity to further improve upon.

1. Take a mindset assessment to see if your tendencies are more toward growth or fixed mindset thinking. Take Dweck's (2007) free assessment at https://mindsetonline.com/testyourmindset/step1.php. Share your results with a trusted advisor and work on shifting your mindset as needed to further develop coaching behaviors in the workplace.
2. Request a 360-degree feedback from your team to determine how well you are currently engaging in coaching behaviors. Utilize your own leaders and trusted peers to review the results and create an action plan that will allow you to play to your current strengths while also working on specific areas of improvement.
3. Create a pulse survey for your team to assess their clarity around the team's current goals and priorities. How clear are team members on their own individual role and expectations? Frequently leverage these short-form surveys to identify areas that may require more clarity on the team. Simple questions such as, "I know where I should be spending the majority of my time this month" or "I know how success will be measured at the end of this project" are helpful barometers of role clarity on the team.

(*Continued*)

(Continued)

4. Get to know your team offline through open-ended questions. Consider a team lunch or offsite to further get to know each team member's working styles and preferences. Taking the time to interact outside of the day–day work will help develop greater trust and allow you to ask more open-ended questions without the distractions of emails and interpretations that often occur in workspaces.

As discussed, the role of the manager resembles more of a long-distance race pace-setter who can provide guidance and coaching along a challenging route. They do this by lending their time to guide an employee's growth through strong coaching behaviors. They identify areas of opportunity to run faster or slow down. They help navigate throughout the race by providing the necessary expertise of potential obstacles to avoid or identifying areas of opportunity to explore. In the end, the goal of the manager as a coach is to guide employees into the process of self-discovery in order to capture benefits toward the organizational objectives. Two specific activities were managers can practice engaging in coaching behaviors are during the goal-setting and performance management process. Each of which offers an opportunity to build greater social capital in teams if the right coaching mindset and behaviors are displayed. Let's explore the opportunities and challenges that arise in each of these two activities.

6.2 GOAL-SETTING: LEVERAGING PERFORMANCE- AND LEARNING-ORIENTED GOALS

Before managers have the ability to effectively engage in performance development activities, it is important that employees understand their goals, priorities, and expectations of what success looks like early on. Goal-setting theory is one of the most studied aspects of management within the organizational behavior literature. In fact, over 1000 studies within the literature demonstrate the connection between goal-setting and one's motivation to exert effort toward higher levels of performance (Mitchell & Daniels, 2003). The primary purpose of a goal is to motivate and set direction for an individual toward a higher level of performance. Goals do this by creating a clear and deliberate discrepancy between a current state and desired future state (Carver & Scheier, 2001). Human beings are inherently wired to help close the gap a goal creates. An inspiring and healthy goal resides in the sweet spot between boredom and causing a state of anxiety. The best goals are those that bring people to their edge without overwhelming them. Goals also act as a marker for one to assess their progress and growth. Research from over 1200 diary entries of employees found those who continually sense progress against a set of goals, even if they are relatively small goals, are much more creative, productive, engaged, and even have better relationships in the workplace (Amabile & Kramer, 2011). The researchers termed this the *progress principle* noting the positive influence progress against goals can have on work performance. Progress, which is measured by a clear set of goals, inherently fuels an employee's sense of achievement. As a result, goal-setting becomes an important activity that managers can leverage to inspire higher levels of performance.

There are two specific types of goals that are well documented with the literature that influence the type of behavior evoked within employees. Goals can be classified as either performance-related goals, eliciting an *extrinsic connection* to an outcome, or learning goals, eliciting an *intrinsic connection* to an outcome (Dweck, 1986). Rational economic theory entirely focuses on the utilization of performance goals, which connect one's efforts to a clear and tangible outcome. For example, a performance goal could be to increase sales revenue by 16% this fiscal year. Typically, an incentive is attached to the attainment of the goal—whether it is simply keeping one's job or obtaining a monetary award upon goal attainment. There is much research and support that shows that a clear and specific performance goal elicits greater performance from individuals than simply asking them to try their best or setting a vague or easy goal to attain (Locke & Latham, 2006). As a result, many researchers make the case for a linear relationship between the difficulty of a goal and task performance for performance goals. The harder the goal, as long as it is attainable, should inspire greater levels of performance. However, as will be discovered, this can also create a blind spot so that people achieve these performance goals at the expense of other important activities. In addition, other streams of research suggest that performance goals can actually impede learning and invoke a sense of anxiety as the emphasis is entirely on the task itself and not on longer term development (Mitchell & Daniels, 2003).

The second type of goal-setting relates to learning-oriented goals. The purpose of these types of goals is to develop greater levels of competency and growth. Whereas performance-oriented goals seek to demonstrate one's current competency by meeting the goal, learning goals are much more likely to be stretch goals that require an individual to acquire a new set of skills to meet the goal set. For example, a learning goal might relate to an individual connecting with other departments to learn how the organization operates or to become more competent in their presentation skills. The emphasis and focus on the outcome centers around the individual's growth and development. Learning-oriented goals are shown to increase levels of performance (Button, Mathieu, & Zajac, 1996), create greater attention on the task at hand along with greater self-set goal difficulty (Payne, Youngcourt, & Beaubien, 2007). And while both learning and performance related goals are effective toward goal attainment, learning goals are better suited when the situation reflects a complex task or requires knowledge acquisition. Performance goals can actually create tension and inhibit the employee from receiving critical feedback during a complex task compared to one who orients their performance toward a learning outcome (Cianci et al., 2010). Learning goals also encourage knowledge transfer, openness to feedback, and greater competency development. Locke and Latham (2006) found that during a complex business simulation, students who received learning-oriented goals kept their businesses running much longer than those who were given specific performance goals. The researcher concluded that the learning goals allowed students to more freely seek out new information, find different ways of accomplishing tasks, and focus on longer term objectives. In today' organizations where intellectual capital development is necessary, learning goals can help keep people developing their skills, encourage greater problem-solving techniques in complex environments, and be more open to new information.

The research is clear. Performance goals are certainly better than not having goals. Learning goals can be better than performance goals in highly cognitive and complex environments. Yet, goal-setting on its own, without the right coaching behaviors to support employees, is not nearly as effective as having goals supported with management coaching. A recent study examining the effectives of coaching on 1246 sales representatives reveals the link between effective goal-setting, coaching, and feedback on an individual's success (Dahling, Taylor, Chau, & Dwight, 2015). The study found that managers who effectively set goals for employees and provided coaching in the form of role clarity and feedback throughout the year, had much more successful employees who attained or surpassed their organizational goals. Employees who had goals, but did not receive the necessary coaching, experienced much less success in attaining their goals. In addition, as a word of caution, the study did find that managers who frequently engaged in coaching behaviors, but were not skilled or providing the right feedback, had the worst results. These employees failed to attain their goals and likely experienced less satisfaction at work as a result of the micromanaging. As this study reveals, the quality of the coaching is just as important, if not more important, than the quantity of coaching employees receive.

Effective goal-setting coupled with coaching behaviors is likely to lead to increased performance across the organizations. The best goals are those that take people to their edge and focus their efforts on learning-oriented outcomes (see Lessons from the field: Patagonia's emphasis on growth through goals). The successful attainment of these goals is most likely to occur under managers who practice coaching behaviors and provide feedback throughout the process. Learning goals that are accompanied by management coaching behaviors are instrumental to knowledge development.

Lessons from the field: Patagonia's emphasis on growth through goals

Patagonia is a US-based retailer of outdoor equipment and clothing that employs more than 2000 individuals. They hire based on three strong missions: to build the best products, to cause no unnecessary harm, and to inspire and implement solutions for environmental causes. While it has historically hired talent around these shared objectives, the company realized that their current goal-setting process needed an overhaul. Today, employees still work with their leaders once a year to set performance goals and expectations. These performance goals are cocreated by both the employee and their leaders. It is a collaborative process to ensure that the employee's goals are aligned to the shared objectives of the organization. However, Patagonia recognized this was not enough to keep employees engaged in their own development. So, Patagonia created a more agile learning-oriented goal-setting process once a quarter. These quarterly goals focus exclusively on employee development and growth. The company asks employees to push themselves and think ambitiously about their learning to attain these goals. The emphasis of these goals is placed on learning, reflection, and growth. Employees are encouraged to share with others their areas of accomplishment, while also discovering what they could have done differently. These quarterly feedback coaching sessions, accompanied with learning-oriented goals, keep employees focused on their own development, while also contributing greater levels of performance toward the organization throughout the year.

6.2.1 The Challenges With Goals: Inattentional Blindness and Irrational Risk Preferences Can Lead to Myopic Decision-Making

While goal-setting is both beneficial and necessary for managers seeking to create both intellectual and social capital throughout the organization, biases can emerge that impede its successful implementation. Ordonez, Schwitzer, Galinsky, and Bazerman (2009) cautions, "goal-setting should be prescribed selectively, presented with a warning label, and closely monitored" (p. 6). This is because people are wired to achieve success through the accomplishment of goals. Unfortunately, this inherent drive to meet goals, can actually come at the expense of others when managers begin leveraging extrinsic rewards to motivate employees. As Ordonez et al. (2009) notes, "Managers are likely to overvalue and overuse goals. Although people recognize the importance of intrinsic rewards in motivating themselves, people exaggerate the importance of extrinsic rewards in motivating others" (p. 11). This happens when managers set high-performance goals and then leverage carrots and sticks (i.e., fear of job loss and the promise of rewards) to motivate employees to achieve them. Consider the following cautionary tale. In the 1990s Sears Auto set very specific performance goals for their staff. The goal was to reach an average of $147 per hour on repairs across all of their centers. The staff worked hard to achieve this target, but at the expense of their customers. It was found that employees overcharged and completed unnecessary repairs to reach this goal. Once it was publicly discovered that employees were engaged in unethical practices, the CEO at the time acknowledged that it was the stretch performance goals that motivated employees to actively deceive customers (Dishneau, 1992). The lesson here is that people are wired to meet goals and will work hard toward their attainment, even at the expense of other considerations such as ethics or longer term successes.

One of the most common biases that arises during goal-setting and explains this type of behavior is the *inattentional blindness* bias. This is the tendency for people to focus too much on one specific thing that they unintentionally ignore all else. Goals cause people to focus so narrowly on a certain outcome that other important features of a task are ignored. This was famously illustrated during Simons and Chabris' (1999) study on the effect of inattentional blindness. The researchers asked participants to watch a video and count the number of passes that the team in white makes. There is another team in black t-shirts passing a ball as well, which the participant is forced to block out. As a result of the intense focus on the task, the majority of participants watching the video fail to notice a man wearing a gorilla suit walking into the middle of the screen, pounding his chest and then exiting the video. Once participants are shown the video again without the burden of intense concentration on a task, they were astonished to realize they missed something so obvious.

Goals can be powerful motivators that evoke an intense and narrow focus on a particular task, but can also create unintentional blindness to other important surrounding aspects. This narrow focus that goals create was well-documented in a study by Staw and Boettger (1990) who asked a group of students to proofread a document. The researchers asked one group to either focus on grammatical issues *or* blatant content errors. The researchers asked another group of students to simply proofread the document and make the necessary corrections. The group that was asked to focus on grammatical errors completely missed identifying some rather obvious blatant content errors. The other group that was focused on identifying blatant content errors almost entirely missed all of the grammatical errors within the document. However, the group that was not primed to narrowly focus on any particular goal was most likely to correct *both* the document's grammatical and content errors. As Bennett (2009) warned, "Goals...might actually be taking the place of independent thinking and personal initiative" (para. 14). While appropriate learning goals can orient one's efforts, high-performance goals that come with extrinsic rewards can actually mitigate positive decision-making.

A recent corporate scandal highlights the dangers of inattentional blindness that performance goal-setting can cause. Wells Fargo set a high-performance goal of eight accounts per customer for each of their branches.

This goal, in hindsight, was nearly impossible and not beneficial to the majority of their customer base. Yet, this goal was set in hopes of having a cross sales organization that leveraged multiple accounts for each customer to obtain higher levels of profitability. Over time, it became clear this was the only goal that Wells Fargo leadership cared about and was used as the ultimate benchmark for high bonus payouts. As a result, both leadership and staff remained narrowly focused on attaining this cross-sale goal.

However, this intense focus on a singular goal created a disastrous culture that encouraged employees to engage in unethical behaviors. Leadership pushed hard for employees to meet this goal of eight accounts per customer and often threatened job loss for frontline employees if they failed to meet their goal. Unfortunately, frontline employees began to create millions of fake accounts to meet this unrealistic goal. At times, customers even knew about these fake accounts, but went along with it based on either personal relationship with the banker or were at times even incentivized to keep these fake accounts opened. This malpractice eventually caught up with the firm and cost them over $185 million in a settlement with federal regulators. Much like the previously discussed Sears auto case in the 1990s, this example shows that even leadership cannot always foresee the consequences that will prevail once an emphasis is placed on stretch performance goals. Without the necessary coaching behaviors in place, inattentional blindness to nearly all else will befall employees, including practicing unethical behaviors and that jeopardize the longer term success of the company.

Additional research showcases the dangers of high-performance goals that leverage extrinsic motivators for their attainment. Wright et al. (1993) found that too much focus on a specific goal decreased extra-role behaviors, such as collaboration or helping out a coworker. Mitchell and Silver's (1990) study suggested that performance goals can promote competition rather than cooperation, which ultimately lowered the performance of the organization under investigation. Cheng et al.'s (2015) work found that companies who set quarterly earnings reports and calls frequently met or exceeded their financial targets for the quarter did so at an expense. These firms were much less likely to invest in longer term needs such as research and development. Other research shows that learning and longer term performance is ultimately hindered when one focuses too narrowly on the pursuit of shorter term performance goals (Ordonez et al., 2009).

Not only do high-performance stretch goals create an inattentional blindness to other important considerations, they can also evoke irrational risk preferences. Knight et al. (2001) found that the higher the performance goal the more likely one would choose riskier strategies for attaining the goal. The research found a direct correlation between higher performance goals and people preferring riskier bets. It was concluded that high stretch goals can actually adjust one's risk preferences, causing them to make decisions with less regard to the potential loss that could occur. The focus becomes so much on obtaining the ends that the means are often overlooked or excused, which ironically can lead to worse performance. Consider the following study on negotiation (Galinsky et al., 2002). A group of participants were given high-performance goals and asked to negotiate with another individual. Other participants were not given a goal and simply asked to engage in a negotiation that would lead to the best outcome. Negotiators with the high-performance goal were much more likely to reach an inefficient impasse rather than reach a profitable agreement. Additional research discovered that this behavior in part was driven by the high-goal negotiators who were more likely to demand larger values and not find creative solutions that resided outside their initial goal.

Goals are an important part of the management process and a necessary step to building social capital in the firm. However, they can pose dangers to managers who may not be aware of the biases that high-performance and extrinsically driven goals can create. To protect against the inattentional bias and adjusted risk preferences high-performance goals can bring, it is recommended that managers create learning-oriented goals that encourage collaboration and leverage intrinsic means toward their attainment. Managers can effectively do this by engaging in coaching behaviors throughout the process and emphasizing the means as much as the ends during project engagements.

Organizations of the future move away from formal goal and performance management systems to self-directed supportive and developmental models

As organizations begin to recognize that annual goal-setting and performance management practices are not frequent enough to keep up with the agility required to remain competitive in today's marketplace, it is becoming increasingly commonplace to shift away from the traditional systems and move toward both agile and self-directed goal-setting and feedback sessions. Recently, academic researchers have also reported on the fundamental shift away from "systems" based management to a more self-directed "supportive and developmental" approach (Segers & Inceoglu, 2012). As a result, some organizations have found that a cadence of quarterly feedback sessions most helpful in lieu of annual performance management reviews. Other organizations, recognizing that too much paperwork and time was being spent on annual goal-setting, which becomes outdated as soon as it is completed, have done away with the goal-setting process all together. Instead, these organizations look to create a few high-level objectives for the firm and ask individual departments and teams to self-direct their own process for obtaining them.

While many of these organizations believe to be more agile and ready for the future, some employees express concern over the lack of clarity, which can exist in these environments. It becomes unclear how one receives a promotion or even awareness around their overall performance. And, as the formal process of goal-setting no longer exists in some organizations, it is now the responsibility of

(*Continued*)

(Continued)

the manager and employee to self-create their own goals. This works well if both manager and employee have a strong relationship and clear sense of direction. However, this can pose many challenges to first time managers who may be struggling how to prioritize their team's work without an overarching set of goals or processes to guide them. In addition, it can also be hard for some managers to practice continuous performance management activities without the necessary organizational systems in place.

As managers continue to encounter more responsibility in the goal-setting and performance management processes, without the necessary organizational level mechanisms traditionally found in top-down organizations, it becomes all that more important for managers to make the time for coaching behaviors. Coaching will increasingly become a differentiating factor for high-performing individuals and teams who will benefit from the agility afforded in the frequency and support that managers can bring outside a formalized annual system. However, this will no doubt, continue to put strain on managers in organizations who will find themselves pressed for time. As a result, their locus of control is recommended to remain small so they can adequately dedicate the needed time to coaching. In addition, the best organizations will substitute top-down mechanisms for supportive practices that foster collaboration across the enterprise.

6.3 A SHIFT FROM PERFORMANCE MANAGEMENT TO PERFORMANCE DEVELOPMENT

Once goals are set the next step in the coaching phase is performance management. Performance management can be one of the more difficult activities of management. It often involves giving transparent feedback, making decisions regarding an employee's performance and even their compensation. Traditionally, performance management has been viewed as an annual activity that is conducted by both managers and their corresponding human resource business partners. One of the most often organizational systems used is infamously referred to as the "rank and yank" or "up and out" process made popular by former General Electric CEO, Jack Welch. This form of performance management requires all employees to receive a rating at the end of the year, and those who are ranked at the lowest levels receive a denial of merit increase or bonus or sometimes can lose their jobs. As a result, organizational leaders spend countless hours debating each individual's performance for the year and are forced to rank each of their team members against one another. As management Prof. Parker (2013) remarks, "An employee could only get high ratings if everyone else fails." This is because the traditional performance management system is built on using the laws of normal distribution found in statistics, which require the majority of individuals to fall in the middle, with few outliers on both high performance and low performance ratings. Many practitioners and scholars have called out this practice as doing more harm than good by creating negative behavior changes in the people who fall outside normal bell curve (Rogers, 2004). If you think about the alterative behavioral assumptions discussed, in particular that people are inherently motivated to cooperate and seek out belonging, this practice runs counter to creating the conditions necessary to do so. In addition, as with hiring decisions, assessing annual performance also comes with a host of biases using their methodology. Most notably is the halo and recency effects, which can cloud the judgment of even the most rational manager. As will be further discussed, the halo effect incorrectly assumes that because an individual is competent in one area they are equally competent in other unrelated areas. The recency effect is the bias to recall more recent or shorter term accomplishments, rather than more holistically consider the longer term performance of an individual. These biases create a lack of accuracy in the data at year-end performance reviews, with one studying finding that 9 out of 10 HR leaders not trusting that the current performance management processes produce accurate talent decision-making (Engler, 2014). Further research suggests that less than 25% of performance ratings correlate back to actual performance in the workplace (Scullen, Mount, & Goff, 2000). This is further evidenced by other research, which found that two-thirds of rated top performers were not the ones making the most contributions to the organization (Rock, Davis, & Jones, 2014). One of the most negative consequences of this is that nearly 50% of employees are "negatively surprised" when they received their rating and compensation at year end (Rock, 2016). This in turn demotivated their performance the following year and encouraged deviant workplace behaviors.

If people were genuinely rational self-interested beings than setting up a system that encourages competition and survival of the fittest may make sense. However, we now know from decades of behavioral research this is simply not the case. How does a behavioral understanding of people change the way managers engage in the performance management process? (see Fig. 6.2 for a comparison on traditional performance management to behavioral coaching and development). To answer this question let's examine a leading company who threw away the old performance management playbook in favor of coaching and development.

6.3.1 Lessons From the Field: Microsoft Reinvents Their Performance Management Systems to Focus on Supportive and Developmental Behaviors

Microsoft had long relied on the use of the traditional rank and yank performance management system within its organization. However, in 2013, it abandoned the model as it felt the use of such a rigid system was crippling collaboration and creativity throughout the organization—which was the

Traditional performance management	Behavioral performance development
Judging performance through competitive assessments	Coaching and development activities to increase learning opportunities
Annual event	Frequent feedback
Top-down, command-control mechanisms	Shared responsibility–both manager and employee building expertise
Individual performance focused–what are the individual's activities and outputs	Network performance focused–how does this person make others around them better
Extrinsically driven–leverage carrots and sticks to motivate	Intrinsically driven–leverage one's need to grow and develop to motivate

FIGURE 6.2 Comparing traditional performance management systems to behavioral coaching and development approaches.

very thing Microsoft felt it needed to regain its footing in the market. They no longer call this process performance management and rather refer to it as *performance development*. What was one of the main motivating factors for this change? Lisa Dodge, Director of Global Performance Programs at Microsoft, notes that the business needed to think differently and faster in light of new products and markets it would enter. The most important change needed was to create higher dependency across the organization, increasing integration and mutual accountability with one another. However, their current performance management approach bred an unhealthy soiled and competitive culture year over year. Microsoft's organizational leaders recognized it had a problem with the way it needed employees to work in the future and the organizational culture and practices it had formerly created. "The current performance management system was not serving us well and we had a strong business case for change" (Dodge, 2014).

Microsoft now focuses their performance development conversation around teamwork, establishing better feedback loops and rewards people based on business contributions, not just individual activities. Individual performance is considered alongside how well that individuals worked with others and the impact made on the collective organization. Microsoft stressed and prioritized that individual success is tied to the way that the individual makes others around them better. As a result, this required a fundamental shift in reward allocation from solely individual inputs and activities, to tangible outputs that impact others and ultimately the organization. To effectively implement a new mindset around performance development, Dodge (2014) notes that the company had to retire distractions that got in the way of healthy collaboration and development, including year-end assessments, ratings, and the infamous bell curve. Instead, the organization looks to their managers and leaders to provide frequent feedback and coach employees toward enterprise impact. Since switching from a performance management system to performance development conversations, employees and managers are more satisfied with the approach. In 2012, under the old system, 40% of employees were dissatisfied with the approach to performance and development, and 45% of management expressed dissatisfaction. However, after moving into the new method, which centers around development, only 17% of employees and 16% of managers reported dissatisfaction in 2014.

And, while the company saw an increase in satisfaction with the new approach to performance development, a more interesting impact happened that centered around employees working together and building social capital. Nearly 89% of all employees now believed that contributing to and leveraging others will increase their own impact. The new approach Microsoft adopted, which encouraged collaboration, focused on reciprocity and the transcendence of rational self-interest toward enlightened self-interest. Employees recognized that simply seeking out for their own interests would do little good in the new culture and environment. These results continue to demonstrate that employees are taught in most business schools that people are self-seeking agents and then enter into organizational cultures, which further foster this mindset by creating competitive cultures that require one to get ahead at the expense of others. This is simply taught or learned behavior, not necessarily what most people prefer. In fact, recent studies suggest that, "human beings are one of the most cooperative species on the earth, because we evolved to sustain cooperation, to put us before me" (Hausmann, 2017). It is now time for future organizational cultures and practices to evolve with this cooperative behavior that is formed around collective gain and enlighten, rather than rational self-interests.

Microsoft is a compelling example of how the infusion of coaching and development rather than judging and competition makes for a more effective workplace environment. And, the shareholders have taken notice on the increased performance Microsoft has been able to achieve with its new culture. In the summer of 2002, the share price of Microsoft was approximately $24.50 per share. By 2012, the stock had only grown to approximately $30 per share, which was well below many of its competitors who were capturing large market share with continuous innovations. However, once Microsoft shifted its culture and focus, their performance has skyrocketed. In November 2017, their share prices were trading at $83.74 per share. Organizations seeking to capture market value must reassess their philosophies around performance management in a knowledge driven economy.

How can managers infuse coaching behaviors into their performance management activities? Kim Scott, former executive at Google, recommends that managers do so in a way that cares personally for their employees, while also challenging them directly. Research shows that the majority of learning and development happens on the job, not in classrooms. Therefore managers providing the necessary coaching and feedback are a core part of an employee's ability to learn and upskill in the workplace. SHRM reported that if managers are not actively involved in the coaching behaviors employee development will remain stunted.

6.3.2 Challenges in Performance Development: The Effects of the Halo and Recency Bias

Without having the guardrails in place during the performance development process, biases can get in the way and lead to discrimination at the individual level, causing detrimental impact on organizations in the form of public lawsuits. In 2002, Ford Motor Company paid out $10.5 million to settle two class action suits, which were filed based on age discrimination during the performance rating process. Other organizations, such as GE and Conoco, also faced and settled lawsuits alleging age, race, and gender discrimination during forced performance review processes. So as organizations begin to drop the forced ranking system, there is an "increased burden on managers to make subjective decisions on employee performance" (Stevenson, 2013). This can further expose managers to unconscious biases that may bring preconceptions to the forefront of decision-making. What are the most common biases that emerge as managers assess an employee's performance? While many biases are likely to emerge during human decision-making, two in particular are present in nearly every performance evaluation.

6.3.2.1 Halo (Horn) Effect

One of the more commonly studied biases in talent decision-making relates to the halo or horn effect. The halo effect is a long-recognized tendency for people to assume that because an individual is good at doing a certain activity, they will also be good at doing other nonrelated tasks. On the contrary, once a negative impression has been made it can be difficult for that person to be seen in a positive manner due to the horn effect. The halo effect was first published back in 1920, when a psychologist studying military ratings found that officers generally judged their soldiers as either being all good or all bad across the board (Thorndike, 1920). In fact, very few of the soldiers were rated as being good in one thing but bad in another. For example, if the solider was considered a strong physical performer they likewise rated high in mental abilities, leadership potential, and even cleanliness factors. The halo created by a strength in one area followed through to nearly all other areas of performance ratings.

In business, a common example of the halo effect is when people are promoted to management positions based on their strong technical expertise. It is often wrongfully assumed that these people will also excel at people management. The halo created by their strong technical expertise presents them as a strong people leader as well. Yet, this may not be the case as people management requires a very different skillset than technical expertise. The horn effect can be as equally as strong during performance reviews. A workplace mishap can follow an employee's career around for years. For example, during a recent promotion meeting a manager put forth a strong candidate who was ready for career advancement. However, another manager sitting on the promotion committee rejected the advancement, citing back to an error the employee had made nearly 3 years ago.

How can a manager overcome the halo or horn effect? One of the best ways to combat this bias is through the use of multiple data points. Consider leveraging 360-degree reviews that ask both colleagues, their direct reports, and other leaders across the business to provide feedback. Reviews that are based on multiple stakeholder feedback can help mitigate the impact of the halo or horn effect. In addition, consider leveraging leadership or competency-based assessments that provide additional data points on the performance potential of employees.

6.3.2.2 Recency Bias

Another hurdle that managers are likely to encounter during traditional performance management processes is the influence of the recency bias. The recency bias refers to the tendency for individuals to judge another person's performance based on shorter term or more recent events, which can be to the detriment of longer term performance evaluations. For example, if an employee completes a highly visible project right before the performance review, it is likely that the managers will more strongly take into account this recent project rather than holistically consider the entire year's performance. It is simply harder to accurately remember longer term performance horizons. So, the employee who may have had an exceptionally strong first quarter is likely to be overshadowed by those who have had more recent successes at the time of evaluation. Likewise, the struggling employee who may have had a strong start to the year is more likely to be penalized due to the recency of their lower performance.

How can a manager overcome the recency effect? It is nearly impossible if a manager is evaluating performance only once a year. However, a more frequent and real-time feedback loop can more accurately provide employee performance assessments to ensure their work is not overlooked due to a lapse in time. Many organizations are beginning to transition to quarterly reviews in hopes of overcoming the recency effect during performance evaluations. Indeed, one of the best ways to combat this bias is to give real-time feedback and ensure that at least once a quarter employees are engaged in a performance management activity.

6.3.3 Lessons From the Field: Overcoming Biases at GoDaddy

GoDaddy is example of an organization who was once riddled with biases in the performance management process and faced declining market share in a quickly commoditized product—webhosting. Their public image, in part driven by their edgy super bowl commercials, which were perceived to be racy, and all too often their internal culture reflected exactly that. It was suggested by former employees that alcohol was prevalent throughout the offices and that gossip was commonplace surrounding interoffice affairs (NY Times, 2017). In addition, sexual harassment lawsuits were brought against the company in 2009. GoDaddy had built both an internal and external reputation that fostered many of the stereotypical biases portrayed in their television ads.

However, a new CEO took over GoDaddy in 2013, and set his sights on creating a more inclusive workplace. In fact, he wanted to create one of the most inclusive technology cultures in hopes of fostering greater innovation, improved performance, and an ultimately better brand image in the market. One of the areas the company started to shift was in the way it practiced performance development activities. The company previously relied on the traditional "rank and yank" style of performance management. Yet, as the VP of Inclusion noted, many of the highly rated employees simply fell into the "like me" resemblances of its current leaders. This common bias, known as the *similarity bias*, was also found to emerge during the employee referral process of hiring. Not only do people often hire in their own image, but also promote and reward others in their image as well. These similarities could be demographic similarities, or even found in shared interests or educational backgrounds. GoDaddy determined that a new method was needed in order to surface hidden gems throughout their organization and change their culture around. Rather than rate individuals on their potential, GoDaddy asked both managers and employees to discuss how well an individual's activities, behaviors, and outcomes reflected the company's desired culture of inclusion, performance, and innovation. Yet, to do so would require a new perspective. As the new CEO remarked, "We had to erase the idea that meritocracy is enough." Lori Mackenzie, Executive Director of the Clayman Institute for Gender Research at Stanford, which consulted with GoDaddy said, "Oftentimes, what keeps companies from shifting is believing the existing system is already fair. The CEO is really committed to undermining that."

To begin, GoDaddy reconsidered the way the company viewed leadership. Rather than promote based on the concept of "I" and aggressive behaviors, they began considering "we" and team accomplishments. They found both introverts and women displaying these newly defined leadership capabilities and began obtaining promotions at a faster rate. In addition, GoDaddy overhauled its entire employee evaluation process to include more specific behaviors and not subjective themes. For example, prior evaluations would ask managers to rate their employees' performance on communication. Traditionally, men rose to the top of the ratings. However, when GoDaddy began asking for specific instances of when an employee shared knowledge with others or collaborated with an outside team, women began to more quickly rise to the top of the ratings.

As a senior VP of the company remarked, "You can't change a place just by hiring more women. You have to create a safe space to talk about the assumptions all of us have. You have to work against the biases" (NY Times, 2017). To help combat the biases that arise, GoDaddy often focuses on what it calls micro-inequalities in the workplace. All too often it was extraverted men who were taking charge in meetings and unintentionally crowding out the voices of others in the organization. In addition, it was all too easy for the louder voices in the room to also take the credit for work done by others. GoDaddy realized these moments that reside outside a formal performance development process matter too. So it is striving to make these micro-inequities a thing of the past. The company now encourages project leaders, not just functional leaders, to lead presentations and become more visible throughout the organization. The company also encourages open discussion around biases and ways that they may be presenting themselves during meetings and projects. These improvements have allowed the company to expand broadly into global markets and innovate at faster speeds.

As with Microsoft, GoDaddy has reaped financial benefits for its changes. The CEO was able to take the company public after the cultural overhaul and has more than doubled its company share value in 2 years. In addition, revenues increased 15% in 2016 to $1.8 billion. Today, the company is valued at nearly $7 billion and a well-respected brand both in the technology industry as well as public eye. The CEO acknowledges there is still a long way to go, but believes the company is now on a path that recognizes the common pitfalls that biases can bring to organizational performance.

6.4 SUMMARY

Coaching behaviors are instrumental toward the continued building of social capital throughout the firm. In particular, managers who are able to leverage these behaviors promote higher exchanges with their employees. To do so requires an orientation toward learning goals and a more intentional shift from traditional performance management to a supportive development approach. Here are four ways that today's managers can leverage the principles of behavioral science to build expertise throughout their team.

1. *Use performance goals with caution, and when in doubt, leverage learning-oriented goals.* A learning goal helps bring knowledge acquisition to the forefront and fosters greater collaboration and knowledge sharing across teams. The individual is much more likely to utilize strategic thinking techniques, while also exploring new ways of approaching a problem. Not only that, but learning goals also allows employees to be more to receiving feedback. It is also much easier to tie back one's intrinsic need of growth to learning goals.
2. *Place an emphasis on the means of goal attainment.* The how should be just as important as the outcome or what. Be aware of the risky and

unethical behaviors that may arise when employees seek after high stretch goals. They may compete rather than coordinate with others throughout the organization. Much attention should be given to the processes and means by which employees seek after their performance outcomes. The journey should be just as important as the final outcome.

3. *Shift from a performance management system to a performance development mindset.* Performance management systems seek to monitor and reward high-performing individuals and punish low performers through extrinsic means. However, a performance development mindset leverages and fulfills individual intrinsic needs by seeking to align their own individual growth with the organizations. Performance development places the emphasis on learning, knowledge sharing, and building expertise. It sees organizational performance as a means to a higher end—human development.
4. *Create a supportive and inclusive environment that fosters collaborative teaming and not competition toward higher levels of performance.* One of the dangers of relying too heavily on stretch performance goals and strong performance management systems is that it creates a highly competitive culture. Rather than having individuals within the same firm compete against one another during performance reviews, place an emphasis on the behaviors and individuals who make others around them better. Reward collaboration and teamwork not simply individual performance.

REFERENCES

Amabile, T. M., & Kramer, S. J. (2011). The power of small wins. *Harvard Business Review, 89* (5), 70–80.

Ames, D., Maissen, L. B., & Brockner, J. (2012). The role of listening in interpersonal influence. *Journal of Research in Personality, 46*, 345–349.

Anderson, J. R. (1982). Acquisition of a cognitive skill. *Psychological Review, 89*(4), 369–406.

Baruch, Y. (2006). Career development in organizations and beyond: Balancing traditional and contemporary viewpoints. *Human Resource Management Review, 16*, 125–138.

Bennett, D. (2009). Ready, aim... fail: Why setting goals can backfire. *The Boston Globe*, C1.

Branham, L. (2005). *The 7 hidden reasons employees leave*. New York, NY: AMACOM, a division of American Management Association.

Button, S. B., Mathieu, J. E., & Zajac, D. M. (1996). Goal orientation in organizational research: A conceptual and empirical foundation. *Organizational Behavior and Human Decision Processes, 67*(1), 26–48.

Carver, C. S., & Scheier, M. F. (2001). *On the self-regulation of behavior*. Cambridge: Cambridge University Press.

Chen, S., Huang, K., & Lao, B. (2015). Is earnings guidance associated with less firm innovation? Available at <http://papers.ssrn.com/sol3/papers.cfm?abstract_id = 2546827>. Working paper, University of Texas and Florida International University.

Cianci, A. M., Schaubroeck, J. M., & McGill, G. A. (2010). Achievement goals, feedback, and task performance. *Human Performance, 23*(2), 131–154.

Cote, J., & Gilbert, W. (2009). An integrative definition of coaching effectiveness and expertise. *International Journal of Sports Science & Coaching, 4*(3), 307–323.

Dahling, J. J., Taylor, S. R., Chau, S. L., & Dwight, S. R. (2015). Does coaching matter? A multilevel model linking managerial coaching skill and frequency to sales goal attainment. *Personnel Psychology*, *69*(4), 863–894.

Dodge, L. (2014). <https://neuroleadership.com/portfolio-items/how-microsoft-transformed-their-performance-management-system-a-case-study/>.

Dishneau, D. (1992). *Sears admits mistakes, takes workers off commission*. The Associated Press, June 22.

Duhigg, C. (2017). If GoDaddy can turn the corner on sexism, who can't? *New York Times*. July 23, <https://www.nytimes.com/2017/07/23/business/godaddy-tv-ads-sexism.html?ref=business&_r=0>.

Dunn, M. (2009). Leadership coaching: The developmental power of the one-on-one. *Employee Relations Today*, *35*, 25–29. Available from https://doi.org/10.1002/ert.20222.

Dweck, C. S. (1986). Motivational processes affecting learning. *American Psychologist*, *41*(10), 1040–1048.

Dweck, C. S. (2007). *Mindset: The new psychology of success*. New York, NY: Ballantine Books Trade Paperback Edition.

Engler, S. (2014). *5 Solutions to performance management challenges*. The Corporate Executive Board. Retrieved from <https://www.cebglobal.com/blogs/5-reasons-your-performance-management-is-a-failure/>.

Galinsky, A., Seiden, V., Kim, P., & Medvec, V. (2002). The dissatisfaction of having your first offer accepted: The role of counterfactual thinking in negotiations. *Personality and Social Psychology Bulletin*, *28*(2), 271–283.

Gavin, D. (2013). How Google sold its engineers on management. *Harvard Business Review*, December 2013 issue.

Hausmann, R. (2017). *The moral identity of homo economicus*. Retrieved from <https://www.project syndicate.org/commentary/homo-economicus-moral-psychology-revolution-by-ricardo-hausmann-2017-11/english>.

Knight, D., Durham, C., & Locke, Edwin (2001). The relationship of team goals, incentives, and efficacy to strategic risk, tactical implementation, and performance. *Academy of Management Journal*, *44*, 326–338. Available from https://doi.org/10.2307/3069459.

Leadership I.Q. (2014). *Optimal hours with the boss study: North America research overview*. <https://cdn.shopify.com/s/files/1/0860/7364/files/Leadership_IQ_Whitepaper_Optimal_Hours_with_the_Boss_Study_2014.pdf?4279660079233060856>.

Lips-Wiersma, M., & Hall, D. T. (2007). Organizational career development is not dead: A case study on managing the new career during organizational change. *Journal of Organizational Behavior*, *28*, 771–792.

Locke, E. A., & Latham, G. P. (2006). New directions in goal-setting theory. *Current Directions in Psychological Science*, *15*(5), 265–268.

Mitchell, T. R., & Silver, W. S. (1990). Individual and group goals when workers are interdependent: Effects on task strategies and performance. *Journal of Applied Psychology*, *75*(2), 185–193.

Mitchell, T. R., & Daniels, D. (2003). Motivation. In W. C. Borman, D. R. Ilgen, & R. J. Klimoski (Eds.), *Handbook of psychology, Vol. 12: Industrial organizational psychology* (pp. 225–254). New York: Wiley & Sons, Inc.

Monahan, K., Chmiola, A., & Roos, L. (2017). How effective leaders drive digital change. MIT Sloan Management Review. Retrieved from <https://sloanreview.mit.edu/article/how-effective-leaders-drive-digital-change/>.

Monahan, K. (2018). (forthcoming). *Meaning in the workplace: A mixed-methods investigation.* Under review.

Ordonez, L. D., Schwitzer, M. E., Galinsky, A. D., & Bazerman, M. H. (2009). Goals gone wild: The systematic side effects of overprescribing goal setting. *Academy of Management Perspectives*, 6–16.

Parker (2013) < http://fortune.com/2013/11/18/microsoft-ge-and-the-futility-of-ranking-employees/ >.

Payne, S. C., Youngcourt, S. S., & Beaubien, J. M. (2007). A meta-analytic examination of the goal orientation nomological net. *Journal of Applied Psychology*, *92*(1), 128–150.

Rock, D. (2016). *The neuroscience of transforming performance and optimizing leadership.* NeuroLeadership Institute, [Webinar].

Rock, D., Davis, J., & Jones, B. (2014). Kill your performance ratings. *Strategy + Business*, *76* (Autumn). Retrieved from <https://www.strategy-business.com/article/00275>.

Rogers, R. W. (2004). Realizing the promise of performance management. DDI Press, Pittsburg, PA.

Scott, K. (2017). *Radical candor: Be a kick-ass boss without losing your humanity.* New York: St Martin's Press.

Scullen, S. E., Mount, M. K., & Goff, M. (2000). Understanding the latent structure of job performance ratings. *Journal of Applied Psychology*, *85*(6), 956–970.

Segers, J., & Inceoglu, I. (2012). Exploring supportive and developmental career management through business strategies and coaching. *Human Resource Management*, *51*(1), 99–120.

Segers, J., Vloeberghs, D., Henderickx, E., & Inceoglu, I. (2011). Structuring and understanding the coaching industry: The coaching cube. *Academy of Management Learning & Education*, *10*, 204–221.

Simons, D. J., & Chabris, C. F. (1999). Gorillas in our midst: sustained inattentional blindness for dynamic events. *Perception*, *28*, 1059–1074.

Staw, B. M., & Boettger, R. D. (1990). Task revision A neglected form of work performance. *Academy of Management Journal*, *33*, 534–559. Available from https://doi.org/10.2307/256580.

Stevenson (2013) < http://fortune.com/2013/11/18/microsoft-ge-and-the-futility-of-ranking-employees/ >.

Thorndike, E. L. (1920). A constant error in psychological ratings. *Journal of Applied Psychology*, *4*(1), 25–29.

Valcour, M. (2014). You can't be a great manager if you're not a good coach. *Harvard Business Review*. <https://hbr.org/2014/07/you-cant-be-a-great-manager-if-youre-not-a-good-coach>.

Weintraub, J. R., & Hunt, J. M. (2015). 4 reasons managers should spend more time on coaching. *Harvard Business Review*. <https://hbr.org/2015/05/4-reasons-managers-should-spend-more-time-on-coaching>.

Wright, P. M., George, J. M., Farnsworth, S. R., & McMahan, G. C. (1993). Productivity and extra-role behavior: The effects of goals and incentives on spontaneous helping. *Journal of Applied Psychology*, *78*(3), 374–381.

FURTHER READING

Stern, L. R. (2004). Executive coaching: A working definition. *Consulting Psychology Journal: Practice and Research*, *56*, 154–162.

Chapter 7

Empowering: Building Reciprocity and Trust

7.1 THE REALITIES OF POWER IN THE WORKPLACE

One of the troubling philosophies found in the traditional style of management, which still resides in many organizations today is that managerial control is one of the best tools to maximize efficiency in the workplace. Many of today's leading MBA programs still advocate and teach that controlling strategic human resources is an effective behavior of management, which is based on the foundational assumptions of rational economic theory (University of Minnesota Libraries, 2017). Controlling behaviors consider people as strategic resources to be leveraged towards maximizing profitable ends, rather than as human beings who seek development and advancement through their work. As a result, the very consideration of controlling another person rests on the assumption that people will inherently deviate from quality work and must be monitored. In addition, controlling behaviors assume that corrective action be taken when stated performance standards are not achieved. While many of the leading scholars who advocate for controlling behaviors presume they should not be done in a manipulative manner, it is nonetheless implied that managers hold ultimate power in the workplace based on their position within the firm and should seek to control employees who may otherwise deviate from the interests of the firm.

This traditional style of management infers an elementary understanding of power, which leverages immature models of decision-making to influence employee behavior in the workplace. For example, controlling behaviors often lead to a micromanaging style of management, which seeks to closely monitor employee activities at the expense of their autonomy. All of the manager's influence rests solely on his position of power or ability to leverage extrinsic rewards, or even punishments onto others. As noted throughout the industrial era, controlling behaviors usually led to taking knowledge away from workers, deskilling employees, and ultimately excluding a diversity of thought in favor of achieving repetitive and predictable outcomes. While many traditional management scholars and practitioners point back to the industrial and manufacturing era when predictive quality outcomes were key to capturing competitive advantage as a justification for controlling

How Behavioral Economics Influences Management Decision-Making.
DOI: https://doi.org/10.1016/B978-0-12-813531-0.00007-8

behaviors, today's leaders should consider the management style and performance differences observed between the 1980s Toyota and American automobile manufacturers (see Chapter 3: Exploring Management Alternatives With a Behavioral Economics Lens case study). Toyota credited much of their success based on their ability to empower its workforce, including those completing repetitive tasks, rather than attempting to simply control behaviors. The focus and emphasis was placed on continuous learning and skill development throughout empowering management behaviors, even for low-skilled workers. And, their company's performance reaped dividends from this management approach. Conversely, in the American manufacturing firms, controlling behaviors often resulted in the very opposite outcomes, including lower productivity and financial performance returns.

Today's managers who seek to create competitive advantage through creativity, knowledge sharing, diversity, collaboration, and higher levels of cognitive thinking can no longer rely on controlling behaviors for doing so. Controlling behaviors often lead to a disengaged workforce who can feel micro-managed or left out of the decision-making process. Gallup research, which has measured employee engagement for nearly 20 years has reported that high disengagement levels have held steady since their measurements began. Unfortunately, more and more employees continue to be actively disengaged from their work (only 32% engagement reported in the U.S. workforce and 16% globally). And, the narrative does not appear to be changing anytime soon. Gallup is forecasting the same levels of disengagement in the coming years. The disconnect created in the employee experience when operating under managers who exert controlling behaviors may help explain why so many employees remain disengaged from their work.

Yet, consider the idiosyncrasy encompassed in this disengagement narrative. As discovered in Chapter 1, The Changing Nature of Work: Macrolevel Considerations for Managers, today's workplaces are made of up the most economically "agreeable" jobs ever done in human history (Gordon, 2016). People are working more comfortably than ever before and reporting less working hours. Mind Gym (2017) reports that people are spending up to nearly 26% less time at work than they did 50 years ago. But, there is a grave disconnect between today's more agreeable jobs and the level of engagement one would anticipate accompanying this work. It is argued that much of this disconnect arises from the "lasting identity with Tayloristic direct control (management behaviors), which often undermines the potential success of empowerment" (Lincoln, Travers, Ackers, & Wilkinson, 2002, p. 285). Additionally, a shift is occurring in support of flatter organizational structures, where much of the direct hierarchal control is removed from management. Therefore managers who were taught to control strategic human resources will have a hard time doing so without the power that once accompanied their positional status in the organization. A leader of a large organization recently remarked,

I now realize after a couple of painful years, I can no longer make anyone do anything in a flat organization. I can only ask them and try to influence their buy-in by also meeting one of their needs in the process. I am now forced to create reciprocal relationships if I want to get work done. I can only use influential power, not positional power in this type of environment.

As this leader's remark suggests, power dynamics are shifting in today's workplaces and simply training tomorrow's leaders to exert control over strategic human resources will do no good. Behavioral science continues to offer newfound insights to unlock greater levels of employee engagement (see Fig. 7.1). Rational economic theory supposes that employees must be controlled through extrinsic levers, while behavioral theory suggests that employees should be empowered through intrinsic means to perform at their best. This difference in theory can best be understood in how these different bodies of literature consider the role of power in relationships. Rational economics considers it a tool to be leveraged towards compliance, while behavioral theory suggests power is best utilized when shared. As a result, one of the keys to unlocking employee engagement in today's workforce is by *empowering* individual and team success. Empowering behaviors fuel an employee's inherent need for autonomy and cooperation. Supporting one's autonomy through the coaching behaviors discussed in Chapter 6, Coaching: Goal-Setting and Performance Management ensures that autonomous employees are equipped with the necessary knowledge and skills to make decisions that further advance the development of the organization.

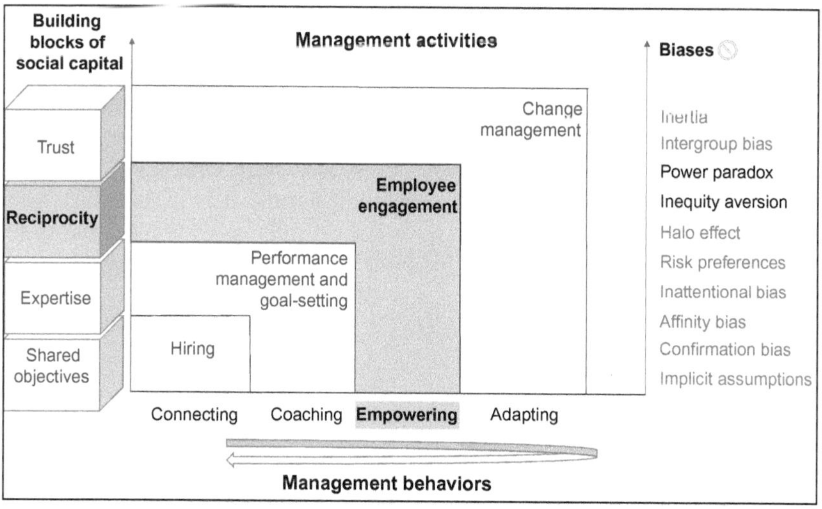

FIGURE 7.1 Empowerment management framework.

7.1.1 Controlling Management Behaviors Rely on an Imbalance of Power in the Workplace

Power, along with affiliation and achievement, is one of the three most basic human needs that McClelland (1988) unpacked in his theory of learned needs. Power is defined as the ability to exert influence over another. According to the theory of learned needs, people are complex and hold varying degrees of these three needs based on their experiences and cultures. The extent to which one is motivated depends in part by their need for power, achievement, or affiliation. The need for power can best be explained by one's need to have influence over the actions of another. Within the workplace power informs, creates or constrains behaviors, provides structure, and establishes operating norms in organizations. Power explains how work is actually done in the workplace. In organizations where power distance is high, such as in traditional hierarchies, there is an accepted understanding of the unequal distribution of power, which resides between leaders and staff. Work is accomplished from a top-down decision-making model, with staff at the lower levels simply responding to the orders given by leadership. Managers use controlling behaviors in these types of environments to ensure work is completed according to a leader's standards.

Scientific management has operated from an unwavering acceptance of power inequity. The aim is to move knowledge away from the worker and into the hands of managers. Taylor, himself, remarked near the end of his life, "I have found it necessary almost invariably to talk but little to men, to go right ahead and make them do what I wanted them to do" (Hoopes, 2003). A strong power distance promotes this mindset of a controlling style of management. It treats employees more like children who have not yet fully developed their cognitive reasoning rather than as adults. For example, a controlling management style can be illustrated in the way parents remark to a child asking for an explanation once an instruction has been given, "Because, I said so, that's why." This statement may then be followed up with, "And if you don't, you can go to timeout." This strong power distance between parent and child does not allow for questioning and leverages rewards and punishments to teach behavioral norms. It is a style that may work well for raising children who have not yet fully reached their ability to cognitively reason, but much less likely to be effective on capable adults in highly cognitive roles.

7.1.2 Power is Relational

It is important to understand that power is not necessarily something that one possesses, but emerges within relationships. Behavioral scholars argue that power surfaces in our interactions with each other and ultimately manifests itself in the actions and responses evoked during the interaction. Power then is not an entity, rather a perception of who holds influence and control based on continued relational interactions, experiences, and consequences (Elias, 1939). Vince (2014) further described power as created and reinforced through emotions, language, status, patterns of blame, and attempts at exerting control. As result, Fleming and Spicer (2004) remarked that power is the implicit understanding, which defines how we experience ourselves in relationship to others. To understand how power works, Frosh (2003) argued that one has to understand both the psychological components, which are formed based on sociological dynamics, and the social aspects, which are informed by one's cognitions. This is in part, what Stacey (2003) meant when he stated that power exists in the act of human relation between two individuals, which either enables or constrains the ability of their interaction and continued development. Strong power variances between individuals will directly lead to less engagement and a restriction of new information emerging during interactions. As behavioral science studies have demonstrated, people will self-censor or exhibit group thinking if a group leader holds too much power, for fear of speaking up. Therefore, the ability of new information to emerge and be freely shared is restricted in asymmetrical power relationships, which controlling behaviors from leaders further create.

Additionally, controlling another person takes away a key motivator to employee engagement—the freedom to choose and feel a sense of responsibility for outcomes. As Bion (1961) remarked, "we are mindful that each time we solve a problem we deprive others of a chance to solve it for themselves. Controlling behaviors can unintentionally take away an employee's sense of pride and responsibility for organizational outcomes and thereby stunt performance. Each time we interrupt the action, we preempt someone else's acting" (p. 158). The majority of workers want to experience a sense of freedom and pride in their work. Controlling leaders directly rob individuals from experiencing the sense of pride that comes from having the freedom to influence an outcome. Weiner's (1979) workplace psychology research found that, "an inability to claim responsibility for (employee) outcomes deprives individuals of many of the benefits associated with success" (p. 490). An employee who achieves success and attributes it directly back to their own work experiences much more pride and efficacy to reach higher levels of performance. The freedom to choose and feel responsible for outcomes are the very things that are necessary to fuel engagement in the workplace.

To summarize, power in and of itself, is neither positive or negative. But it is how power is leveraged, and to what end, which makes power either beneficial or harmful to others. Nonetheless, power is inherently needed in all organizational life in order for work to be accomplished. It would be foolish to fully remove power from leadership and remains essential to effective management and engagement of the workforce. However, there may be a better way to leverage power over simply resorting to controlling others through hierarchal position that will engage today's employees.

7.1.3 Five Forms of Power in Leadership Positions: Not All are Created Equally

Social psychologists French and Raven (1959) identified five forms of power that leaders display within organizations (see Fig. 7.2: Five forms of power). Not all of these forms of power are created equal in the formation of social capital. Some styles will diminish the ability of people to engage in healthy relationships, while others will enable effective human relations in the workplace. While formal styles of power have traditionally been leveraged in both political and organizational settings, there exists compelling evidence, which suggests that a softer, or informal, style of power to influence others may be more beneficial to organizational level outcomes (Nye, 1990). For example, hard power, which overly relies on tangible sources of influence, such as through rewards or threats, has been previously linked to negative job satisfaction, an increase in burnout and absentee rates, lower productivity, and ultimately lower self-confidence at work. Whereas softer forms of power, as those found in referent and expert styles of power, which influences others through intangibles such as trust, empathy, or expertise, are linked to employees experiencing higher levels of job satisfaction, performance, and greater confidence in their work. The fundamental problem with leveraging hard power in organizations is that it arouses fear, which drawing from the behavioral research discussed in Chapter 3, Exploring Management Alternatives With a Behavioral Economics Lens, hinders one's ability to be creative and effectively collaborate with others in the workplace. In addition, behavioral research shows that employees who work under fear will end up causing more harmful consequences for the organization over the long term.

Consider the following scenario to illustrate this point. Bridgette was an emerging leader, who oversaw an operations group within a financial services firm and seemed to have the ability to connect with all of her employees. She displayed courageous empathy towards her staff by connecting

Type of power	Behaviors used	Ability to create social capital
Reward power	Leverages extrinsic rewards in exchange for compliance	Low
Coercive power	Uses fear and punishment to ensure compliance	Very low
Legitimate power	Uses status and position to influence the behavior of others	Low
Expert power	Uses their knowledge and experience to guide others	High
Referent power	Influences others based on respect, admiration, friendship, and loyalty	Very high

FIGURE 7.2 Five forms of power.

personally with their needs. In the office, Bridgette was often seen hosting educational sessions or handing out candies to keep employees motivated during the holidays. She had an open-door policy and did not position herself as above her staff, but rather as working right alongside them. She led almost entirely from a form of referent power that leveraged trust and empathy to influence others. Even her department's employee engagement results were strong year over year in a function that historically achieved large levels of turnover and absenteeism. Bridgette was able to keep employees more engaged and longer in their positions than her predecessors.

But, Bridgette recognized that her ability to solely manage her growing staff of nearly 100 employees was limited, so she hired a well-known tenured operations leader, Katie, to help manage the group. Katie thought Bridgette was spending too much time connecting and coaching staff and not enough time monitoring and enforcing quality. Katie led by her positional power created a strong power distance between herself and the staff. While quality temporarily increased, longer-term employee engagement began to suffer. Turnover began to increase and absenteeism became a growing problem. Yet, Katie began to double-down on her leadership style, as the decreasing engagement and lack of prosocial behaviors, only reinforced her perception that people needed to be closely monitored and controlled. She created more layers within the department and asked her managers to adopt a zero-tolerance policy for errors. Fear and distrust eroded the years of social capital that once powered the team's success.

A department that once thrived now resembled the same characteristics common in Taylor's firms in the 1920s—a highly short-term efficient, but miserable workplace. And, a surprising downstream consequence that had firm wide impact began to emerge. The operations function had been one of the largest recruiting pockets for other functions in the firm. Because of the strong training and connections Bridgette provided to her staff, her employees often moved onto other parts of the organization and became successful contributors in new functions. This reinforced a positive internal talent development narrative that further fueled employee engagement across the firm. But, now with turnover increasing, employees were looking to leave the firm, not grow within it. In particular, the finance and sales teams began to struggle finding internal talent and had to turn to the external market, which was both costly and less effective due to the amount of training that was now required to bring employees up to speed. While one quality metric increased in the short-term, longer-term consequences eclipsed the efficiency gain. This story illustrates a compelling point. While controlling behaviors may lead to short-term quality and efficiency increases, their long-term impact may be much more harmful to broader firm wide initiatives in surprising ways.

Empirical research supports the findings discussed in this illustrative example. Consider the following studies that cut across industries and context. The Ken Blanchard companies sought to determine the most effective style of power to engage a workforce. Their study analyzed data from over 650 employees to determine which form of power was most beneficial to employee engagement and performance. It was found that referent (beta = 0.367) and expert power (beta = 0.357) were by far the most effective at positively engaging the workforce. Both legitimate and coercive power, which had strong multicollinearity, led to negative emotions in the workplace and active disengagement. In particular, coercive power was significantly related to a lack of prosocial behaviors and intent to exert effort. Reward power (beta = 0.073) was positively related to engagement, but had a much lesser effect compared to referent and expert styles of power. Rewards are still a powerful motivator, but should be used sparingly based on their capability to crowd out more meaningful motivators, such as trust, empathy, and expertise. As this study suggests, most people prefer to follow leaders who exhibit strong expertise and empowering behaviors. Therefore the traditional command and control styles are likely to evoke negative emotions and spark disengagement throughout the workforce.

Other studies conducted have sought to determine the impact empowering leadership styles would have on overall medical team performance. In many medical environments, there is a strong hierarchy between doctors and their medical teams. As a result, less empowered staff, such as nurses or medical assistants, do not usually question a doctor's authority, even if they sense a concern. This strong power distance can create devastating patient outcomes, as less empowered employees are less likely to report adverse events. Reporting adverse events is one of the very first and necessary steps in identifying and rectifying patient safety outcomes. However, two studies confirm similar results (Appelbaum et al., 2016; Hanna, 2014). Medical teams working for doctors who exerted formalized power, which created high power distance, were much more susceptible to making errors and the doctors were less likely to find out about adverse events, ultimately lowering the quality of care a patient received. As this medical study shows, trying to exert control and influence through authoritative position can backfire. Research continues to show that people are less likely to share information under command and control styles of leadership as shown within medical hierarchies. The results of this study should raise concern for any organization still leveraging fear-based systems with strong hierarchies as information flow and performance is often hindered.

One last study to consider, regarding the use of power in organizations, as it relates to manufacturing. A team of researchers examined the productivity of 308 manufacturing companies, over a period of 22 years, to determine the consequences of empowering leadership behaviors on company performance. Traditionally, it has been assumed that leadership behaviors more commonly associated with total quality control will lead to better company performance in the manufacturing context (Birdi et al., 2008). Informal styles of power were measured assessing the level of empowerment, training, and team-based work employees experienced in their workplaces. Operational management practices were measured using the adoption of total quality management, just-in-time management, implementation of advanced manufacturing technologies, and supply-chain partnering. It was hypothesized that each of these management styles – one leveraging formal power through control, while the other leveraging informal power through trust and training, would lead to higher company performance. The researchers were surprised to report that their hypothesis of operational management techniques was not supported. In other words, managers who practiced more formalized operational techniques did not experience a lift in productivity. In addition, company performance was not found to correlate back to traditional operational management behaviors. However, the researchers did find a statistically significant relationship between empowerment and company performance. The researchers reported that employee empowerment and training led to a 9% increase in value added per employee. This finding that "softer" management behaviors compared to "harder" styles of management directly led to increased company performance has found much support within the strategic human resource management literature, suggesting that engagement, training, and teamwork are all vital components of competitive advantage for a firm. Softer forms of power may have always benefited organizational performance, but it is now becoming more commonly recognized and expressed as behavioral sciences continues to shed new light on management. Empowering employees may unlock the key towards competitive advantage for organizations operating in flatter structures and more complex environments, which require higher order cognitive thinking and collaboration to achieve its ends.

7.2 EMPOWERING EMPLOYEES FOR COMPETITIVE ADVANTAGE

Empowerment is ultimately experienced during relationships whereby the person with power, utilizes it to share resources, information, and actively engages in the development of others. As Lincoln et al. (2002) noted, the etymology of empowerment reflects that the, "acknowledgment of power to achieve an end rather than as an end in itself" (p. 273). Management power should be used to create and develop efficacy in others, not take it away, which many formalized styles of power end up doing. Softer forms of power, either through expertise or relationship building, allows managers to more freely use power as a means, not an end. Empowerment should lead to higher skill development, knowledge sharing, and shared responsibility between a manager and their team for organizational outcomes. Empowered employees possess the knowledge and skills, as well as the responsibility, to successfully achieve the shared objectives they were hired into the organization to achieve.

The very antithesis to empowerment is a sense of powerlessness. Managers empower their staff through the removal of organizational conditions that foster powerlessness, such as a lack of information, development, or inclusion necessary to attain success (Conger and Kanuungo, 1998). Often, well-meaning managers create a sense of powerlessness by overstepping and involving themselves in another's work. This over involvement shifts the responsibility for an outcome from the individual back to the leader. As a result, powerless individuals may experience impulses towards dishonesty, stealing, and an overall lack of loyalty towards the organization (Charness, 2000). Therefore, part of the empowerment process involves what Peters (1988) described as the difference between "letting go" and "really letting go". Really letting go involves removing oneself both physically and psychologically from the task, so the employee is in control, yet impressing upon the employee the high standards and efficacy required to do the task well. Empowerment allows the employee to drive towards the outcome, while managers providing the support and development needed to be successful.

Empowerment is best realized when employees have the necessary skills, knowledge, and psychological safety to bring their best to work each day. Managers who are actively engaged in coaching behaviors are already providing the necessary opportunities for employees to develop their skills and acquire the right knowledge to do their jobs well. Acquiring skills and knowledge, while relying on others, tends to be an individually experienced phenomenon. Empowering management behaviors must now foster the inclusive environment for individuals to apply their skills while not believing they will reap negative group-level consequences for doing so (Edmondson, 2014). Managers do this by fostering *psychological safety* amongst its team members—an experienced group phenomenon. Psychological safety is simply the belief that an individual can share their skills and knowledge with others in the group without fear of repercussion. Within every relationship and team a psychological contract exists, which comprises of the often-unspoken expectations that exists between each other (Morrison, 1994). Psychological safety is present when the unspoken expectations manifest themselves in feelings of trust and respect between individuals.

A climate of empowerment recognizes that each individual member brings something unique and necessary to achieve organizational level goals, and as a result provides the necessary platforms for individuals to express their ideas. Empowering individuals to speak up and have a voice in the discussion allows them to feel respected and valued, which further ignites their engagement at work. Psychological safety is best experienced in low-power distance relationships and inclusive environments. Managers who lead from referent or expert power are much more likely to create psychologically safe environments for employees to actively engage with others in the workplace. Managers who create high-power distance environments through coercive or legitimate positions of power are less able to engage the workforce in a way that adds value to the organization. This is because formalized power usage leaves little room for individuals to experience the necessary safety to express themselves. Much like the medical team studies showed, doctors who distanced themselves from their staff, were much less likely to know and react to adverse events. A lack of psychological safety can lead to not only a disengaged workforce, but a less valuable organization.

Managers who empower their teams through active skill development and create a psychologically safe environment for individuals to express their knowledge, are much more likely to experience better organizational level outcomes. Consider the following findings from research on empowerment:

- *Empowered employees are more likely to feel a sense of personal responsibility for their work and take ownership of outcomes.* Employees who sense responsibility assume ownership of the outcome and are much more likely to attend, care, and ensure positive results, than those who are simply perceived as following orders. In addition, responsible employees are much more likely to care for others in the workplace and exhibit prosocial behaviors (Weiner, 1979; Monahan, 2015).
- *Empowering others reduces the costs of supervision and other indirect costs.* Monitoring employees is costly and shows up in hidden ways, such as through employee quit rates, lower performance, and higher training costs. A research study that examined a national representation of call centers found that both turnover rates were lower and sales growth was higher in companies where managers practiced empowered behaviors (Batt, 2001). Empowering employees with autonomy, supporting with skill development, and creating collaborative opportunities can save firms money in the long run.
- *Empowered employees are more likely to find innovative solutions.* Research shows that employees who are given autonomy are much more likely to find new ways of solving a problem, leveraging a wider range of critical thinking. This not only allows for greater individual skill development, but the organization also advances as its collective workforce begins to develop and share their new knowledge and skills throughout the firm workforce (Leach, Wall, & Jackson, 2003).
- *Empowered employees focus more on their own skill development.* Employees who find themselves in empowering environments are more likely to further develop their skillset, which leads to higher quality organizational level outcomes, innovations and a greater ability to adapt to change in the most cost-effective way (Senge, 1990).
- *Empowered employees experience higher performance as a result of reduced anxiety and enhanced self-efficacy.* Empowerment is built on the

building blocks of trust and reciprocity and as a result lowers an employee's anxiety by mitigating fear, while also equipping them with the necessary efficacy to do the job well (Parker and Price, 1994). Empowered employees experience positive emotions towards the organization, which in turn leads to greater commitment and likelihood of displaying discretionary efforts, leading to higher organizational level performance outcomes.

- *Empowered employees are more likely to share knowledge and collaborate with others.* One of the greatest impacts of empowerment is that it encourages employees to openly share knowledge and collaborate with others. In a research study of 64 work groups comprised of 537 members, empowerment and psychological safety directly led to increased knowledge sharing amongst team members (Wei-Li & Yi-Chi, 2017). In controlling environments where everyone may be looking over their back and keeping information relatively close, empowering environments free people to trust each other and proactively seek out connections with others.

It is important to note that managers who empower their employees are not practicing a laissez faire style of leadership. Rather, the process of empowering requires high managerial involvement as autonomous employees rely on supportive environments to experience their greatest levels of performance. Patterson, West, and Wall (2004) found that simply empowering employees without providing the right training, development, and collaborative environment can lead to disastrous outcomes and even chaos. Therefore, high involvement management prioritizes the empowerment of employees and considers employee development a key component to organizational performance (Lawler, 1986). High involvement managers actively connect, coach, and empower individuals to succeed in organizational environments. Empowering and high involvement management can only occur once trust and reciprocity, two of the key building blocks of social capital, accumulates.

7.2.1 Behaviors Leaders Use to Empower Others

Empowering employees can take much time and commitment on the part of managers. As noted previously, empowerment is commonly associated as an outcome of high involvement management. As managers begin to contemplate where this additional time will come from, Wellins, Byham, and Wilson (1991) advocate that managers should actively seek to transition any time spent on directing and controlling behaviors, which can take up a considerable amount of time, to facilitating and empowering behaviors. The following are key behaviors that managers can actively practice, which empowers their workforce towards higher levels of performance.

1. *Actively share information.* Wellins et al. (1991) research suggests that managers should be spending a significant portion of their time, sharing knowledge with employees. Managers who practice effective communication, such as openly communicating financial results, the firm's strategy, and setting clear goals are much more likely to empower employees to achieve more within the organization (Avolio et al., 2004). Often employees may simply feel left in the dark on where the firm is headed, which dims their own vision on how their efforts fit within the boarder organization. Managers who empower have mastered the art of letting go of information.
2. *Develop their own moral competency.* In the process of empowering, mistakes and conflict will at some point be experienced. Managers who develop a strong moral competency, defined as the ability to handle conflict and resolve problems based on moral principles through deliberating and discussing, rather than by force, are more likely to effectively reap the benefits associated with empowerment. Empirical research by Kim and Kim (2012) found that a leader's moral competence was positively associated with employee empowerment and performance. The higher the manager's moral competency, the more likely their staff achieved better results in the workplace. Managers who try to offer empowerment without the necessary character to back it up runs the risk and "probability that empowerment will be experienced and assessed as a patronizing act of false charity bestowed upon employees" (Willmott, 1995, p. 93). Managers high in moral competency have mastered the art of letting go of failures and pushing towards creative resolutions in the midst of conflict.
3. *Practice humility.* Hoopes (2003) discovered that one of the most necessary traits of effective leaders in power is humility, which combats the inherent thorns that arise in positions of power. Claxton, Owen, and Sadler-Smith (2015) argue that hubris, or excessive pride, is one of the chief perils confronting leaders in powerful positions. Leaders who rely on harder forms of power, such as those that come from position, rely on their hierarchical position to influence others. This can come across as arrogant and assertive towards those they try to influence. Bennis (1979) discounted power that came from fear, irrationality, or coercion, arguing it leads to resisting change and dehumanized irrational conflicts. However, humility allows leaders to lead from a position of empathy and trust, which promote rationality, knowledge sharing, and collaboration. Shaw (2002) eloquently explains humility as the acknowledgment that, "The whole precedes the parts...I cannot be me without you" (p. 156). Leaders who lead with humility recognize the interdependency their own power has with others. Employees who see managers willing to admit to mistakes and lead alongside, not over others, are much more likely to be willing to exert more efforts towards organizational outcomes. Managers who lead with humility have practiced the art of letting go of position.

7.3 BIASES EMERGE IN THE PERCEPTION OF POWER

While power is an inherent need that many people do strive for, it comes with a host of complications when exercised in the workplace. Hoopes (2003) describes the paradox of management power in American society as such.

> *Management power is an American paradox, a vital necessity of our economic well-being and an obvious contradiction of our democratic values. . .Free people want to feel as free at work as they do elsewhere in society. As much as we can, we ignore the fact that we check many of our freedoms at the workplace door. (p. 2–3).*

Yet, in order for organizations to operate effectively, management power is needed, but should be exercised with much humility and moral competency. But, two biases pose challenges for even the best intended managers looking to use power, regardless of its form, to influence others. These biases may be two of the greatest inhibitors for the successful building of social capital, which hinges on both, a sense of reciprocity and trust.

7.3.1 Inequity Social Aversion Bias: Power That Promotes Inequality Will Lead to Irrationality

One of the biggest inhibitors at this stage in the process of building social capital through effective behavioral management is the perception that a manager's power is being used to give preferential treatment to others in the workplace. The behavioral economics literature refers to this as the *inequity social aversion bias*. Humans are wired to strongly prefer equality and avoid inequality, and when inequality is perceived, it brings a host of irrational behavior. Payne (2017) writes, "When the level of inequality becomes too large to ignore, everyone starts acting strange. Inequality affects our actions and our feelings in the same systematic, predictable fashion again and again. . .Inequality divides us. . .eroding our trust in one another. It generates stress and makes us all less healthy and less happy." (p. 3). A lack of fairness violates the human desire for reciprocity, which is one of the necessary building blocks of social capital. Behavioral research shows that people will actually forgo gain in order to prevent someone else from obtaining a superior reward (Fehr & Schmidt, 1999).

Employees do not perceive their status within the organization in a vacuum, but in relationship to others, especially by those who are perceived to have power. The inequity social aversion bias was captured in a classic experiment, "Monkeys reject unequal pay." Within the experiment monkeys were incentivized with cucumbers to hand over pebbles to the researcher. Each monkey was able to see the exchanges taking place amongst the other monkeys and the researcher. The experiment began by giving equal exchanges, which left all the monkeys satisfied with their cucumber. However, as the experiment progressed, the researcher randomly gave one monkey a grape in exchange for the pebble. Grapes were one of the monkeys' favorite treats. When the researcher went back to the other monkeys and continued to give them cucumbers in exchange for the pebble, they were furious. They rattled their cages and threw the cucumber back at the researcher. It was discovered that monkeys care deeply about fairness (Brosnan & de Waal, 2003).

Research on human beings shows that this same level of dislike towards the perception of inequality occurs as those cucumber throwing monkeys. For example, data shows that "air rage" from passengers on flights is four times more likely to occur if the plane has a first-class cabin. The separation and preferential treatment received by some passengers as a result of the first-class cabin, increased the risk of a passenger disturbance as much as a nine-hour delay. Other economic research shows that some of the best performing baseball teams are those with lower pay inequality ranges for players on the team. It was reported that teams with higher equality in pay performed much better. Payne (2017) writes, "Higher inequality seemed to undercut the superstar players it was meant to incentivize, which is what you would expect if you believed that the chief effect of pay inequality was to reduce cooperation and team cohesion." Even the superstars performed better when their teams experienced more equal pay.

Van Dijke et al. (2010) demonstrated that the use of authority and power dramatically shapes employees' perceptions of organizational fairness. If an employee believes they are being treated unfairly, they will be more likely to engage in deviant workplace behaviors. For example, a meta-analysis (Colquitt et al., 2001) shows a significantly strong relationship between fairness and employee organizational citizenship behaviors. This is because a sense of fairness sparks a sense of reciprocity. If an employee feels respected and valued, which a sense of equality provides, then they are more compelled to give back to the organization in a respectful and valuable manner.

When a perceived sense of intentional inequality is perceived as a result of a person in power giving preferential treatment to another, the relationship experiences an immediate erosion of trust. Inequality evokes irrational thinking and promotes a competitive environment amongst team members who actively seek to bend the rules towards their favor. When people can no longer trust each other, survival of the fittest takes over. However, leaders who enact decision-making procedures in a fair manner promote cooperative employee behaviors that include engaging in prosocial behaviors with each other in the workplace. One of the best guardrails to employ to avoid the perception of inequality in management decision-making is to establish a clear, consistent, and transparent set of rules and processes for how rewards, projects, and resources are allocated across the team. Any hint of abuse of power will emote irrational decision-making as well as behaviors among teams.

7.3.2 Power Paradox: Power Blind Managers From Displaying Reciprocity in the Workplace

The problems of power have been well documented throughout the centuries. It was Lord Action in the 19th century that first warned, “absolute power corrupts absolutely”. Power is often associated with this notion that it can cause the individual who holds it to behave in a manner contrary to socially acceptable norms. For example, imagine you are in the following scenario. You are tasked with leading a team of three individuals who are responsible for revising policies in your organization. Your job is to supervise the team and ensure the project stays on track. The team is huddled around a conference room discussing the progress of the project when a plate of five cookies is delivered to the room. Everyone eagerly takes a cookie and welcomes the much-needed break. Unbeknownst to you, you are chewing with your mouth open and spilling crumbs on the table. The other team members take notice, but do not say anything. After a few minutes, the work begins again and one cookie remains on the plate. Without much conscious thought, you immediately reach for the last cookie on the plate.

Do you think you would have really taken the last cookie? Chewed with your mouth open? Science suggests if you were in a position of power, probably so. This experiment has been conducted numerous times with different participant’s randomly being assigned the position of power. Over 75% of the time the person in power reaches for that last cookie. Nearly 100% of the time they chewed with their mouth open and spilled crumbs. It has been famously named the cookie monster experiment—representing the way people change even when given hypothetical power.

The Stanford Prisoner experiment is another classic and more extreme example of power gone wrong. Within this experiment researchers assigned some participants fictitious power as a guard over the other participants who were labeled prisoners. They were then placed within a jail-like scenario and asked to assume their respective roles. Within days the whole thing had to be shut down, because the guards were abusing their position of power—overstepping common social norms of behavior and mistreating the fictitious prisoners.

There is an innate human tendency towards power. Yet, gaining it fundamentally changes the way you see others and react to the world around you. Recent research has referred to this phenomena as the *power paradox* (Keltner, 2016). The power paradox shows that people utilize empathy to gain leadership positions, and then once power is obtained, people lose their sense of empathy for others. The very thing that raises people up to power is the formation of social capital, but the irony is, that once it is achieved, leaders will unwittingly make decisions that are contrary to these very principles.

The power paradox carries over to more than just taking the last cookie. It may surprise many individuals to learn that the group most likely to shoplift in America is the wealthier and higher-powered people of society. The most likely to speed through a pedestrian zone with people in the walkway? Those with higher power and wealthier cars. These surprising research studies show an inverse relationship between power and observing social norms. For example, the assumption of power results in a lack of ability to empathize with lower powered individuals (van Kleef et al., 2008). Powerful positions also cause individuals to lose the ability to hear others' point of view. Research has shown that powerful people tend to be hyper-focused on themselves (van Kleef, Oveis, Homan, van der Lowe, & Keltner, 2015). For example, research suggests that leaders are inspired by their own stories and lose interest when others start talking. A feeling of power may actually blind one to recognize the need for reciprocity and to display empathy for others around them.

7.4 SUMMARY

Managers must increasingly rely on informal uses of power, such as expert or referent forms of power, to foster creativity, collaboration, and knowledge-sharing behaviors in the workplace. In addition, the key to engaging employees is through empowerment. To successfully accomplish this, managers must be willing to grant autonomy and share credit for workplace successes. This is a deviation from the traditional command and control style of leadership often advocated for in the theory of business administration. One of the tools managers can leverage is to engage in reciprocal relationships that are marked by high levels of exchanges and a sharing of power and information. Reciprocal relationships are the mutual and cooperative interchange of exchanges that resemble a balance of power. While asymmetrical power dynamics lend themselves more frequently to perceptions of inequality and the power paradox. All too often organizations rely on an organizational chart for decision-making rights, rather than bringing in those with the most expertise. Employees across all levels who are actively engaged in management decision-making are much more likely to freely give information that will benefit the end outcomes. Effective reciprocity occurs when managers give autonomy and social support to employees thus practicing the behavior of empowerment. Empowered employees in return actively seek to make decisions and act in the interest of the organization. This creation of reciprocity through empowering relationships allows trust to further develop, which managers will need in order to successfully engage in the next behavior of management—*adapting* through change management activities.

REFERENCES

Batt, R. (2001). The economics of teams amongst technicians. *British Journal of Industrial Relations*, *39*, 1–4.

Birdi, K., Clegg, C., Patterson, M., Robinson, A., Stride, C. B., Wall, T. D., & Wood, S. J. (2008). The impact of human resource and operational management practices on company productivity: A longitudinal study. *Personnel Psychology*, *61*(3), 467–501.

Brosnan, S. F., & de Waal, F. (2003). Monkeys reject unequal pay. *Nature*, *425*, 297–299.

Claxton, G., Owen, D., & Sadler-Smith, E. (2015). Hubris in leadership: A peril of unbridled intuition? *Leadership*, *11*, 57–78.

Fehr, E., & Schmidt, K. M. (1999). A theory of fairness, competition, and cooperation. *The Quarterly Journal of Economics*, *114*, 817–868.

Frosh, S. (2003). Psychosocial studies and psychology: Is a critical approach emerging? *Human Relations*, *56*, 1545–1567.

Gordon, R. (2016). *The rise and fall of American growth*. Princeton, NJ: Princeton University Press.

Hoopes, J. (2003). *False prophets: the gurus who created modern management and why their ideas are bad for business today*. Cambridge, MA: Perseus Pub.

Keltner, D. (2016). *The power paradox: How we gain and lose influence*. Penguin Press.

Lawler, E. (1986). *High-involvement management. Participative strategies for improving organizational performance*. San Francisco: Jossey-Bass.

Leach, D. J., Wall, T. D., & Jackson, P. R. (2003). The effect of empowerment on job knowledge: An empirical test involving operators of complex technology. *Journal of Occupational and Organizational Psychology*, *76*, 27–52.

Lincoln, N. A., Travers, C., Ackers, P., & Wilkinson, A. (2002). The meaning of empowerment: The interdisciplinary etymology of a new management concept. *International Journal of Management Reviews*, *4*(30), 271–290.

McClelland, D. (1988). *Human Motivation*. Cambridge University Press.

Monahan, K. (2015). *Personal responsibility in the financial services industry: The cognitive antecedents and behavioral consequences of an employee's sense of responsibility in organizations*. ProQuest Dissertations Publishing, [Dissertation].

Patterson, M. G., West, M. A., & Wall, T. D. (2004). Integrated manufacturing, empowerment and company performance. *Journal of Organizational Behavior*, *25*, 641–665.

Payne, K. (2017). *The broken ladder: How inequality affects the way we think, live and die*. Viking Publishers.

Senge P.M. (1990). *The fifth discipline: The age and practice of the learning organization*. London: Century Business.

Shaw, P. (2002). *Changing conversations in organizations: A complexity approach to change*. London: Routledge.

University of Minnesota Libraries. (2017). *Principles of management*. Retrieved from: http://open.lib.umn.edu/principlesmanagement/.

van Kleef, G. A., Oveis, C., Homan, A. C., van der Lowe, I., & Keltner, D. (2015). Power Gets You High. *Social Psychological and Personality Science*, *6*(4), 472–480.

van Kleef, G. A., Oveis, C., van der Lowe, I., LuoKogan, A., Goetz, J., & Keltner, D. (2008). Power, Distress, and Compassion Turning a Blind Eye to the Suffering of Others. *Psychological Science*, *19*(12), 1315–1322.

Weiner, B. (1979). A theory of motivation for some classroom experiences. *Journal of Educational Psychology*, *71*, 3–25.

Wellins, R. S., Byham, W. C., & Wilson, J. M. (1991). *Empowered teams*. San Francisco: Jossey-Bass.

FURTHER READING

Becker, B. E., & Huselid, M. A. (2006). Strategic human resource management: Where do we go from here? *Journal of Management*, *32*, 898–925.

Manz, C., & Sims, H.P. (1990). *Superleadership: Leading others to lead themselves*. New York: Berkley.

Chapter 8

Adapting: Building Trust During Change Management

8.1 MANAGING CHANGE: MOVING BEYOND PREDICTABLE PLANNING ACTIVITIES

If successful management in the 21st century requires the building of social capital by connecting people through shared objectives, coaching with and towards expertise and empowering employees with autonomy, it will also in part, depend on the manager's ability to foster trust during times of change. Organizational survival in complex markets depends on constant adaptation, which requires employees en masse to positively react to fluctuating market demands (D'Aveni, 1994). This includes evolutions in employee interactions, processes, roles, relationships, and culture, all of which form during the stages of connecting, coaching, and empowering. Managers will now be required to ask individuals and teams who are connected and empowered to adapt to changes in the environment. At this stage, much like in Tuckman's (1965) classic group development model, which comprised of the stages of forming-storming-norming-performing-adjourning, individuals can choose to adapt and reconnect in new ways with their teams, or they can choose to adjourn and connect elsewhere in the ecosystem of the organization or marketplace. The very nature of change presents a pathway to learn and adapt to new ways of working, or it presents an immovable barrier that causes individuals to opt-out and seek connections elsewhere.

Consider the following example. In 2013, Zappos, an online retailer, decided it needed to change the way it was operating in order to remain competitive in the rapidly evolving e-commerce space. Rather than rely on traditional management practices, which leadership felt was slowing their ability to innovate and respond to customer needs, the organization decided to upend its entire management model and implement self-managing teams. In essence, management roles would be removed and repurposed, leaving individuals responsible for ensuring the success of their work and teams. This was a substantial shift in operating norms, roles, and overall culture. Some employees eagerly adapted to this new way of working, which left them feeling more empowered. However, others were much more skeptical and even uncomfortable with the new way of working. While the shared

How Behavioral Economics Influences Management Decision-Making.
DOI: https://doi.org/10.1016/B978-0-12-813531-0.00008-X

objectives by which they were hired into the organization did not change, the way in which they were to go about achieving them certainly did.

By 2015 nearly 2 years later, only 85% of the Zappos employees had fully adapted to the new operating model. This was causing recognizable friction between those who began practicing self-management and those who remained in the "old way of doing things." Leaders at Zappos recognized that in order for the new cultural norms to fully take effect, they would have to provide an opportunity for employees to fairly opt-out. In April 2015 the CEO of Zappos, Tony Hsieh, offered the following to the employee population. Embrace self-management or take a 3-month severance package and use that time to find another organization that may better align with the individuals' preferred working style. Within a month, nearly 14% of the organization took the CEO upon his offer and left the organization. That meant that one in seven employees decided not to adapt to the new self-management system.

Tony Hsieh believes that employees perform best when they are integrated into Zappos cultural norms, which he fully recognizes are not for everyone. It is why according his leadership philosophy he encourages employees to walk away from Zappos if they are unable to adapt. Within the first month of being hired, employees are allowed to quit and be compensated up to $2000 if they decide Zappos is not for them (Feloni, 2015). Notwithstanding the decision to upend the management model was very controversial, but the Zappos CEO understands the necessity of adapting in order for organizational survival. Allowing employees an opportunity to opt-out with compensation can create trust in those whom remain as well as for those who decide to leave. Rather than forcing people to adapt to change, as many traditional command and control management styles suggest, Zappos recognizes employment as a reciprocal relationship by which some will accept and others not, and provides generous packages for those unable to adapt. The opting-out process allows for greater team cohesion for those who decide to stay, which allows shared objectives, empowerment, and autonomy to more quickly rise amongst team members.

But change can be messy and complex. Not all employees will or want to adapt. Yet when facilitating large scale changes, such as a technology implementation or sizeable cultural changes as noted in the Zappos example, many managers and consultants alike turn to process maps, workflow documentation and milestone Gantt charts to plan a course of action. Successful change efforts are typically measured by numbers, metrics, and data points, commonly referred to as key performance indicators. These traditional change management behaviors are grounded upon the planning activities proposed in the theory of administrative management. It supposes that change can be captured in punctuated equilibrium models with change occurring across a long period of small incremental changes, which are then punctured by small periods of radical change (Rosenkopf & Tushman, 1994). Over time, these patterns of change can be predicted and planned for as it ultimately returns to equilibrium. These types of narratives within organizations often focus on whether a change initiative is on-time or on-budget. Rarely, do these conversations around change include narratives around personal and group identities, a sense of anxiety or even feelings of shame. Even less likely to occur in this dialogue is the emotional complexity of grief, which accompanies many of the change initiatives in the workplace. Even Tuckman (1965) would later refer to the last stage of team development as "mourning" after a team's dynamics no longer are suitable for future needs. Tuckman (1965) recognized the need to create a time and space, albeit short, for employees to mourn the loss of the cohesion and accomplishments as incurred as a team before dissolving and moving onto the next deadline and activity.

The need for change is likely to only grow given the market forces discussed in Chapter 1, The Changing Nature of Work: Macro-Level Considerations for Managers. As Brown and Eisenhardt (1997) note change is relentless and continuous for the majority of firms competing in today's markets. "For these firms, change is not the rare episodic phenomenon described by the punctuated equilibrium model, but, rather, it is endemic to the way these organizations compete (p. 1)." Planning for such changes may prove to be of little value for managers seeking to navigate the complexity that accompanies many of the realities changes bring to people within an organization. Rather, drawing on the fields of complexity theory and evolutionary science may prove to be a better starting point to understand how managers can create the capacity for people to effectively adapt in today's organizations. As the Zappos story illustrates, asking employees to adapt is a complex endeavor, and while not all will choose to do so, effective management can still build trust even in the midst of challenging circumstances.

8.2 THE COMPLEXITIES OF CHANGE

Building and sustaining trust demands a considerable amount of time. It requires the already existing building blocks of social capital to be present and activated through the behaviors of connecting, coaching, and empowering (see Fig. 8.1). For many individuals and teams this process can take months and even years to fully develop, and yet it only takes one irrational event to destroy. Managers must be vigilant in their quest to build and infuse trust throughout their teams. Noting back to Chapter 4, The Manager's Evolving Role, we found that building trust required four core facets. The first required engaging in honest and authentic communications. Consider the following scenario that occurred in an organization to illustrate how important this element is to building trust in organizations especially during

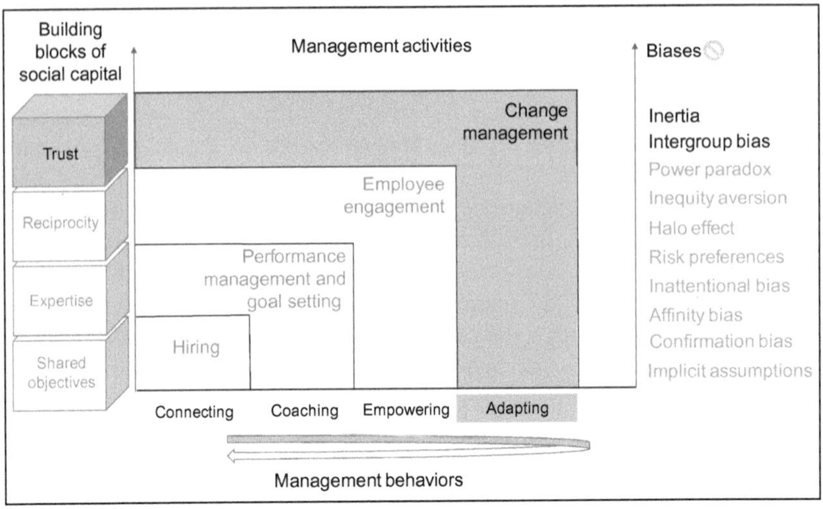

FIGURE 8.1 Management framework adapting behaviors.

times of uncertainty. Employees at a large services firm who worked at the satellite office location began to sense a change was upon them. Their office's travel was restricted, budgets were tight, and hiring freeze for open roles all marked the start of the fiscal year. Yet there was little to no transparency on why this was the case. Historically budget decreases and hiring freezes only occurred during financial downturns, however, overall business appeared healthy and strong at the firm.

The restraints on travel and hiring continued into the first couple of months of the new fiscal year. Much of the office staff grew anxious, and even began lashing out towards management, who were also unaware of the large transition that was about to take place. As it turned out the headquarter leaders were quite frankly uncomfortable communicating the negative changes that were to impact this satellite office. A decision was made, for a variety of economic reasons, that it would be better suited for the firm to close down the satellite office's operations. But, rather than clearly communicate the new business strategy and allow employees the time to adapt, the leaders simply avoided it. However, one manager, recognizing that maintaining business as usual was nearly impossible in light of the uncertainty the staff was facing called their leader and asked for a straight answer. The manager implored that their staff was well-equipped to handle whatever would come next, but that not knowing was becoming unbearable.

Soon after, leaders from headquarters visited the office and communicated honestly where the firm was headed, and that the new strategic direction would result in the office's closure in approximately 9 months. Leadership anticipated strong pushback and were surprised when the employees expressed relief for the transparency. This honest communication allowed employees the necessary time to begin to prepare for both the transition of the business as well as their own professional careers. While leadership thought that high turnover would immediately cripple the daily operations of the office, the opposite occurred. Employees came to work much more focused and ready to begin the transition as well as the next phase of their working careers. The sense of anxiety that came from uncertainty was actually worse than preparing for the office closure. As one employee remarked, "I want to end my tenure at the firm on a high note. I appreciate that I have nine months and transparency from leadership to effectively prepare." As this real-life story depicts the best policy during times of change is honesty and authenticity. Hiding and avoiding change activities can head organizations to chaos, the very thing they are trying to avoid.

Trust also hinges upon fairness, which was examined in Chapter 7, Empowering: Building Reciprocity and Trust. As discovered the root cause of much irrational behavior in the workplace can often be attributed to the perceived sense of inequity captured in the inequity aversion bias. As a result, managers who strive towards fair and consistent decision-making rules and processes are able to create needed engagement during times of uncertainty and change. Lastly, successful managers who create this type of engagement are able to operate from a place of enlightened self-interest. These managers genuinely care about the well-being of their employees as the upcoming change besets them.

While building these critical components of trust can be challenging, even in the best of circumstances, unique challenges are presented; For one, change is emotional and can immediately evoke a sense of anxiety, fear or even grief. Looking back to Chapter 3, Exploring Management Alternatives With a Behavioral Economic Lens, we remember that one of the worst emotional states for rational decision-making comes when people operate from a position of anxiety and fear. Learning is stunted and the ability to adapt nearly impossible. Therefore managers must consider the emotional toll that change can bring upon the individual being asked to conform to their shifting environment. Secondly, change is personal. Many individuals attribute much of their personal identity from work and organizational changes can threaten one's identity causing an inability to accommodate. Effective managers who practice adapting behaviors will recognize how organizational change can pose a significant impact on personal work identities. Thirdly, change is social. The ability for one to accept change directly depends around the health and functioning of the broader group and collective organization. As a result, change is relational and highly dependent upon the ability of others to successfully adapt to changing norms. Effective managers who successfully navigate team transitions leverage the social aspect of change for the benefit of the individual.

8.2.1 Change is Emotional: Mitigating Feelings of Anxiety and Shame

Stacey (2003) remarks that change and learning, "inevitably give rise to anxiety... It becomes important then to pay particular attention to how people respond to anxiety because defensive ways of dealing with anxiety inevitably close down learning processes" (p. 9). Asking people to change is not simply a rational exercise that only appeal to one's own cognitions, but also must give way to one's emotional response that change inherently invokes. Without paying considerable attention to the emotional side of change, it will not only slow down the speed to which one can conform, but also impede the learning process necessary for one to effectively evolve.

Consider the following example of how a technology implementation turned into an exercise of managing individual's emotions rather than organizational processes. The CIO of a large technology firm was thrilled when a cutting-edge financial reporting software was approved by the CEO to be installed throughout the firm. This new automated technology platform would save the organization not only millions of dollars by mitigating human error and unnecessary time during the reporting process, but it would also free up capacity for employees to work on broader strategic initiatives and projects. Therefore the CIO was shocked when the financial reporting teams within the organization refused to leverage the new software. The employees continued to work in their previous state. Headstrong the CIO began to closely monitor usage of the new platform and sent out scolding emails to the entire department making a rational appeal as to why this technology was so important to the firm's long-term strategy and success. However, the majority of employees simply deleted the emails and continued on with their routine. A month later, with only 10% of the workforce adopting the new technology, the CIO decided to run a contest and offered an iPad to the employee who spent the most amount of time on the new software. In addition, he sent out weekly peer reports highlighting who had logged into the software and those who had not. After a few weeks the technologies adoption had only rose to 25%.

Frustrated, the CIO turned to his human resource business partner to investigate what the resistance to the new technology was all about. He had tried to use monitoring behaviors and even rewarding behaviors to motivate the adoption of the technology, but to no avail. The HR team conducted numerous interviews throughout the department and quickly began to identify the real problem. Employees indeed understood how the software worked and even recognized the rational need for the firm to adopt this new technology. But, emotionally they felt anxiety and worried they lacked the competency to engage in the strategic tasks that their job would now require once they had capacity. Many of the employees had spent years in technical school and training on how to manually calculate the financial reports and less time on interpersonal strategic conversations. This created not only a sense of uncertainty on what the future held, but also a sense of embarrassment in their loss of perceived expertise. The best thing the CIO could do was encourage and foster the efficacy in this department to engage in a different skillset. Rather than train on the technology platform, these employees needed training on creative thinking, communication, and presentation skills. Only when their competency increased in these new skills could they then overcome the emotional hurdle of anxiety and shame that the new technology represented.

As this story illustrates, more often than not, it is not that employees do not recognize the rational appeal of change, but it is the emotional side that gets in the way of successfully complying with new opportunities. Change, even when positive, can cultivate a general sense of anxiety from having to move from one skillset to another. It can also mean a perceived loss of competency and efficacy to acquiring a new one. The most effective managers respond to this emotional need by digging deep into the emotional state a change may bring and craft creative solutions for bolstering efficacy throughout the workforce. As Aram (2001) notes, not knowing, especially in a social environment such as a high-performing organization, can be deeply shaming. Individuals are social beings as discussed in Chapter 3, Exploring Management Alternatives With a Behavioral Economic Lens, and often derive their sense of pride from the perception of others. Asking employees to evolve without providing the appropriate safety net to ensure their good standing amongst their peers will remain intact can be devastating. Trust then forms once employees realize that managers are directly dealing with anxiety by preparing employees to be ready and competent in the future, saving them from the risk of embarrassment that would accompany incompetence. The appropriate change message should focus not only on what the upcoming change means for today, but also how it actively bridges the present skillsets with those needed in the future. The question managers should ask how does this required change upend an employee's previous know-how and how do I create the environment that allows them to successfully engage in continuous learning? Phrasing change initiatives by embracing the sense of loss experienced while also compelling individuals through their inherent desire for growth and good standing with their peers can be much more powerful than a solely rational appeal to change. Since the majority of workers inherently do not want to get left behind, they will need the right supportive environment to begin to engage differently in the workplace.

8.2.2 Change is Personal: Understanding How Change Upends Personal and Collective Identities

Every employee's identity is not just expressed as an "I," but encompassed as a "we" in organizational settings. Elias (1939) research showed how indistinguishably linked "we" identities are too "I" identities. Every employee's identity is in some way entangled within their role, work or relationships at the organization. There is truly no such thing as separate personal and professional lives—they are all simply one person who expresses and manifests themselves differently depending on the circumstances. As a result, Stacey (2003) advises that change can shift one's individual and collective identities, which ultimately can be threatening. This is why territory wars so often occur within organizations, even though departments and individuals are all on the same team. These emotions might also cause internal transfers to become difficult for managers to support, due to the shift from "my" to "yours" within the organization. The shift in identity evokes a sense of emotion that can stunt the best of change efforts. Consider this story of how a seemingly positive leadership transition went awry as a result of the emotional shift in identity it caused.

Ryan was a rising star within his organization. He worked hard and connected well with his peers and leaders. Within a couple years he moved up the ranks and managed an entire department within the operations group. He went from managing only two individuals to now having a team of thirty. This was a large learning curve, but one that Ryan embraced. However, his identity slowly began to solely focus on the status of his position within the firm and less on his actual performance or relationships. Ryan would lead off nearly every conversation with his title and how many people he managed. His leader tried to coach him that the quantity of staff did not matter as much as the quality of the relationships and output of work within the department, but it largely fell on deaf ears. After a year the department began to show signs of struggle. Interpersonal dynamics began to bubble up and a loss of productivity occurred. Leadership began to recognize that having 30 people report directly into Ryan may have been a mistake. No leader, no matter how strong their business acumen, could think strategically and effectively build social capital among that size of a group at the same time.

Leadership discussed and came up with a positive structure change to support the group. Clearly Ryan was talented but needed help to handle the daily scope of the role. Luckily, Ryan had previously hired a chief of staff, Kim, who had great experience in the industry and could easily step in and assist in the daily management of the group. The leadership team called Ryan into their office and were excited to tell him that they were going to offload half of the department to Kim so they could bring him into more strategic meetings and conversations. Ryan was stunned and remained silent. He walked out of the leadership meeting with his head down and decided to take the rest of the day off.

He returned to work the next morning and requested a meeting with leadership where he pleaded that they not formally announce this change. Perplexed the leaders began to reinforce, "Ryan, this is a fantastic opportunity for you to get out of the weeds and build greater strategic capacity. If you are worried about messaging, this is all positive and will be communicated as such." Ryan, however, now felt lost without his lead role in the organization. He had prided himself as head of the entire 30-person staff, and now felt that he had to share part of that identity with Kim, who was helping colead the day-to-day work. He had wrapped himself up so much in the size of his department that he was unable to recognize the opportunity before him. As a result the identity shift was too much for Ryan to handle. The once rising star left within 3 months of the change and ironically took on a much lesser role within another organization.

This story illustrates how powerful roles, identities, and relationships resonate within individuals in organization. A shift that requires one to adapt and even adopt a new identity can be difficult, even if the change is largely positive. Irrationality can mark the behaviors of people trying to cope with role and identity changes. Therefore, remember as a manager, when crafting change communications the impact it will have on role identities in the workplace. Some people may pride themselves in titles or positions on the organizational chart. Others may simply find their identity by their individual niche they have carved out within the firm. Regardless of what it is, adapting, which will be required to survive in the future of work, will create at times turmoil and cognitive dissonance for those employees seeking to reconcile past identities with the required future role. Managers who are able to build trust during this time do not shy away from these challenging conversations and fully recognize the power of identity. Instead they actively continue to coach and provide opportunities for employees to more fully find the identity that is best suited for future organizational needs.

8.2.3 Change is Social: Relationships Determine the Extent of Adapting

Stacey (2003) writes, "To claim that it is only individuals who learn is to continue with the major Western preoccupation with the autonomous individual and to ignore the importance of social processes" (p. 2). Employees are social beings whose needs are inherently connected to the needs of others around them. People want to be liked, respected, and valued by their peers. Change can threaten this perceived standing with their peers. As Shaw and Stacey (2003) remark, change is highly relational and depends on the social dynamics of the group. If people are connected to others in the organization and believe their own individual learning and adapting to change activities will benefit others, they are much more likely to participate in adapting behaviors (Friedman, 2014). Many employees want to help their peers succeed and successful change often results from shared social learning experiences. Furthermore research finds that in order for change to be meaningful there has to exist a connection for the well-being of others. This creates a tremendous opportunity for managers to ensure that change is not just connected to processes, task lists and deadlines, but is also connected to the human element behind those tasks.

Consider the following true story of a large manufacturing firm. The finance department had found a more effective way to keep track of inventory and ordering new parts for the organization. They implemented the new system and specifically reached out to the research and development (R&D) department to adopt this new process and policy for inventory tracking as they ordered and maintained the largest supply of inventory at the firm. However, adoption rates were incredibly low the first month. Thinking the R&D teams just needed more in-person training, the finance department held additional learning sessions to explain the new inventory tracking system and the money it would save the organization for complying. Yet even after the trainings, the R&D group failed to leverage the new inventory tracking system, to the determinant of the finance department employees who were staying late to reconcile the variances.

The finance leadership team had a different idea. Rather than continue to make rational appeals for the change they decided to make this change a social experience. They invited both members from the R&D group along with the finance organization to an offsite location. At the offsite they visually represented the entire process and highlighting the pain points the finance employees were experiencing. In addition, employees from finance shared the personal impact this was having—picking up their children late from school, missing out personal obligations after work, and feeling burned out. The R&D team members were shocked to see the impact their negligence was having on this group and how a relatively simple adaption to a system would fix the majority of the problems surfaced. It was not until faces were put to processes did the team fully recognize the impact this change would have. Managers seeking to change should remember that it is a human and social experience rather than a top-down ask and initiative. Leveraging the innate desire to connect with one another will be much more beneficial than hours spent reviewing data points and rational explanation on change.

8.3 THE NEED TO ADAPT: A COMPLEX INTERWEAVE OF THE PERSON, ENVIRONMENT, AND RELATIONSHIPS

This book illustrates, and has exposed, a new business narrative based on behavioral sciences that will be required to navigate and compete in today's markets. Rational economic thinking has run its course in its ability to prepare managers for leading in today's complex and nonlinear environments. In addition, the behavioral sciences have shown the importance of human psychology in the workplace and the opportunities and challenges that deviations from rationality create. This may be no truer than in the conversations surrounding change management. It is not only naïve to assume that managers have the ability to properly plan and control for a predictable future that leverages rational actors, but it can lead to devastating outcomes for both employees and customers. Well-intended, but faulty change efforts can dehumanize the entire employee experience, while also jeopardizing organizational performance. Consider this illustrative example.

Two large retail organizations sought to increase sales during the holidays. Overall consumer electronic sales were sluggish in the market with both retailers' reporting disappointing profits year to date. To help boost sales, each retailer decided to introduce a new sales process. The new sales process required a completely different approach to selling and came with a steep learning curve for employees. However, to encourage employees to adapt to this change, retail organization A decided to boost employees' motivations through intrinsic levers. For example, leaders coordinated catered lunch and learns, while providing ample training opportunities for all employees to ensure they felt empowered as experts to sell the new products. The leaders also built and communicated a business case for the new sales process based on the positive impact it would have on the consumer experience. While this new process would likely boost profits, it was not seen as the end goal for adaption, but rather the leading message centered around the ability to better help others. In addition, to create a sense of teaming, the leaders created regional competitions, which required team members to collaborate with one another at the store level to try to win gift cards and additional paid time off. Lastly, the leaders made an intentional effort to thank employees for their long hours worked during the trainings and made sure they started each day publically sharing a consumer success story from the day prior.

However, retail organization B took a page right out the traditional change management playbook to implement the sales change. Leaders remained huddled in a conference room with outside consultants determining the best approach to roll out the new sales process. Leaders were busy with their heads down creating process maps, slide decks, and a communication plan on who would receive training and when. It was determined, in an effort to save money on training, that the top sales associates would become change agents for the new sales process. These selected associates would go through the in-depth training and then would be responsible for training the rest of the employees while on the job. But, this created an overall sense of anxiety on the retail floor as many employees anticipated a major change coming, but felt left in the dark on what exactly that change may be. In addition, the organization took their top performing sales associates off the sales floor for a week on train-the-trainer activities with the hopes they would become the experts and train others. But, when the top performing sales associates returned to the floor, they did not focus on training, as the leaders hoped, but rather got back to selling. They had lost a week's worth of commission on training and were bound and determined to make it up. Lastly, the leaders created a business case for the news sales process based on how much additional dollars this would save the organization with vague communications about bonuses being higher if the new sales process was fully adopted.

Also, in an effort to boost performance, retail organization B began publically tracking individual sale associate numbers. Any employee could now log into the system and see how their own individual performance staked against another. This created a very competitive environment with employees trying to "steal" consumer sales from each other. The individual focus on sales ultimately diminished the customer experience as the focus no longer was on the customer's needs, but rather on who could attain the greatest number of add-ons to the customer ticket. After the holiday season, retailer A posted a profitable year and maintained a strong public brand image. However, retailer B struggled to retain customers, lost brand reputation in the market, and ended up closing their retail operations by the following holiday season.

This illustrative example shows that asking employees to adapt to change can be complicated. Even the best intended efforts can backfire without a proper understanding of human motivation and behavior. Eoyang (2011) remarks, "organizational change deals with conceptual, relational, and cultural entities whose "weight cannot be measured with scales" (p. 322). Turning to spreadsheets, numbers, and making rational change appeals based on profits, while ignoring the very real human side of change causes a miss in many strategic initiatives. Many mainstream business reporters and scholars remark that the majority of change initiatives fail, some noting that nearly 70% of changes do not meet their goals (Kotter, 2006). The question is, why? Eoyang (2011) suggests that organizational change has all too often been prescribed as a straightforward process of unfreezing the current state, creating processes and incentives to move towards a desired state and then simply refreezing that desired state. Much of this thinking and work has been grounded on both rational assumptions of people and even predictable models drawn from the field of physics. The language and frameworks created around change rely on the functioning of open and closed systems, inertia, time, and processes. The traditional role of a manager is to successfully predict, plan, and implement organizational change as a process that can be controlled. Yet this is often not the case for how change actually works in real organizations. This thinking improperly assumes that management and human behavior can be likened to physics, a hard science, which as discussed in Chapter 2, Rational Economics and the Administrative Theory of Management, does not follow the principles of a double-hermeneutic. Rather, management more closely resembles unpredictability and complexity. Remember, when one of the leaders of Microsoft described the product innovation process akin to navigating white water rapids? As a result, some scholars today are turning from predictable models to describe organizational change and instead drawing on the learnings found in complexity sciences that examine butterfly effects, self-organization, fractals, and emergent networks (Eoyang, 2011). The realities of organizational change may be better understood by drawing from the ecological and evolutionary theories of change and adaptation. Change is not a one-time process that can be easily planned for, but rather an emergent response that occurs between people seeking to influence their environment. As a result, change management can better be captured in today's organizations as a continuous process of evolution.

8.3.1 Defining Adaptation

Adaptation is defined as the way a living organisms changes their internal make-up to improve fit within their environments. "More generally, when agents in a complex system adjust their internal characteristics to better fit with external agents to improve survival, their change processes can be characterized as co-evolution" (Eoyang, 2011, p. 326). Adaption occurs as the environment and organism coevolve together. Bandura (1986) described this process in human behavior by the theory of *reciprocal determinism*, which explains human behavior by the influence and interactions of both personality factors and social environmental factors. According to reciprocal determinism the person is constantly trying to adapt to their environment, while at times, also trying to exert control over their environment. At any given time or place a personal factor or social environmental factor might be stronger and thus create a change in either the person or environment. The reality of change management can better be explained as asking people in organizations to continuously evolve, or become suitable to both present and future environments, which over time slowly involves people and environmental factors becoming all together something different.

This framing of change understands that behavior can only be understood at the interplay between cognitive, social, and environmental conditions. This means that understanding behavior as unidirectional is not fruitful for understanding change events. Rather, human behavior is much more complicated and affected by repercussions, which can create challenges for managers trying to predict and adequately plan change events. In addition, the work of Manz and Sims (1984) found that a leader's own behavior could only be understood by also looking at the behaviors of their subordinates and their performance. In other words, individual action is not simply based on a set of intentions that function in isolation apart from the environment. Rather, people act in response to the environment and the behavior of others around them. As a result, eventual change is a social experience that is best reflected in the interplay of one's own cognitions and the social environment.

With this newfound understanding of change as an emergent experience in the person and environment, one can now view change as a learning activity captured when a person responds differently to the environment. Change is successfully realized when interdependent people learn and influence their environment to do something new (Stacey, 2003). For example, employees learn when they take on a new role within the organization or implement a new process throughout the firm. Adaptation can be observed in the, "self-organizing patterns of conversation" that occur between employees and the broader organization (Stacey, 2003, p. 8). Learning can best be understood by examining the behaviors that occur between the way people interact with each other and their environment. Therefore instead of trying to change people, it may be better to leverage the natural inclinations of employees who seek after growth, development, and purpose to continuously adapt to changing organizational and market dynamics. Rather than avoid or force change, managers should seek to creatively design projects and environments that require continuous learning and growth, which helps employees explore opportunities in dynamic environments. Schwisow (2015) explains it as such,

> *Adaptation management will mean creating a steady stream of quality projects that either look to improve the business, develop and operationalise innovations or respond to changing market conditions. The organisation's employees won't need to be made to buy into these projects – they will be the source of them. Staff won't need to be cajoled into accepting the business changes that come from these projects – projects will become the business's new normal. Adaptive projects will no longer be met with resistance from the team – they will bring the team together and be the source of motivation and engagement (p. 1).*

8.3.2 Adaption in Practice

Consider the following empirical study to illustrate this understanding of change and adaptation. Brown and Eisenhardt (1997) sought to understand why some organizations were successfully adapting to the convergence of telecommunications and consumer electronics industry in the mid-1990s, while other organizations struggled to survive. Some organizations were able to quickly adapt and morph into something entirely new, while others were unable to make the transition into the new markets. The researchers conducted multiple field studies, leveraging a mixed-methods inquiry, by collecting data based on interviews, surveys, observations and secondary sources. A total of six US company case studies were created with the following learnings.

Effective change managers were those who relied more on *dynamic learning interactions* with their employees rather than following a formalized change processes. These managers did not perceive change as a one-way activity, but rather leveraged communications and feedback to steer clear of chaos, while also providing employees the freedom and support to learn and improve the organization's current product offerings. The researchers describe it as finding the sweet spot between chaos and control, which can only be found in both fluid and frequent interactions across the firm. This type of management style has been well supported throughout the literature. For example, firms with "fluid job descriptions, loose organizational charts, high communication, and a few rules may be conducive to innovation because they free developers from constraints allowing them to change flexibly and create novel ideas" (Brown & Eisenhardt, 1997). Freeing oneself from formalized processes may actually enhance the interaction between managers and employees during times of change as it allows for greater fluidity and flexibility in actions. In addition, this holds a key lesson for managers seeking to create change. They must allow capacity and freedom for employees to continuously learn and adapt to their environment. Too often change is approached as a one-time event moving from one state to another in linear fashion guided by flow charts and process maps, without ever fully allowing employees the space and time to learn and adapt over time.

Effective change managers *experimented* often and did not overly rely on their initial plan for change. Rather than rely on their initial and static strategic plan, even if the environmental conditions no longer supported it, effective change managers crafted multiple plans through the use of low-cost experimentation. There was not a one-size-fits all approach to the change, but instead managers leveraged a variety of inputs to determine what the best course of action may be. What worked yesterday, was not assumed to work in the present, let alone the future. This learning requires today's managers to act more like design thinkers rather than strategic planners. Many times, teams devise a plan and view any other activities or strategies as competing. However, within this research, successful managers actively sought out divergent ideas and created alternative pathways to the future. As a manager, think of this as writing your plans in pencil rather than permeant marker. Managers must be willing to erase and sketch new versions rather than allow their initial thinking to mislead them as the environment demands further adaptation.

Successful change managers created a *rhythmic transition process* between current and future states, thus fueling a relentless yet manageable pace of change. The status quo was avoided by an environment that prized prototyping, experimentation, and learning. Chaos was avoided by ensuring a continuous loop of feedback and ensuring lines of accountability were clearly drawn when necessary. This required high involvement from managers to ensure people were working at the right things at the right time. At times, it may require employees to drop what they are doing and move onto something else quite rapidly. It also means becoming more comfortable with the unknown. While planning activities thrives on prediction, adapting activities thrive on uncertainty. Vaill (1996) describes this key difference as "learning as a way of being," further explaining an adapting organization as one who is able to navigate a world of permanent white water. Learning as a way of being requires a mindset that sees uncertainty as part of the journey and does not seek to plan or control for it. Rather, Vaill (1996) asserts,

> *It is the non-explorers who rather naively assume that once they have a clear sharp picture in mind of where they are going, they can trust that picture through to the end. To be an explorer is to not know where, precisely and concretely, one is going.... The explorer feels your uncertainty and your fear and even sometimes your fury. However, he or she does not think these states of mind can be escaped. Instead, they are part of what the explorer explores (p. 45).*

As this research suggests, managers who practice high-involvement interactions with their employees, experiment, and adopt an explorer mentality, are much more likely to build the necessary capacity to adapt and evolve to changing market conditions. Indeed, adapting is a complex endeavor that requires the interplay of both person, environment and relationships. As the retailer case study illustrates, even the best intended plans can backfire without the right understanding of human behavior during times of change. This misunderstanding often occurs because of the heuristics, or biases, which arise and are inherent in many human responses to change.

8.4 BARRIERS TO CHANGE: INERTIA AND INTERGROUP BIASES

By this point in the management process, social capital should be relatively high amongst colleagues. However, one of the most challenging biases to overcome when there is too much social capital is the tendency towards organizational inertia. This is especially likely when the team or organization has not faced many challenges or been forced to adapt to external market pressures. This lack of pressure to evolve can create a sense of familiarity with one's roles, habits, and relationships at work. A strong culture often forms around traditional ways of doing things. Norms go relatively unchallenged. This overall lack of adaptation built into some organizational cultures leads to less learning and more comfortability and even pressure to uphold the status quo. This can create a major blind spot at the organizational level for capturing new opportunities that demand adapting.

For example, the automotive industry can represent the tendency to keep leveraging what has traditionally worked in the past. From 1945 to 1975 the car industry was dominated by large car manufacturing, namely American, which consumers demanded during this time. However, a great market shift happened in the late 1970s that forced larger automobile manufacturers to also make smaller, more fuel-efficient vehicles. Unfortunately the majority of US manufacturers had never prepared for alternative strategies and lacked the necessary resources and assets to execute on this shift. As a result the Japanese auto companies could capitalize on an historically dominated American made market. They captured this newfound market need and began swiftly building strong brand loyalty, which to date has proven difficult for US auto makers to capture back.

The pull towards the status quo and more broadly towards organizational inertia can be strong. Behavioral economic research shows that the majority of individuals will not proactively change their 401k contributions or existing health care plans unless nudged to do so (Thaler, 2016). For whatever reason, many will not actively seek out adaption unless they are in a supportive environment that demands doing so. This pull towards maintaining similarity and comfort can also give rise to the intergroup bias, which actively seeks to protect what the group knows at the expense of others, which further restricts the ability of the firm to adapt.

8.4.1 Intergroup Bias: Forming an "Us" Rather Than "We" Narrative

A small group of individuals were selected within a large organization to lead an innovation lab. The whole purpose of this team was to create compelling insights and innovative solutions that would help keep both the firm's image as well as product offerings on the cutting edge. The individuals selected to participate in this group were highly qualified and skilled in both technical and interpersonal skills. As a result the group cliqued fast and quickly formed social capital amongst its team members. Within a couple of years this group was well-respected not just within the firm, but in the external market as well. The individuals were sought after for keynotes at leading industry conferences. As time progressed though something began to happen that puzzled the broader firm leadership. This group became territorial and guarded with their materials. They were often perceived as going rogue by other functional leaders who became increasingly frustrated by their lack of cohesion across the broader organization. This group's productivity began to slowly diminish as the years went by. They had erected walls so high that few were able to truly connect and utilize their innovations in a useful manner. What had happened to such a highly skilled innovative group of people? The answer lies in an understanding the intergroup bias.

Remember the study that Brown and Eisenhardt (1997) conducted seeking to understand why some companies were able to navigate the complex convergence of the telecommunications and consumer electronic industries in the mid-1990s? These researchers found that companies that struggled bringing products to market on time and in a way, which met customers' needs could be explained by the internal dynamics of teams within the firms. Previously unsuccessful firms often fell victim to the intergroup bias. For example, a struggling organization within their study was marked by individuals exhibiting high communication only within their own group, remarking that "It's not cool to withhold information" (p. 12), but essentially failed to communicate between cross-project teams. Working across teams was not a priority or seen as critical to the team's success. As one leader remarked, "We are very compartmentalized because we are all so focused on our own tasks" (p. 12). Contrary, organizations that thrived during this time intentionally created cross-functional team meetings and communication platforms to allow knowledge sharing to extend one's own team.

Intergroup bias can be defined as the tendency for one to show favoritism towards in-group members, often at the expense of the out-group. It is found in the narrative that forms between group members that a "us" versus "them" exists, even if it is with others within the same organization. The case study illustrated earlier shows a highly innovative group that began to view others in the organization as outside their concern. They began to display behaviors that were exclusive and territorial, which favored their own interest and not those of the broader firm.

How can groups protect themselves from developing such high social capital amongst this own team members that it comes at the expense of others in the organization? One of the surest ways to protect against intergroup bias from clouding the judgment of team members, according to an extensive metaanalytical review, is to more frequently interact with members outside one's group. Frequent interaction with others can reduce bias while increasing empathy for others (Pettigrew & Tropp, 2000). Further research in laboratory settings has found that interpersonal interactions are far more effective at reducing intergroup bias than task focused communications (Bettencourt, Brewer, Rogers-Croak, & Miller, 1992). The best thing highly cohesive groups can do is actively seek out associative connections across the organization, rather than achieving a distinctiveness in their identity (Hewstone, Rubin, & Willis, 2002). Leaders of teams should actively seek to practice their connecting behaviors in the first phase to protect against teams failing to adapt to changing environments as a result of the intergroup bias.

8.5 ADAPTING CONTINUOUS LEARNING: BEST PRACTICES FOR ESTABLISHING TRUST

As discovered change management is a complex activity that requires managers to build the capacity throughout their workforce to adapt through continuous learning behaviors. One of the surest ways to ask people to adapt is by forming trust that their identity, emotions, and social dynamics will be taken into consideration. As soon as individuals perceive threat or fear biases will likely impede their ability to adapt. The following are provided as recommended actions for managers who are seeking to foster trust while also encouraging adaptation through continuous learning.

1. *Create intentional time and space for learning and adapting in the workplace.* All too often employees are bogged down chasing after the day-to-day that they simply stop evolving and taking time to notice the changes

that begin to happen around them. Adapting is a continuous behavior that requires both cognitive and emotional capacity to participate in. Encourage employees to pay attention to the broader marketplace and engage in active dialogue around what is working or not working. Reward those with a critical eye on the present state and push towards an alternative future. In addition, ask employees to attend industry conferences, networking events, and participate in continuous learning activities that promote the awareness to keep adapting to the changing environment around them.

2. *Leverage cross-functional teams and projects.* It can be easy for managers to spend so much time building and developing their own teams that they lose sight of the broader organizational narrative taking place around them. By leveraging other team members and engaging in cross-functional dependent work encourages employees to stay connected to shared objectives while also protecting against the intergroup bias that may emerge at this phase in the management lifecycle. In addition, working across teams keeps change activities as social experiences that are based on interdependent relationships with others across the firm.
3. *Do not let the ink dry on planning activities.* Keep an open and creative mind to allow alternative pathways to emerge for attaining organizational objectives and performance. All too often managers feel compelled to stick to a plan once it has been formalized. Yet the most effective change management activities are fluid in nature, which allow for constant adaption of shifting environmental factors.

8.6 SUMMARY

Change management may be one of the most difficult of all the management activities to participate in. It requires considerable amounts of cognitive capacity to evolve and adapt to frequently changing social dynamics in organizations and external shifts in the broader market. However, managers who have successfully engaged in connecting team members, coaching them with and towards expertise and empowering decision-makers across the team are much more likely to have the capacity in their teams to effectively respond to changes. The best of managers will do this by infusing trust throughout the process and guarding against common biases such as the intergroup bias, which can mitigate a team's ability to acclimate. In addition, successful managers who recognize that change is emotional, personal, and social, can leverage these needs to further create the necessary social capital that lowers the costs of working together in the workplace. Adapting can certainly be difficult, but is also the very essence of being human. Its presence is key and even fundamental to the continued growth and evolution in both individuals and organizations.

REFERENCES

Aram, E. (2001). *The experience of complexity: Learning as the potential transformation of identity, unpublished thesis*. University of Hertfordshir.

Bandura, A. (1986). *Social foundations of thought and action: A social cognitive theory*. Englewood Cliffs, NJ: Prentice- Hall, Inc.

Bettencourt, B. A., Brewer, M. B., Rogers-Croak, M., & Miller, N. (1992). Cooperation and the reduction of intergroup bias: The role of reward structure and social orientation. *Journal of Experimental Social Psychology*, *28*, 301–319.

Brown, S. L., & Eisenhardt, K. M. (1997). The art of continuous change: Linking complexity theory and time-paced evolution in relentlessly shifting organizations. *Administrative Science Quarterly*, *42*(1), 1–34.

D'Aveni, R. (1994). *Hypercompetition: Managing the Dynamics of Strategic Maneuvering*. New York: Free Press.

Elias, N. (1939). *The Civilizing Process*. Blackwell, Oxford.

Eoyang, G.E. (2011). Complexity and the dynamics of organizational change. In: Allen, P., Maguire, S., & McKelvey, B. (Eds.), *Sage Handbook of Complexity and Management*. London: SAGE.

Feloni, R. (2015). Inside Zappos CEO Tony Hsieh's radical management experiment that prompted 14% of employees to quit. *Business Insider*. Available from http://www.businessinsider.com/tony-hsieh-zappos-holacracy-management-experiment-2015-5.

Friedman, R. (2014). *The Best Place to Work: The Art and Science of Creating an Extraordinary Workplace*. New York: Penguin.

Hewstone, M., Rubin, M., & Willis, H. (2002). Intergroup bias. *Annual Rev. Psychology*, *53*, 575–604.

Kotter, J. (2006). *Leading Change*. Cambridge, MA: Harvard Business Review Press.

Manz, C. C., & Sims, H. P., Jr (1984). Searching for the unleader: Organizational member views on leading self-managed groups. *Human Relations*, *37*, 409–424.

Pettigrew, T.F., & Tropp, L.R. (2000). Does intergroup contact reduce prejudice? Recent meta-analytic findings. In: Oskamp, S. (Ed.), *Reducing prejudice and discrimination*. Taylor & Francis Group, pp. 93–114.

Rosenkopf, L., & Tushman, M. (1994). The coevolution and technology and organizations. In J. A. C. Baum, & J. V. Singh (Eds.), *Evolutionary dynamics of organizations* (pp. 403–424). New York: Oxford University Press.

Schwisow, J. (2015). Adaptation Management in the New Change Management, LinkedIn, https://www.linkedin.com/pulse/adaptation-management-new-change-jeff-schwisow/.

Shaw, P. & Stacey, R. (2003). *Experiencing spontaneity, risk and improvisation in organizational life London: Routledge.*

Stacey, R. (2003). Learning as an activity of interdependent people. *The Learning Organization*, *10*(6), 1–10.

Tuckman, B. W. (1965). Developmental sequence in small groups. *Psychological Bulletin*, *63* (6), 384–399.

Vaill, Peter B. (1996). *Learning as a way of being*. San Francisco: Jossey-Bass Inc.

Thaler, R. H. (2016). *Misbehaving: The making of Behavioral Economics*. W.W. Norton & C.

Afterword

Within the fictional superhero comic book series, Ben Parker advises the young and struggling Spiderman, "With much power comes much responsibility." Entering into the management profession brings a greater sense of responsibility for organizational outcomes. Management, while filled with many opportunities, also presents challenges unfounded at other levels within the organization. It may be no wonder then that a recent Pew Research Center (2014) study found that only 39% of employed adults wanted to become a boss or top manager some day. It is not a position that all employed individuals strive toward. Yet, the role of manager today is as instrumental to organizational outcomes as it was at its inception. Getting the management role right is necessary for firm survival. Yet, the usefulness of many of today's dominant assumptions that underpin leading management behaviors and practices have proven to be antiquated at best, and at worse, harmful to longer term value creation.

For those who are either entering into the management profession for the first time or for the seasoned manager seeking a new paradigm, the contents of this book sought to bring an alternative perspective to the dominant discourse surrounding many of today's leading management practices. The traditional management discourse subscribes to the activities proposed in the theory of business administration, which is largely based on rational economic assumptions of how people make decisions and behave in organizations. As discovered, rational economic theory is less helpful to inform our understanding of the way people actually behave within real organizations. The lack of usefulness in rational economics informing management theory is partly based on the complexity and unpredictable markets firms seek to compete in today, and in part, based on the fact that people are not as self-seeking as many of the rational models presume.

Within an alternative narrative, the behavioral sciences are leveraged to form a new paradigm on the role of management in today's firms. This new paradigm marks a profound departure from the time and place where the theory of business administration and management was first considered—in environments that relied on efficiency, routine and low cognitive skills. Therefore, this book proposes that the role of manager moves from one who administers tangible resources in a predictable and controllable fashion to the one who adapts to the complexity of both the environment and people they manage. Rather than relying on command and control styles of leadership to mitigate agency costs, today's managers may be better off leveraging the inherent desire for people to grow, develop, and belong by building social capital to lower the costs of doing business and align interests. As a result, the role of manager departs from one who plans, organizes, controls, and directs tangible resources to one who connects, coaches, empowers, and adapts to people and relationships across an ecosystem. This frees the manager from engaging in the command and control style of leadership, which is averse to the development of knowledge and people in today's workplaces.

This new behavioral paradigm of management also requires a newfound understanding of human behavior and the irrationalities, such as implicit assumptions or the power paradox, which can mitigate one's ability to effectively build social capital in the workplace. As discovered, social capital is built upon a manager connecting employees to shared objectives during the hiring process, coaching with and toward expertise during goal-setting and performance management activities, empowering through reciprocal relationships to foster employee engagement and adapting during times of change. As a result, the manager's newfound role in organizations consists of both highly cognitive, emotional and relational activities. As Scott (2017) remarked, many of today's leading management theorists undervalue the emotional toil and labor managers face each day working with people. In addition, to further complicate matters, managers are not immune to the many heuristics that impede rational decision-making in the workplace. While the majority of this book has focused on the importance of engaging in effective talent management through a more thorough understanding of behavioral sciences, it is also important to consider how managers can create their own time and space for development, growth, and a sense of belonging to the broader organizational narrative.

CREATING SLACK FOR MANAGERS TO FLOURISH IN THE NEW PARADIGM

Embracing this new way of leading people in the 21st century requires a new understanding of the role of *slack* in a manager's day. All too often, slack or simply building in time to think is overlooked and seen as a "nice to have" or luxury in a manager's schedule, rather than a necessary component to effectively lead today's workforces. In practice, many managers lament their never-ending schedules, hectic pace, and navigating the overwhelming amount of data and emails that flood their inbox daily. Even as the manager role further evolves to place an emphasis on talent development, the manager will still be responsible for their own work streams and continued maintenance of their own expertise. All of these pressures require greater capacity to make trade-off decisions to lessen the cognitive load required to be an effective manager in today's complex marketplace. A *trade-off decision* involves evaluating a set of alternatives against one another to determine a course of action. The trade-off decision process involves having to decide to give up one thing in order to pursue or attain something else. Rational economics presumes a cost–benefit analysis would be completed, with the decision-maker accurately choosing the option which would maximize their own interest. Yet, we now recognize from behavioral sciences, that relationships, for example, can trump rationality, or that a fear of loss will cause one to prefer a less optimal option. As Simon (1956) remarked, one can only hope to satisfice among a choose of alternatives. The question is how can managers create greater capacity to make better trade-off decisions and maximize their time spent investing in both themselves and their teams? The answer lies in the creation of slack.

Mullainathan and Shafir (2013) use the following analogy to illustrate the importance of having slack in one's day to make better decisions. They provide the following scenario.

> *You and your friend decide to take a road trip across the country. You are given a very small carry on size luggage to pack your items. However, your friend is given an oversized extra-large suitcase. As a result, your friend has room from not only what he needs for the trip, but also throws in some frivolous items just in case you encounter a rainy day on the journey. But, you are forced to make many trade-off decisions as you have no room for extras. In fact, you barely have room for what you may need on the trip. For example, do you pack the umbrella and rain boats or forgo these potential necessities and hope for no rain?*

Mullainathan and Shafir (2014) remark that the size of the suitcase either enables or constrains your ability to make good decisions that will benefit yourself and others. As a person with the smaller suitcase, you are required to make predictions about future needs—which behavioral research suggests people are not very good at. However, the slack capacity afforded by your friend's larger suitcase dramatically simplifies their planning (and ultimately enjoyment) relative to yours for the same trip. Managers are all too often trying to pack in more than a day's worth of activities in a 24-hour time block, and as a result they lack the necessary slack to make good decisions and develop people in the workplace. The question this illustration poses is, how much space is left in your suitcase at the end of the day? Do you have enough room to make rational decisions and not fall victim to the influence of the many heuristics that can get in the way? Today's management more closely resembles a long-distance marathon, which requires one to have both the capacity and sustainability to engage in longer term decision-making.

Therefore managers must aggressively seek to simplify the more they face complexity in the workplace. One of the best ways to accomplish this is through the creation of slack in the system. In order to adapt to change, think creatively and manage effectively, slack is a necessary component in the new paradigm of management. The harder one runs at maximizing efficiency during the day-to-day execution of tasks, the more costs they will likely encounter at an expense to future growth, development and adaptation. In order to effectively engage in the management behavioral activities described throughout this book, the following management tips are provided.

1. *Proactively build in buffer times when deciding on timelines, deadlines and meetings.* You are likely to be overly optimistic on the team's ability to accomplish a task, make decisions and engage in productive meetings. A simple way to help plan for the unexpected, and allow the team necessary time to think, is to build in slack time into one's calendar in order to effectively transition from one activity to the next. Rather than schedule back-to-back 30- or 60-minute meetings, schedule 20 or 45 minutes to allow for slack time. You can then use this intentional slack time to properly reflect and transition into the next activity.
2. *Tackle your high priority items at the start of the day.* As time progresses your ability to fight back decision-fatigue is going to wane. So, rather than save your coaching and development activities to the very end of the day, do them right upfront. Your best energy and ability to behave rational is when few decisions or actions have been completed. Do not wait until the end of the day to build the necessary social capital required with your team to sustain their performance over the long-run.
3. *Make time for your own development that is free of distraction and interruption.* Emails and the sound of constant pings from employee instant messengers can highjack the best of intentions. Managers must not be afraid to disconnect—literally—from their technology to reinvest in their own development. This allows employees to act autonomous and be free to make decisions, while allowing you the necessary time to recharge and come back with your best foot forward.

The role of the manager is likely to grow in its complexity the more markets and organizations evolve to meet the changing needs of the 21st century consumer and workforce. The manager's ability to effectively build social capital to lower the costs of business transactions will be instrumental to building and sustaining competitive advantage. Historically, a manager only had to concern themselves with planning, directing, controlling, and organizing resources to achieve this end. Today, managers need to become experts at connecting, coaching, empowering, and adapting. The proper utilization of these skills hinge upon a behavioral understanding of human psychology and behavior. Managers who are able to recognize the humanity within their team by building environments that allow for cooperation and active knowledge sharing, will not only achieve greater organizational success, but also reap the benefits associated with the development of others. Indeed, managers who make decisions based on enlighten self-interest for the development of others will outperform the rational economic manager simply seeking to control divergent self-seeking agents in the workplace. This of course requires slack in the system to learn, grow, and adapt.

A question to consider, as you contemplate the research and new paradigm presented in this book is, *who would you rather work for?* The behavioral manager seeking to leverage your innate desire to achieve success and connect with others in the workplace, or the command and control manager simply out to maximize their own interests and mitigate the agency costs you as an employee pose to the firm's shareholders? Lead in the way you would want to be led—leveraging the very best in humanity at work, while also creating the necessary behavioral guardrails for better talent decision-making. Tomorrow's workplaces depend on it.

REFERENCES

Mullainathan, S., & Shafir, E. (2013). *Time Books*. New York, NY: Henry Holt & Company LLC.

Mullainathan, S., & Shafir, E. (2014). *Scarcity: The new science of having less and how it defines our lives*. Picador Publishing.

Pew Research Center. (2014). *Why it's great to be the boss*. Retrieved from http://www.pewsocialtrends.org/2014/01/09/why-its-great-to-be-the-boss/.

Scott, K. (2017). *Radical candor: Be a kickass boss without losing your humanity*. St. Martin's Press.

Simon, H. A. (1956). Rational choice and the structure of the environment. *Psychological Review*, *63*(2), 129–138.

Index

Note: Page numbers followed by "*f*" and "*b*" refer to figures and boxes, respectively.

D

E

F

N

O

P

R

S

T

Kolibri 360 GmbH
Ferdinand-Jühlke-Straße 7
99095 Erfurt, Deutschland
produktsicherheit@kolibri360.de